Cavalcade of Broadcasting

By Curtis Mitchell

A Benjamin Company/Rutledge Book

Follett Publishing Company
Chicago

Acknowledgments:

Excerpts from pages 71-72, DAVID SARNOFF: A BIOGRAPHY
by Eugene Lyons, 1966, reprinted by permission of Harper and Row.
Excerpts from "Broadcasting" Magazine Volume I, Number 1,
1932, reprinted by permission of "Broadcasting."
Excerpts from "TV and Your Child—In Search of an Answer,"
reprinted from TV Guide®, November 29, 1969 issue from
'What Television Should Be Doing to Safeguard OUR
GREATEST NATURAL RESOURCE—OUR CHILDREN' by
Neil Hickey. Copyright © 1969 by Triangle Publications, Inc.

A Benjamin Company/Rutledge Book
ISBN: 0–695–80208–9
Copyright © 1970 by The Benjamin Co. and Rutledge Books, Inc.
Prepared and produced by Rutledge Books, Inc.
This book is available at discounts in quantity lots
for industrial or sales-promotional use through
The Benjamin Company, Inc.
485 Madison Avenue
New York, New York 10022
Library of Congress Catalog Card Number 78–121733
Printed in the United States of America

Follett Publishing Company
1010 West Washington Boulevard
Chicago, Illinois 60607

Contents

Foreword

by Bob Hope

4

Even though I hate to let work interfere with my true profession—golf—broadcasting has been my home away from home for at least half my life.

Before most people could pronounce "Bing Crosby" I was brushing my teeth with Pepsodent for the National Broadcasting Company. That was in 1938. And twelve years after we started on radio, television became inevitable, and in the spring of 1950 I did my first television show only a few blocks from where I had started in the Broadway theater in the 1930s.

It is now twenty years and several million miles later, but the memory of that first show is indelible. Now, for the first time, millions of Americans could watch and hear—and switch you off with your mouth open.

Of course, the real high spots in my television seasons have always been our Christmas tours, enabling us to visit with tens of thousands of American youngsters around the world who are at lonely outposts defending our way of life so that the rest of us can enjoy the privileges of this great country. They tell me we have traveled more than five million miles since we started these Christmas tours—and I figure I have covered at least one million just driving to and from the airports. We have been to Germany, Alaska, Korea, Greenland, Okinawa, Japan, Hawaii, Greece, Turkey, Libya, Crete, Italy—to name just a few—and for the last few years we have been allowed to entertain our valiant troops in South Vietnam.

Incidentally, while we were on tour in the South Pacific recently, I heard words of praise from the son of a soldier whom we had entertained in North Africa in 1942. I said to him, "I hope your great-grandfather caught me at Appomattox."

Thanks to radio and television, we have been able to travel around the world, bringing entertainment to the farthest reaches of the globe. And I have had more thrills than a fellow should be allowed in addition to the sheer privilege of coming into American homes week after week for all these years.

But let's face it. We're just starting. With the satellites and all the other new communications devices coming off the drawing boards, television has become a truly international medium, capable of bringing the great American dream into millions of homes around the world—and capable also of bringing other cultures to the attention of our people. This may have been a gleam in somebody's eye when I first walked up to a microphone thirty-five years ago, but now it is a reality. And this is the really exciting challenge of the years ahead. A great force for good, television—and radio, too—already has had greater impact on the lives of the citizens of this world than any other communications medium known to man in the past. We will use it wisely. And I, for one, hope to be a part of both TV and radio for the next fifty years as I have fortunately been in the past.

Introduction: "Managing a Miracle"

Consider the impact of modern broadcasting. After fifty years of gestation, after an endless stirring together of wires and tubes, greed and altruism, genius and stupidity, time has produced a miracle.

What broadcasting is, so are we. Its images and sounds have entered our eyes and ears until we citizens of the '70s are constantly aware of its symbols and think in living color.

The world has never seen the like of its potency, its view of life—and its pressures on the mind of man.

Its dimensions are awesome and its compulsion almost irresistible. We had better learn all we can about it:

Ninety-seven percent of the American people own one or more radios.

Ninety-five percent own television sets.

Every day, 100 million persons in the United States listen to radio.

Every day 100 million persons watch television.

In all history, no other medium of communication comes close to those figures. Newspapers cannot touch them. Neither can magazines. All the books published in the Western world in a year reach only a fraction of the people reached by broadcasting *in a single day.*

"Broadcasting stands as the most successful and universally

Opposite: Richard Nixon, the first person in history to talk to a man on the moon. While whole nations watched, technology scored its greatest triumph, laying the groundwork for miracles.

FIRST STEP ON
THE MOON
WHITE HOUSE
LIVE FROM MOON

accepted business enterprise in history," says Vincent T. Wasilewski, president of the National Association of Broadcasters.

And how people listen. Take·radio first. Researchers tell us that nine out of ten radio families listen an average of nineteen to twenty hours each week. In television, the figure is over twenty-one hours—three hours per day. Least hooked are the teen-agers. They listen only about nineteen hours per week.

Senator Thomas Dodd of Connecticut puts it more dramatically. "By the time the average high school graduate enters college," he says, "he has spent twenty thousand hours viewing television."

People listen everywhere! With integrated circuits smaller than a grain of rice beginning to replace transistors, the newest sets are going into stuffed toys, rings, wristwatches, sunglasses, hats, purses and ladies' hair driers. When a station asked its listeners to tell them of the place in which they were listening, they got answers from maternity wards, treetops, sewers, prison cells, church cloisters and outhouses, as well as bedrooms, living rooms and kitchens.

A few years ago, radio was supposed to turn up its toes and surrender to television. Quick-draw economists called it another buggy-whip industry, destined to be replaced by progress. Not so! "We have become a nation wired for sound," says Newton Minow, former FCC commissioner. "Radio has become America's roommate."

Most authorities see this as a great responsibility. Archibald MacLeish says: "Broadcasting matters more over the long run . . . than what anybody else does because [it is] more persistently shaping the minds of more people than all the rest of us put together."

Leo Cherne, director of the Research Institute of America, says that broadcasting determines "the way we perceive and the way we think, and most importantly, what we think well of."

Professor Dallas Smythe, researcher in communications, calls broadcasting "the agenda setter for society."

Professor Stanley T. Donner, of Stanford University, says: "I should rather admit that I had no music or books in my house than to admit that I had no television set."

On the other hand, some critics are stirred to angry diatribe. Norman Cousins, editor of the *Saturday Review,* has called broadcasting "an assault on the human mind . . . an invasion against good taste . . . a series of plodding stereotyped and low quality programs" having a "grinding lack of imagination and originality." And he concludes ". . . all speculation over the future of TV must begin with

the hard truth that right now it is being murdered in its cradle."

Carl Sandburg, the poet, said, "The rocket named television has lost its course."

Walter Lippmann wrote: "While television is supposed to be free, it has in fact become the creature, the servant and indeed the prostitute of merchandising."

Whatever it is that broadcasting does or is supposed to do, its basic charter consists of seven words imbedded in the law of the land. Radio and TV stations are licensed to operate "in the public interest, convenience, and necessity."

That legal proclamation controls the thoughts and actions of approximately 100,000 executives, technicians, entertainers, newsmen and others in the industry. They speak daily over 6,728 radio stations and 871 television stations. The end product of their labors can be heard over our 250 million radio sets and seen on our 60 million television receivers. Their effect has been to create the most powerful medium of mass communications ever known. Its power has changed America and Americans.

Left: Arte Johnson and bride-to-be Ruth Buzzi became instant stars on "Laugh-In." Top: A slim Jackie Gleason (almost) joined Audrey Meadows and made "The Honeymooners" a popular parody of married life on "The Jackie Gleason Show." Below: Funny girls are a rarity on TV; here Carol Burnett (right) joins Lucille Ball on "Here's Lucy."

TV has turned every home into a sports arena, while psychologists continue to argue over whether such programs release or encourage human aggression. All agreed it made superb looking and listening. As program material, sports costs the networks millions of dollars annually.

More facts:

It has changed entertainment. Broadcasting killed vaudeville, the traveling stock company and the tent theater. Nor has Broadway escaped. Until 1930, an average of two hundred plays opened every year. Today the number of productions is closer to fifty.

Before television, movie admissions soared to 90 million each week. Today movie audiences are one-fourth as large. And Hollywood studios are making more TV serials than theatrical releases.

Enjoyment of sports has changed. Once, big league baseball monopolized the sports pages and World Series games were the big radio events of the year. Now, we have football, basketball, hockey, track, skiing, auto racing, horse racing, bowling and golf, each with its "world series" and its immense following.

Newspapers and magazines have changed. Newspapers now carry more cartoons, columns and features. Because so many readers get their news from network radio or TV, newspapers now concentrate on local events and "follow-up" features that explain broadcast headlines. Fiction was once the surefire ingredient that sold women's magazines. Not now. Editors realize that the female appetite for fantasy is supplied by daytime serials, so they fill their pages with nonfiction articles about diet and family problems and with celebrity biography. Even picture magazines have added essays on national problems as a counterbalance to the TV documentary.

Personal behavior and personal relationships have changed. According to scientific surveys, after a family buys its first TV set it spends less time at the movies, lodge meetings, cocktail parties and sports events. And the lady of the house is less likely to go visiting next door or to gossip over the back fence. She also sees less of her relatives.

The power of broadcasting has served Americans well. The U.S.A. is the land of "causes"—Heart Fund, Red Cross, Boy Scouts, YMCA, Girl Scouts, Muscular Dystrophy, the list is endless. Broadcasters have organized themselves into a free distribution agency for the messages of these organizations. In cooperation with national advertising agencies, more than a hundred campaigns are broadcast each year. It has been estimated that the total value of all these local and national contributions by broadcasters amounts to more than half a billion dollars annually.

Disaster service is a unique function of broadcasting. A graphic example was the great power blackout of 1967. Electric power failed over all New Engand, including some of our greatest cities. Nothing that was driven by electric motors worked that night

—not trains, elevators, traffic lights, signals, phones, home TV sets. Eight hundred thousand passengers were trapped in New York subways. At a standstill, on the edge of panic, the Northeast turned to transistor radios and to receivers in automobiles. They got the news as soon as authorities learned what had happened. Pillage and panic were prevented. In a unique and unprecedented sense, law and order were maintained.

"Cyclone Alley" was a death trap across the Middle West until the government and broadcasters combined to provide a permanent cyclone watch. Now communities are warned of cyclone conditions and of the approach of any twister. In one instance, a mobile unit was touring through farm country when an unanticipated tornado blocked its way. The men in the unit reversed their course, contacted their station and broadcast an emergency warning as they raced ahead of the big wind.

In 1969 Mississippi was invaded by Hurricane Camille with winds up to 200 miles per hour. "It will be recorded as one of the major disasters of all time," *Broadcaster South*, a trade magazine, said later. "Camille '69 slammed into the U.S. mainland at the Biloxi-Gulfport area . . . taking over 150 lives and causing damage estimated in excess of one billion dollars." In two counties, 5,000 homes were destroyed, 9,000 seriously damaged, and 22,000 more manhandled by the tempest.

As Camille charged across the Gulf of Mexico, local broadcasting stations urged people to flee. During her approach, the air was full of familiar voices naming escape routes and sanctuaries. After she passed, not a sound rose from the desolation. Local radio towers had fallen like tenpins: WROA and WGCM Gulfport, WRJW Picayune, WVMI Biloxi. A dozen stations had been knocked off the air. The studio and transmitter of WLOX Biloxi had been in a hotel a stone's throw from the water. The transmitter failed when the first tidal wave swept through the hotel.

The storm's aftermath saw broadcasters struggling to get back on the air. All of them had lost some or most of their equipment. General Electric rushed a new transmitter to WLOX. Civil defense generators were borrowed. Everybody helped everyone else. Incredibly, the station returned to the air within hours to undertake the grim duty of sorting out families, reading long lists of known dead, describing unidentified bodies.

The area was without water, food, shelter, clothing, electricity, gas and medical and sanitary facilities. Transistor and car radios were long since dead.

Help came in two great surges. First, broadcasters began a statewide appeal for baby food, milk, water, food, clothing and transistor radios. Unlimited air time was given to Red Cross and government officials.

The second wave stemmed from a swiftly organized "We Care" drive. Within a week, a statewide TV-AM-FM network began a daylong appeal for funds. The goal was $1 million. Stars came from Hollywood, celebrities and VIP's offered their services. Banks, city halls and broadcasting stations were named as depositories. Contributions began to come in at once. By sundown, one station had received $150,000. By midnight, the goal was surpassed. $1 million was in the fund.

One of broadcasting's most singular characteristics is *immediacy*. Some time ago, a broadcaster in Iowa went on the air with news and bulletins at 8 A.M. At two minutes after air time, he read a bulletin giving a description of a stolen car with its license number. Miles away, a motorist, tuned to the station, pulled up at a stoplight, directly behind the stolen car. He found a policeman and the car thief was arrested two minutes before the newscaster finished his quarter-hour broadcast.

Even a period of profound sorrow can be made bearable and inspiring. After television and radio had covered the funeral of former President Eisenhower and presented documentaries of his life, James Reston, then the executive editor of *The New York Times*, wrote: "It demonstrated how national television can bring before the people the things that touch their nobler instincts. . . . The old soldier gave us a glimpse of nobility, and through this remarkable instrument of television, the people responded with a solemnity and sincerity no cynic could deny."

Broadcasting is a mover. Professor Paul Lazersfeld of Columbia University makes this point frequently in his many studies of audience influence. He says broadcasting moves people and things because it "bestows prestige and enhances the status of individuals or items by creating a favorable impression."

Early in 1970, Cleveland lawyer Howard M. Metzenbaum decided to run for a vacant senatorial seat. His opponent for the Democratic nomination was astronaut John H. Glenn, Jr. Metzenbaum was unknown; Glenn was famous around the world. "You haven't a chance," Metzenbaum's friends said.

The campaign started with the usual speeches. Then spot announcements began appearing on TV and radio stations across the state, showing a friendly guy talking to housewives, laborers, students, old people and his family. Across the tube, in bold, confident letters was the name, METZENBAUM. Glenn's modest TV campaign was overwhelmed. During the last week of the campaign, Metzenbaum visited Cleveland TV homes sixty-five times.

When the votes were counted, he had won by a nose. He had snatched victory, as *The New York Times* said, "from the most beloved and famous of all the astronauts—John H. Glenn, Jr."

The spots cost the victor $85,000 plus $300,000 for air time. Critics claimed Metzenbaum had "bought" the nomination with commercial announcements. "Without TV, I couldn't have won," Metzenbaum admitted, "but how did Mr. Glenn get his name? He enjoyed a free $3.5 million TV spectacular when he orbited the earth, and the taxpayer was footing that bill."

In the Great Debates of 1960, between candidates Nixon and Kennedy, television moved enough people to vote for Kennedy to elect him President. In 1968 it moved a majority to support the image of Richard Nixon over that of Hubert Humphrey. Several accounts of the TV aspect of the latter campaign have been published.

In politics, the quest is for listeners. Pollsters say that the average television audience for the Nixon-Kennedy debates numbered about 71 million, and that a total of 115 million tuned in to at least some part of the four encounters.

When a questionnaire asked state governors and state chairmen of both political parties what they thought of broadcasting as a political tool, 63 percent of the governors called it "crucial." More than 80 percent of the state chairmen agreed.

Reporters with the Kennedy-Johnson party in Dallas in 1963 recall that Johnson, upon hearing those fateful words, "The President is dead, Mr. President," thought immediately of reassuring the nation and showing its citizens the orderly transfer of power. "We must have continuity," he said over and over. "We must show that the government is in firm control." On the plane returning to Washington, he wrote the few words that would best help to achieve that end. On arrival at Andrews Air Force Base, he went immediately to a microphone and TV camera to show himself, sorrowing but in command. His brief declaration gave the promise that the nation would be safe "with God's help."

Broadcasting moves merchandise, too. Ten years ago, new products were introduced to the buying public at the rate of two thousand per year. Today the rate is well over six thousand. This ability to move products, especially packaged products, is not new. Back in the heyday of "Clara, Lu, and Em" in 1933, a special offer for

Colgate's Super Suds drew 600,000 responses. Another offer by General Mills, requiring a Bisquick boxtop and a dime, pulled 485,000 orders.

Other examples are visible every day in any supermarket. FCC Commissioner Nicholas Johnson has mentioned two of them in his book *How to Talk Back to Your Television Set*. "The manufacturer of the bottled liquid cleaner Lestoil undertook a $9 million television advertising program and watched his sales go from 150,000 annually to 100 million. . . . The Dreyfus Fund went from assets of $95 million in 1959 to $1.1 billion in 1965."

Economist John Kenneth Galbraith says: "The industrial system is profoundly dependent upon commercial television and could not exist in its present form without it."

The world's nations have adopted various kinds of television systems. Some are government monopolies, operated and programmed by government officials. Others have parallel systems operating side by side, one public and one private. Ours is run by private enterprise.

Three reasons have been given by authorities for the superiority of what is called "the American system of broadcasting."

First, the American system of private enterprise collects an annual sum of more than $3 billion each year from advertisers, which makes available vast sums of money for programming, plus a profit for the entrepreneurs.

Second, the American system of competition pits station against station and network against network so that programming becomes a constant search for something better.

Third, the American system of checks and balances opposes the unrestrained use of the airwaves with a watchdog organization called the Federal Communications Commission, thus assuring commitment to public interest.

In essence, American broadcasting is the result of a circulating or self-perpetuating effect. Because it collects such huge audiences, advertisers spend vast sums to reach those audiences. Because advertisers spend such vast sums, programs are constantly being created to collect those huge audiences.

Under this system, the spiral of competition rises.

According to the A. C. Nielsen Company, 53 million TV homes (93.9 percent of all TV households) watched the Apollo moon landing mission in 1969, the largest U.S. audience ever attracted to a single event. Each home reportedly watched for an average of fifteen hours and thirty-five minutes.

A somewhat higher percentage of homes—96.1—tuned in

Vice President Lyndon B. Johnson taking the Presidential oath shortly after the assassination of President Kennedy. Because TV showed every detail of an orderly transfer of power, a troubled nation soon calmed its fears and surrendered quietly to its grief.

President Kennedy's funeral, several years earlier, but the total audience was smaller because fewer sets were in existence. The time a family spent before its TV receiver during that week was thirty-one hours and thirty-eight minutes.

When the American TV signal was relayed overseas, the audience grew to astronomical figures. Wilson P. Dizard, in *Television: a World View,* says: "Never was a single emotion shared by so many people as on that day in November 1963, when 300,000,000 persons on four continents watched the televised funeral of a martyred American president."

Another unity of emotion was achieved in April of 1970 when hundreds of millions of viewers watched the crippled Apollo 13 as it splashed down. Live pictures, carried by satellite, were fed through Great Britain to the Soviet Union and twenty-two countries of the European Continent and North Africa. At Geneva, a spokesman for the European Broadcasting Union said, "This looks like the biggest broadcast of all time."

Access to TV's outsize audience comes high. A run-of-the-mill one-minute spot on a program of average popularity costs about $40,000. What may have been a record price for a single minute of time was charged for participation in the Super Bowl game of 1967. On that program, the price was $150,000.

To buy a full hour of time between seven and eleven o'clock on a network costs about $300,000. Few advertisers can make such an investment week after week, which accounts for the absence of such famous old favorites as "The Firestone Hour" and "The Telephone Hour."

Television magazine estimated the weekly production costs of network programs for the 1968–1969 season as follows:

On ABC:

Peyton Place—$89,000; Mod Squad—$170,000; Bewitched—$87,000; Judd—$170,000; Lawrence Welk Show—$105,000; Sunday Movie—$750,000.

On CBS:

Carol Burnett Show—$190,000; Doris Day—$85,000; Red Skelton—$199,000; Beverly Hillbillies—$105,000; Thursday Movie—$750,000; Jackie Gleason—$239,000; Ed Sullivan—$200,000.

On NBC:

Laugh-In—$160,000; Monday Movie—$750,000; Julia—$80,-000; Kraft Music Hall—$190,000; Ironside—$180,000; Get Smart—$90,000; Walt Disney—$195,000; Bonanza—$196,000.

Today many advertisers buy "participations" in an on-going series, thereby reaching (in theory) the same listeners week after week. Sometimes, sponsors buy alternate weeks. Other sponsors buy an occasional "special," which is a one-shot idea, depending upon a galaxy of stars or a dynamic idea to lure extra listeners.

Whatever the cost, exposure on television reaches so many people with such persuasiveness that a wide variety of products is sold profitably. If the American economy did not support this means of distributing advertising (in competition with magazines, newspapers and billboards), it would wither away and vanish.

In any dialogue about the merits of the American system, the question arises: How can a broadcaster's concern for the public interest survive such intense competition for audiences and income?

The unlikely answer is, simply, that it does.

Examples are seen in the way networks handle unusual news stories. When Pope Paul visited the United States in 1965, his unprecedented journey created tremendous public interest. The nets planned their coverage to show every papal activity, from arrival at Kennedy Airport to the Mass at Yankee Stadium. To clear their facilities for this coverage, they canceled dozens of commercial broadcasts and rebated $5 million to sponsors. Then they sent camera crews

Above: One of the great news stories of recent years was the 1965 visit to America of Pope Paul VI. Networks canceled dozens of commercial programs at a cost of millions in order to serve the public. Below: Super Bowl football attracts a huge audience. Advertisers pay a king's ransom for a single commercial minute.

to points of vantage where, throughout the day, they could project the Pope's activities. That cost another $1 million.

Covering space shots has long been a costly venture. Each time NASA shoots a rocket at the moon, regular programs are canceled, refunds given and sky's-the-limit checks signed in order to dispatch personnel and equipment to choice locations. The price tag for a single shot is about $1 million.

The biggest news story of recent decades was the assassination of President Kennedy. Broadcasters covered it for four days of continuous reportage. The out-of-pocket expenditures for the nets was estimated at $10 million. Additional expenditures were incurred by affiliated stations, which canceled all their local programs. Total estimated loss to broadcasters was about $32 million.

Such expenditures represent projects in the public interest. In the real world of finance, they represent a curtailment of corporate profits. In the real world of broadcasting, they represent the investment in public service. No other nation has such partnership ties among its citizenry, its government and its business.

Although the contributions of local stations to the public interest, convenience and necessity will be detailed in later chapters, one local service program of note in 1970 deserves mention here. It was the twenty-four-hour marathon about drugs and their abuse that WPIX New York put on the air on May 9.

Stirred by the epidemic of drug use that was crushing so many young citizens, the WPIX management planned its own blockbuster to provide understanding and, hopefully, to stimulate action. "D-D Day" was the name of the program—"D for Drugs, D for Don't!" The basic package was six hours long. The station repeated it four times—for twenty-four consecutive hours.

Full-page ads in New York newspapers first addressed the public, presenting "An Open Letter to All Parents About Drugs." The ad stated that WPIX had canceled its programs and commercials for the entire day and night. Twenty-five telephone lines would be kept open, manned by experts ready to answer any question. "This information is vital," the ad said. "Plan your Saturday around it."

The point is that somebody at WPIX perceived the extraordinary need of the New York community for an authoritative supply of information about drugs and their use. And that some executive committed the station's personnel, prestige and technical facilities to distribute that information.

The first decision was a moral-ethical-social one. The second was, at bottom, financial. Together, they represent the kind of thinking to which more and more modern broadcasters have come.

Much room for improvement remains, but the good news is that change has taken place and is taking place, and this change is healthy. William Paley, president of CBS, described it: "The public's voluntary sifting of the worthwhile from the shoddy is an evolutionary rather than a revolutionary process. It is admittedly inefficient but it cannot be speeded up. But once accomplished, it has a validity, a force, and a permanence that no government edict or citizens' committee or monolithic industry action can ever bring about. It may be the hard way but it is the only way that promises ultimate progress and at the same time guarantees our freedom."

The prognosis is favorable. Most freebooters and freeloaders have been weeded out of broadcasting and have been replaced by a new breed of executive who balances his social trusteeship with the economics of the hard sell.

Time is a deliberate physician, but the healing of broadcasting has never stopped.. As broadcasters and audiences grow up together, through self-testing and self-knowledge, small increments of progress are achieved. Pebbles washed in a running stream slowly become smoothed and rounded. Broadcasters, FCC commissioners, intellectuals and just plain Joes have rubbed against each other now for several decades. With each passing day, the electronic stream picks up speed and power, promising still greater miracles.

1

Crackpots, Kooks and Geniuses

To create the wonderful world of broadcasting, a series of brilliant young geniuses (often called crackpots) built upon one another's ideas in a most astounding fashion. Later they were succeeded by entrepreneurs (also called crackpots), who employed their gifts of organization and administration until, step by uncertain step, the edifice of the American way of broadcasting reached its present height.

This report tells their story, from broadcasting's now nostalgic past to its great future.

Anyone following the trail of the liberated electron down through the ages must have noted several phenomena:

• Its discoverers and liberators were usually young, often unbelievably so.

• They were often "loners," working against the tides of so-called authoritative opinion and of public indifference.

• They had to fight to establish the validity of their ideas.

• They were supported financially by their families or by educational institutions, rarely by commercial interests.

• Contrary to popular opinion, most inventors are not dreamers. They are thinkers and experimenters, do-it-yourselfers using the process of trial and error, a method not unknown to the science of any era.

• Finally, a new idea is worthless to society until some enterpriser sees in it the possibility of turning a profit.

STOPPING CONDENSER
CRYSTAL
DETECTOR SWITCH
COUPLER
SECONDARY SWITCH
SECONDARY CONDENSER

The American system of free broadcasting is no accident; it is the end result of many inexorable pressures. Perhaps a review of a few milestones will illuminate the point.

Set your mind back to man's pre-electric age. No smokestacks rose above industrialized cities. Wheels were turned by muscle. Boats were driven by wind. Messages were delivered by men on quivering legs or astride lathered horses. But already something significant had happened.

A Greek philosopher, Thales of Miletus, had worn a jeweled bauble made of amber. By accident, it rubbed against the sleeve of his robe, and immediately attracted to itself such small objects as lint, straw and bits of paper. The philosopher made note of this mystical attraction, not suspecting that he was perhaps the first citizen of the electronic age.

For centuries, magnetism was a mystery. Thales explained the attraction of his amber jewelry by asserting that it had a "soul." Already, lodestone—a variety of the mineral magnetite—was being used to create bulky compasses. The Chinese, ancient documents say, even mounted them on their chariots. Sailors declared that whole mountains of lodestone existed in the Far North and were so powerful that they pulled the nails right out of passing ships.

By the year 1600, eight autumns before Pocahontas saved the life of Captain John Smith at Jamestown, Virginia, a court physician to Queen Elizabeth had written a learned dissertation on magnetism. It was exhaustive, scholarly and of no significance whatever except to investigators who would be informed by it two hundred years later. In Queen Bess's day, the public preferred to think of magnetism as magic.

Then came Professor Hans Christian Oersted of Denmark. Several scientific happenings had long intrigued this Dane. One of these was a report from Johann Georg Sulzer of Zurich (1720–1779) that he had "tasted" electricity. Up to that time, electricity had been a far-out phenomenon tossed by Thor across the sky, accompanied by thunderclaps. Sulzer asserted that he had placed his tongue between a strip of silver and a strip of lead. Attaching a wire to one end of the silver plate, he touched its opposite end to the lead plate. Forthwith, a warmish, wiggly sensation suffused his taste buds and his moist tongue.

An allied event was the bizarre behavior of a number of frogs' legs as reported in 1780 by Professor Luigi Galvani, of Bologna, Italy. Having amputated the legs of several frogs, he ran copper wires through their thighs and hung them from an iron railing. Immediately, the leg muscles began to twitch, so that the legs executed an eerie, airy dance. It won for Professor Galvani the title of "The frog's dancing master" and opened up the field of animal electricity.

A third clue came in 1800 when Count Alessandro Volta brought lightning down to earth by suggesting that electricity could be induced by the chemical action of moisture and two different metals. A pile he built to demonstrate his ideas became the great-great-grandfather of all batteries.

These matters were much in the mind of Hans Christian Oersted of Copenhagen as he lectured his dozing students. He had devised an experiment in 1807 to test his theory that electric current could create a magnetic field around a wire. His experiment, however, had failed. Now years later, in 1820, he was trying again. This time he placed the wire—accidentally—parallel with instead of across the compass needle. When the current was turned on, the needle moved. Thus, in a dreary classroom, magnetism and electricity were paired by the leaping imagination of Professor Oersted. For months, he could think of little else. Magnetism was a mystery. Electricity was a mystery. But now he knew that somehow they were kin.

In 1827 an English chemist and physicist named Michael Faraday published his discovery that a wire moving through a magnetic field somehow created within itself a current of electricity. Four

Even after all these years, nobody knows what electricity is—but Hans Christian Oersted was the first to show what it did—like creating a magnetic field around a wire carrying the magic "juice." Left: His demonstrations established the science of electromagnetism and lifted the lid on Pandora's box.

Alexander Graham Bell (top), holding his first telephone, carried forward the ideas and inventions of Samuel Morse and others (above), explaining his electrical telegraph to skeptical moneymen.

years later, another Englishman used this principle to build the first true electromagnet. Following suit, researchers devised spinning gadgets of wire coils and iron magnets from which they eventually produced a reliable electrical current.

As every schoolboy knows, the inventor of radio was an Italian youth named Guglielmo Marconi. So say all the school books, encyclopedias and popular periodicals, passing over the point that any invention is merely the uppermost rung of a lengthening ladder of discovery. Without the lower rungs, no man can climb.

As a prototype of his breed, however, Marconi is almost perfect, and his life-style is well worth modern scrutiny. He came to maturity in an age of intense intellectual interest in the newly demonstrated atmospheric phenomenon known as "hertzian waves." These waves were invisible. They could pass through ocean fog or prison walls. To scientists of 1892, they were as exciting as the 1969 landing on the moon was to us.

Born in 1874, Marconi, the introverted and privately educated son of a well-to-do Italian family, lived with his parents and a brother in a country house called the Villa Grifone at Pontecchio near Bologna. As a teen-ager, he became interested in electricity and a student of the experiments of Benjamin Franklin. Before he was twenty-one, he had experimented with equipment of his own design and construction.

A vacation trip to the Alps accidentally lighted a fire that was to burn with unprecedented fierceness. At leisure one day, looking for reading matter with which to pass the time, he selected a magazine containing an article about hertzian waves.

But perhaps we should start back at the beginning, if there is a beginning. Accept the fact for now that machines have already been invented which can produce large quantities of electricity and are being used for telegraphic purposes. Utilizing this standard source of power, the American physicist Joseph Henry took a modest first step toward making radio waves useful when he ran a current of electricity through a coil of wire and discovered that it magnetized steel needles up to 200 feet away. No wires connected the devices. It was a puzzling phenomenon. He called it "induction at a distance."

Other scientists soon became interested, including Sir Oliver Lodge, Lord Kelvin and Thomas Edison. It was clear to them that when a spark jumped a gap to complete an electric current, something happened besides the emission of light.

Michael Faraday, who had discovered the unity of electricity and magnetism, speculated on the mystery but got nowhere. Then another Britisher, the great physicist James Clerk Maxwell, converted the enigma to a mathematical formula which proved, at least to him, that light waves and electrical waves were the same kind of energy.

Now we arrive again at Heinrich Hertz, the Hamburgian, whose mother's ancestors had been Lutheran ministers and whose father's progenitors went straight back to ancient Israel. His home was an intellectual oasis in which he learned to speak English, French and Italian. Like Marconi, he had turned one room into a junk-shop laboratory. By the time he was twenty, he had read all of the Faraday-Maxwell reports in their original language. A close friend, physicist Hermann Helmholtz, said to him, "They've given us theories. You prove them."

Young Heinrich did so, discovering the mystery of wavelengths and how to measure them, and finally how to control the invisible flow until the waves could be focused like a searchlight. He called them "invisible light" and said that they resembled the disturbance caused by a stone thrown into a pond, except that the hertz waves travelled at 186,000 miles per hour. By the time he was thirty-four, Hertz was trying to shoot invisible beams in all directions. He died at age thirty-seven.

Reading about these things during his vacation in the Alps, young Marconi felt the first hot spark of a determination to complete this work. Grabbing a pencil, he began. Back home, he built equipment according to his new calculations. His workshop was a room at the top of his father's mansion. No one was admitted, not even his mother, who brought him meals which she left on the floor before his locked door.

One day he invited her to a demonstration. She watched, white-faced, fearing the worst. Guglielmo adjusted wires, closed switches, patted coils into exact position and lo! in the distance, a bell rang weakly.

"No wires?" she asked.

"No wires."

Now Marconi Senior became involved. He found his son's experiments fascinating and began to think of ships in distress and of battleships talking to each other as they deployed against an enemy.

As further experiments progressed, all the Marconis waited anxiously. Surely, among all the world's famous scientists, someone must be making the same discovery. Young Guglielmo carried part of his equipment into the fields. He inserted a key into his sending circuit, explaining, "I aimed at breaking up the emissions into long and short periods." Now telegraphy without wires was his passion.

In turn, a teen-ager in Italy named Marconi read up on every experiment he could find, added his own insights and succeeded in propelling (and sensing) electrical waves through the air. By 1897, he was doing it with this homemade wireless set.

27

Month by month, "emissions" from his third-floor lab reached across the hills. At the receiving end, he rigged a loop of wire to a tall pole. It was the world's first antenna and it brought in signals astonishingly loud and clear.

The time for action had come. With help from the parish priest and the family physician, Marconi Senior composed an announcement of Guglielmo's miracle and offered it to the Italian Minister of Post and Telegraph. His leisurely reply said that His Majesty's government was not interested.

The family held a council of war. What other nation might be interested? The answer was, obviously: the empire on which the sun never set. Madame Marconi had close ties with the British empire. She was pure Irish, the daughter of an aristocratic Dublin family who, at the age of twenty-one, had eloped with Guglielmo's father. "We'll go to London," she decided. As she packed hats and gowns, her son put his precious gadgetry together in a black box.

They sailed for England in midwinter, 1896. In America, women were shortening their skirts to one inch above the ankle and anchoring the hems with lead weights; it gave them more freedom when riding their bicycles. Only a year had passed since the first patent had been issued for an engine to power those horseless vehicles called automobiles.

Arriving in England, young Guglielmo—wearing a high stiff collar and funereal suit and carrying his black box—was stopped by customs officers. "What do you have there?" He answered readily, truthfully—and they seized his treasure. A machine for wireless telegraphy, indeed! Two years earlier, an Italian anarchist had murdered the president of neighboring France. This could be a plot against their own Royal Family. This Italian youth had the eyes of a fanatic, and the beautiful woman with him spoke English with an Irish accent. Surely, *that* was peculiar. So they smashed the black box until its coils and batteries and wires were a shambles.

Once past customs, however, the Marconi prospects brightened. A relative found an honest patent attorney. Guglielmo bought new parts and reconstructed his black box. He was given an appointment with Sir William Preece, chief engineer of telegraphs in the British Post Office, who by chance was also a wireless buff but had been unable to send signals for any distance. Of all the men in London who might have been approached by young Marconi, Preece was the one to understand.

Government-sponsored tests were ordered on Salisbury Plain. The reconstructed black box dutifully emitted its waves on command.

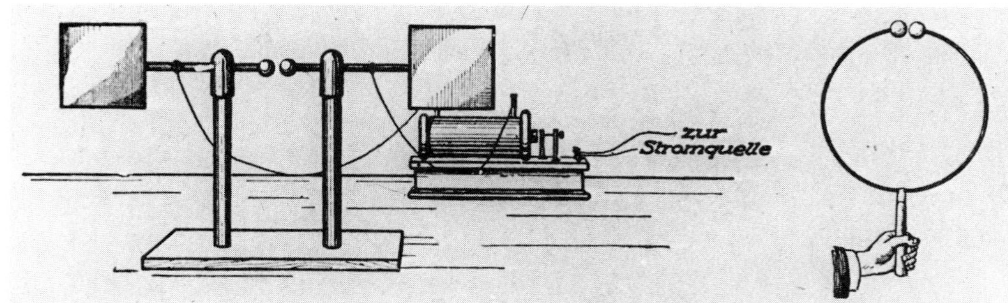

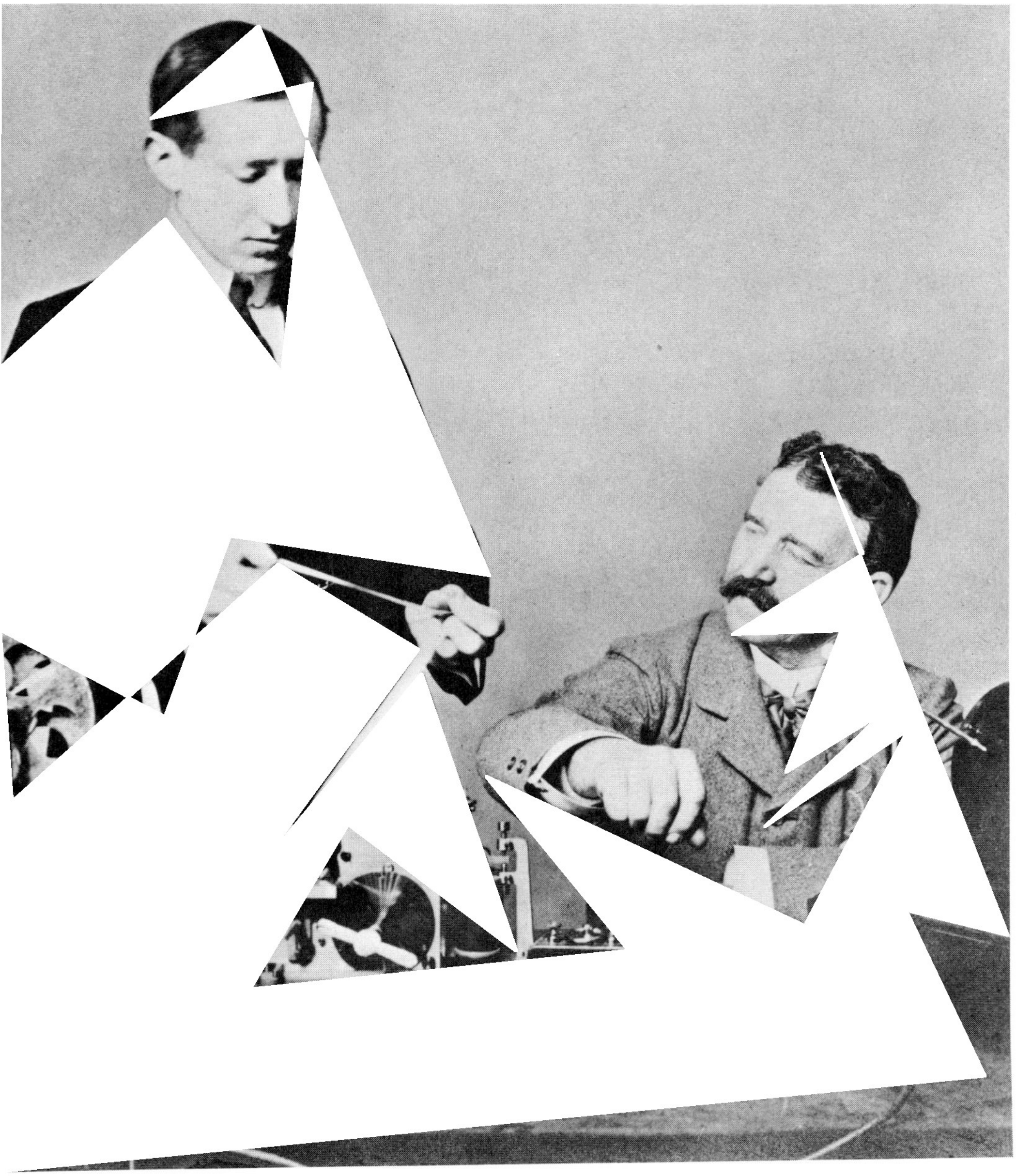

Top: Making gadgets like these is child's play to any schoolboy, but when Heinrich Hertz of Germany put them together in 1886–1889, they were black magic—for the waves they created went through walls and London fog. Later, Marconi (left) utilized them to cover the miles without wires—and founded a British communications company that still endures.

Marconi's signals crackled across 1 mile, then 4 miles, finally 9 miles. As the word spread, the shy youth became a celebrity. Soon the British government gave him a patent.

News of the Marconi magic reached Italy. Officialdom in Rome had second thoughts and begged him to return his black box to his native land. He took a ship to La Spezia and easily established communications with warships miles away at sea. Hastening to Rome, he lectured King Humbert and Queen Margherita on wireless telegraphy.

Back in London, sympathetic commercial interests were planning his future. Young Guglielmo had fallen into the hands of good advisers. They knew the worth of what he had devised, and they knew how to turn it into treasure, so they attached themselves to him and his destiny in a most acceptable way. They organized a company that would soon be known around the world as the Marconi Wireless Telegraphy Company. In addition to giving him a job and half of the company's stock, they deposited in his bank account the equivalent of more than $100,000. He was twenty-three years old.

Lightships off the British coast were presently equipped with Marconi radio transmitters. When a steamer smashed into one of those lightships in 1899, the wireless brought prompt help. Thus, by saving lives, broadcasting began its long career in the public service. But another performance was equally important. An Irish newspaper in Dublin hired the Marconi company to give an eyewitness account of the famous Kingstown Regatta. Marconi followed the wind-blown yachts in a steamer trailing a 75-foot antenna. In Dublin, newspaper extras announcing the winner were on the streets before the vessels reached port. Nobody called it news coverage but that is what it was, the first of countless sporting events to bring reality into the world's parlors and playrooms.

After the fleets of England and Italy had committed themselves to use his device, British brains began to think of the U.S. Navy, engaged just then in a duel with Spain's Asiatic fleet. In the meantime, a yacht, the *Shamrock*, owned by Sir Thomas Lipton, was to race an American craft named *Columbia* off the New York shoreline. An alert Manhattan editor invited Marconi to repeat his radio reportage. So the youthful Italian took passage to the New World.

America was emotionally ready for the young genius and his invention. Its Navy had just won a series of victories over Spanish men-of-war in Cuba and the Philippines. A doctrine called "manifest destiny" was being preached by editorial writers. Suddenly the United States considered itself a great power.

When the invading *Shamrock* was defeated by the *Columbia*, Marconi's wireless reports from the scene of the race caused a sensation. Again, men with pencils and eyeshades decided that it was time to exploit this latest gift of science.

One month after the international yacht races had imprinted the name of Marconi on millions of minds, the Marconi Company of America was founded in New Jersey. Capital of $10 million was authorized, represented by 2 million shares. The British parent company retained 365,000 shares. Others were purchased by English and American financiers. And Guglielmo Marconi was assigned 600,000, worth $5 each. At the age of twenty-five, he was a millionaire.

The feat that won Marconi the scrutiny of history, however, came in 1901. Having built a towering transmitter in Poldhu, England, he sailed to Newfoundland and installed his coils and batteries at St. John's. A kite antenna lifted a thin wire into the clouds. A precise transmission schedule had been laid out. In England, at a certain time on a certain day, a man pressed his telegraph key in a trio of stuttering dots. In North America, Marconi and his friends waited, watches in hand. Faintly, the distant spark spoke to them across the immensity of the Atlantic. Not a message but a symbol of what one day would be a thousand million messages, all begun that day with three staccato dots, the letter S of the Morse alphabet.

Young, rich and honored, Marconi piled one triumph on top of another. Within a few years, his inventions were whisking messages from Ireland to the Antipodes, India and South America. His subsequent career matched that of his youth. At the time of World War I, his services were commandeered by both the Italian army and navy.

Much earlier, British enterprise had consolidated its control of world communications. When Admiral George Dewey defeated the Spanish fleet in Manila in 1898, the U.S. had received the word via British cables. To some, proposals of the Marconi company seemed an extension of this monopoly. In particular, many were offended by the policy of renting out instead of selling equipment even though the compay offered a package including a trained operator and shore stations open around the clock.

The times were unique. The United States had just humbled a great European power, depriving Spain of her overseas empire. The gawky nation from the wrong side of the tracks now saw itself as an international swashbuckler. To many citizens, renting Marconi's foreign gear seemed close to treason.

Another aspect of this policy upset many U.S. humanitarians. The Marconi company had gone to great expense to build shore stations with which to serve the ships using their equipment. In the beginning, their stations accepted all calls that came their way. Suddenly, they asked why they should respond to ships using German or Italian or other rival gadgetry which, likely as not, was operating in violation of basic Marconi patents. Henceforth, they decreed they would respond only to messages transmitted on bona fide Marconi hardware. Softening a little, they added, "except in emergencies."

Cries of "British monopoly" rose throughout the land. Chauvinists conjured up pictures of Yankee seamen sinking beneath the waves while hardhearted Anglo-Saxons ignored their pleas for succor. In the midst of the tumult, young Marconi scuttled home. Later this policy would be changed and he would return. For the moment, however, the field was open to his rivals.

It must be noted that nineteenth-century Europe had enjoyed no hammerlock on scientific ingenuity. Though most American efforts would not come to light until later, one experimenter, a Professor Amos E. Dolbears, of Tufts College, had already chalked up one small miracle. Ten years before Marconi obtained his first patent, he had sent and received radio waves through the air. To get distance, he had attached a wire to a gilt kite and sailed it aloft, the same device that Marconi would use later while receiving the first signal across the Atlantic. Dr. Dolbears, using an old receiver from a Bell telephone and a homemade microphone, had been able to understand speech over a distance of a half mile.

Another pre-Marconi pioneer was Dr. Mahlon Loomis, holder of what is probably the first United States patent for wireless transmission. He operated on two peaks in the Blue Ridge Mountains, lifting his antennas into the clouds with giant kites. Peak-to-peak communication was established, but Dr. Loomis was ahead of his time.

Following the introduction of Samel F. B. Morse's dot-and-dash telegraph in 1844, many investigators had tried to send the human voice along a telegraph wire. About the time our Union was dissolving in 1861, a German named Philipp Reis first described an electric telephone to the public. Alexander Graham Bell's breakthrough did not come until fifteen years had passed and conditions were right to make telephone lines commercially practicable.

Similarly, Marconi's success in transmitting code messages through space inspired a host of experimenters to transmit the human voice. One of the first was Reginald A. Fessenden, a professor at the University of Pittsburgh, who had worked for Thomas Edison at Menlo Park, New Jersey, and then for Westinghouse.

By 1900 he was in the service of the U.S. Weather Bureau

of the Department of Agriculture, because the government had decided to serve its farmers by issuing weather information.

Historian Erik Barnouw in *A Tower in Babel,* a masterly account of the birth of broadcasting, describes his achievement: "Fessenden . . . proposed a heresy. The wave sent out must not be—as in the Marconi system—an interrupted wave or series of bursts. Instead, it must be a continuous wave, on which voice would be superimposed as variations or modulations. This heresy became the foundation of radio."

Fessenden's work produced a series of successes that attracted financial backers. With their money and the know-how of General Electric scientists, he put together a transmitting station at Brant Rock, Massachusetts. By Christmas of 1906, he was ready to broadcast.

With each passing year, more and more amateurs had joined the army of listeners. At sea hundreds of operators on merchantmen and naval vessels formed a worldwide audience. On duty, they always wore their "cans"—slang for the earphones needed to pick up code signals. One memorable night they were startled to hear a brisk voice speaking. A woman took over, singing sweetly. A man read slowly and with feeling. Next, a violin solo. Finally, a talk. It was Fessenden and his friends in a historic experiment. Fessenden himself had played the violin and read several verses from the Bible. Later, there would be a New Year's broadcast.

Top: Army wireless experts of World War I included Major Guglielmo Marconi (second from left) who served Italy as a communications expert. His British company provided a majority of all Allied experts. Above: Tubes were the blood of wireless distance—so tubes got bigger, producing more power. Dr. Irving Langmuir of GE holds the world's biggest—good for an unheard-of 20 kilowatts—circa 1915.

Touring executives of the United Fruit Company, hearing words pouring out of the ether, perceived a commercial use for them. If a ship at sea could be directed to the port where the highest prices prevailed—it was an idea! So presently, science merged with commerce, and Fessenden equipment began to guide a fleet of bulging banana boats on more profitable voyages.

Another event, of no apparent importance at the time, was the Marconi company's hiring of an intense, skinny youth from the New York slums. His position was that of a humble office boy. His name was David Sarnoff. Within a year, he would be carrying Guglielmo Marconi's briefcase, running errands for him during his 1907 visit and taking the first steps in one of the most amazing careers in the history of American business.

The name of Lee De Forest has vanished from Radio Row, but it was much discussed in the early days of broadcasting. De Forest was an authentic, home-grown genius. A few called him pushy. Many called him a crackpot for reasons that will become obvious. Without question, he was a gadfly with a dream plus an abundance of scientific savvy.

Though born in the Middle West, he was raised in Alabama where his clergyman father presided over a Negro college. He got his education from the Bible, from reading the *Patent Office Gazette* and from his years at the Sheffield Scientific School at Yale University, where his classmates voted him both the nerviest and the homeliest member of his class.

Old-fashioned in many ways, De Forest often entrusted his secret thoughts to a diary. One entry said: "What finer task than to transmit the sound of a voice of song to one a thousand miles away. Oh, if I could do that tonight."

More than any others, he understood that tinkering in a garret was less profitable than tinkering in public. Having an understanding of the physics of his craft, he also remembered that Alexander Graham Bell had introduced his telephone to the public through personal appearances at Philadelphia's Centennial Exposition in 1876. Further, he knew that Marconi himself had won his first public acclaim reporting a yacht race.

Providentially, a yacht race would be run soon between Long Island's south shore and Sandy Hook, New Jersey. The year was 1901. De Forest's signals were already being heard around the rooftop in Chicago where he worked. "Emboldened," as he put it, he approached the New York *Tribune*. They had made other arrangements for coverage. He hurried to the Associated Press. They, too, had signed with

a wireless man. Finally, he made a deal with an almost unknown outfit called Publishers Press Association.

Friends loaned him $1,000 with which to build sending and receiving equipment. Skipping meals and rarely sleeping, he and his associates completed their assignment, but De Forest collapsed and was rushed to a hospital. Just then an anarchist assassinated President McKinley and the races were postponed. This reprieve allowed the inventor time to recuperate and when the first race was re-scheduled he was there to cover it. But his report never got through. Three rival transmitters along the route hit the air simultaneously and their competing signals turned the impulses to chaotic caterwauling.

Still, all was not lost, thanks to the newspapers that had hired him. Having announced that they were getting direct reports by radio, those editors would not be denied and published the results, which the press association delivered, as "Radio Flashes." Feature stories told of the remarkable De Forest radio service and inventive skill.

One reader was a smooth promoter named Alexander White. He had Wall Street connections and a magnetic personality. When he contacted young De Forest, he led him straight to the mountaintop, promising the world. "My associates and I will back you," he said. "We'll capitalize our company for $3,000,000 and sell stock to the public. We'll manufacture whatever equipment you design and sell it to governments around the world." Departing, he pressed a $100 bill upon the dazzled inventor.

Flattered and reassured by the prospect of having research funds for once, De Forest threw himself into the new enterprise, called the De Forest Wireless Telegraph Company. He got a fat chunk of stock—it would soon be worthless—and a salary of $20 per week.

Suddenly, life was beautiful. The U.S. Army's Signal Corps made a purchase and so did the Navy. Promotor White now turned Publicist White, with De Forest as his willing assistant. They bought a new 1902 automobile, filled its back seat with coils and batteries and drove it about New York City, its spark gap crackling. Each afternoon it rolled up before the Stock Exchange, got the closing prices from a runner and blasted them into the ether while crowds blinked in amazement. It made no difference that nobody was listening to the new "radio." At Coney Island, a slender mast soon pierced the sky, and the company announced that this was the first of a globe-girdling chain of De Forest stations. Stock sales rose so fast that Financier White, living it up with the social set, recapitalized the company for $15 million.

At the St. Louis World's Fair, Lee De Forest and his wireless tower were irresistible attractions. "The staccato crackle of our spark," he wrote, "brought them swarming." And the stock sold and sold.

Currents were sweeping twentieth-century America. Nothing seemed impossible. Teddy Roosevelt, speaking not so softly, wanted a Panama Canal—and he got it, some said, by fomenting a revolution. The Wright brothers had flown, wearing their high stiff collars, at Kitty Hawk, North Carolina. Movies were catching on and "The Great Train Robbery" had made a star of a man called Bronco Billy. In Detroit, an ex-mechanic with odd ideas was beginning to turn out an endless stream of black automobiles called Fords.

But in wireless telegraphy, progress had come to a crashing halt. To realize its destiny, "wireless" transmission had to compete with cables, which spanned every ocean and continent, day or night, without fail. Current radio equipment, everyone soon realized, was inadequate. The problem was to get more power, a lot more!

Clever minds began to work at it, De Forest's among them.

A kind of scientific three-horse parlay solved the impasse and illustrates the up-the-ladder movement of science. Years earlier, an Englishman, William Crookes, had built a glass bubble with charged wires at opposite ends. When he pumped all the air out of the bubble, an electrical current flowed between the wires and the inside of the glass glowed. What was that stuff flowing between the wires? Hanging a small metal plate inside his tube, he saw that it cast a shadow. Obviously, the flow was composed of particles of some sort. Today, we call them electrons.

This initial step encouraged a 1903 experiment by a fellow Englishman, Professor John Ambrose Fleming, a Marconi company man. He remembered an electrical principle that had been noticed and abandoned by Thomas Edison, and he added it to the Crookes tube. His result was a new kind of detector of radio signals. He called it a diode valve. It was another step forward, but it still fell short of what was needed.

Meanwhile, Lee De Forest, by 1906, had resolved the problem. "The difficulty of unsufficiently powerful reactions was overcome by a little three-electrode tube invented by the writer and called the Audion," he explained later. "This revolutionary device, used as an amplifier, strengthened by astronomical ratios the ears of radio and the eyes of television, and made possible the clear reception over great distances which we have today."

His contribution was a third element, a "grid" suspended in the stream of electrons flowing through the tube, with a variable current of its own to regulate that flow. In his diary, De Forest wrote: "I had discovered an Invisible Empire of the Air."

What had De Forest done? He had found a way to multiply an electric current billions of times. Engineers called his Audion a little giant. Technically, it was a thermionic valve with three elements: anode, cathode and grid. With it, he would conquer the world. Interestingly, he remained the romanticist and thought of it in poetic terms. "My present task," he wrote, "is to distribute sweet melody over the city and the sea so that even the mariner far out across the silent waves may hear the music of his homeland."

But trouble was brewing. Alexander White, De Forest's Wall Street backer, began one more financial manipulation. He and his associates suddenly formed a new concern which they called the United Wireless Telegraph Company, capitalized at $20 million, to which they sold their controlling interest in the De Forest company. The inventor and his friends were left holding the bag.

But De Forest also held the Audion patent. It could be worth millions or worth nothing, depending on luck and litigation, but it became the basis of a second De Forest operation. Facing a bleak future, he decided on a powerful publicity crusade. Step one was to start broadcasting from a New York studio to amateur set-builders. Most experimenters had used phonograph records. De Forest varied his radio fare by inviting speakers to his microphone.

The general public and the press remained indifferent, but hundreds of amateurs wrote letters of appreciation. Slowly, the money that sustained the operation was used up. Providentially, the federal government announced a round-the-world goodwill tour of its fleet consisting of sixteen battleships and twelve thousand men. De Forest huddled with the admirals and his Audion won an order for enough equipment to outfit every vessel. His company was saved.

What else could an inventor do to attract attention? A comely pianist named Nora Blatch lived in the next apartment. De Forest met her, fell in love and married her. His excitement about broadcasting was contagious and she became a fellow promoter. Together, they discussed possible exploits. The one sure way to an editor's attention was to make a new distance record. But how? A balloon, a kit, a mountaintop—these had been done. But in Paris, left over from an earlier World's Fair, was the Eiffel Tower, which stood 984 feet tall.

Hurrying to the French capital, De Forest and his bride wangled permission to make a voice broadcast from the tower's top. Their talent consisted of a Pathé phonograph and a large selection of records. On the appointed night, they went on the air, taking turns at changing until the next day's sunrise. Cannily, De Forest had installed receivers in various homes and hotel rooms to which he invited journalists and editors.

Reception was perfect and the French press raved. The De Forests became instant celebrities. Cards and letters came from all over France—one from 500 miles away.

Back home again, De Forest sought other opportunities to arouse the public. Two years passed before he found the event he needed. On January 13, 1910, the Metropolitan Opera Company would present an extraordinary double feature: *Cavalleria Rusticana* and *Pagliacci,* starring Enrico Caruso. De Forest got permission to broadcast direct from the stage of the world-famous Metropolitan Opera House.

His transmitter was in a room just beneath the roof. His antenna was copper wire suspended from two bamboo fishing poles. Two microphones were installed, one on stage, another in the wings. Nobody knew how they would work.

At the appointed time, De Forest's guests arrived in the offices and apartments in which he had foresightedly installed batteries of earphones. "Listen and pass them on to the next person," they were told.

Caruso came on the air and his audience held their breath. His tenor boomed magnificently for a few moments, faded away, and was succeeded by snarling dots and dashes. It was like that all evening. Neither De Forest nor *The New York Times* was pleased. Still, it was the first time ever that an opera had been broadcast from the Met.

Critics in his audience told De Forest what was wrong. So did old telegraph and telephone hands. They said he was trying to use "wireless" for something beyond its capacity. Given time, it might win a place alongside other reliable methods of communication, but even in that field, its future would be limited. Who would send a private message that all the world could hear? What business concern would trust its secrets to a message service that trumpeted them through the air?

As for popularizing music, concerts and opera via radio waves—forget it.

De Forest went back to his experiments. He remained convinced that a way must be found to achieve his goal of transmitting beautiful melody and speech to the ears of his most distant countrymen.

2
Enterprisers and Amateurs 1911-1918

America the beautiful slumbered in the springtime sun. Electric runabouts and four-cylinder Fords were bouncing along ever-lengthening gravel roads. A noisy musical vogue called ragtime was inspiring a host of "animal" dances: the fox-trot, bunny hug, camel walk, chicken scratch and turkey trot. Business was good, and all was well with the world.

What of wireless? "A plaything," learned men said.

Overseas, John Bull was patting himself on the back over his empire's latest triumph. Britain's White Star Line had just sent the world's largest, fastest, safest ocean liner on her maiden voyage. A floating city, she carried almost 2,500 of the Anglo-American world's most notable people. Two famous radio names had been on the original passenger list, those of Signor and Signorina Guglielmo Marconi. But business had needed him immediately in America, so he had booked an earlier sailing.

Now, music and laughter echoed in the wake of the ship as her skipper followed the more dangerous but shorter course along the Grand Banks. Another liner, the SS *California,* had wirelessed that icebergs lay ahead.

At Cape Race, Newfoundland, a seventeen-year-old Marconi operator named Charles B. Ellsworth was working the dogwatch. Shortly after midnight, he intercepted a message.

"CQD SOS from MGY. Come at once! We've struck a berg," it said.

TITANIC

Stunned, he refused to believe that the SS *Titanic,* that brand-new queen of the seas, could be in trouble. It had to be a joke. "The boys are hazing me again," he decidèd. A quick check showed that all the other Marconi men were asleep in their bunks. He woke the chief operator and asked him to listen. The message confirmed, they relayed the news to all who might be listening. Other steamers quickly acknowledged, and headed toward the wounded *Titanic.*

The *Carpathia* was closest. Other vessels, farther away, wanted to help. Ironically, the *Carpathia,* the ship that could have helped most—she was only 58 miles away—carried but one operator and he had gone to bed. When the *Carpathia* finally awoke to the peril and arrived at dawn, the unsinkable *Titanic* had foundered and the sea was littered with bodies and crowded lifeboats.

Sitting at his key in the Marconi station atop Wanamaker's Department Store in New York, young David Sarnoff heard the faint rustling in his earphones that was not quite silence but not yet a signal. Straining every faculty, he managed to decipher the thin stirrings as they clustered into dots and dashes. The *Olympic* was talking from 1,400 miles away, relaying the message she had received from the *Titanic.* Sarnoff called the newspapers, a traditional courtesy to the press, and then returned to his instruments.

The New York Times of April 15, 1912, reported: "At 12:25 tonight the White Star Liner *Titanic* called CQD [SOS had not yet become generally accepted as a signal of distress] to the Marconi station here and reported having struck an iceberg. The steamship said that immediate assistance was needed."

For the next three days and nights, young Sarnoff would never leave his post as he copied down the names of survivors picked up by a half-dozen mercy ships. During those crucial hours, he became the one link between the rescued and a waiting, agonizing world.

The ultimate count of those drowned was worse than anticipated. More than fifteen hundred persons had gone down with the *Titanic.* Thanks to wireless, however, more than seven hundred were saved.

The sinking of the *Titanic* is an oft-told tale, but it is meaningful to broadcasting because it was the first national demonstration of the power and the glory of the tamed electric spark. For days, news of the disaster held the nation spellbound. One swift consequence was Signor Marconi's own spirited reaction. After questioning his Marconi men aboard various rescue ships, he ordered experimental work started in many directions.

The position given by the *Titanic* had been miles from where

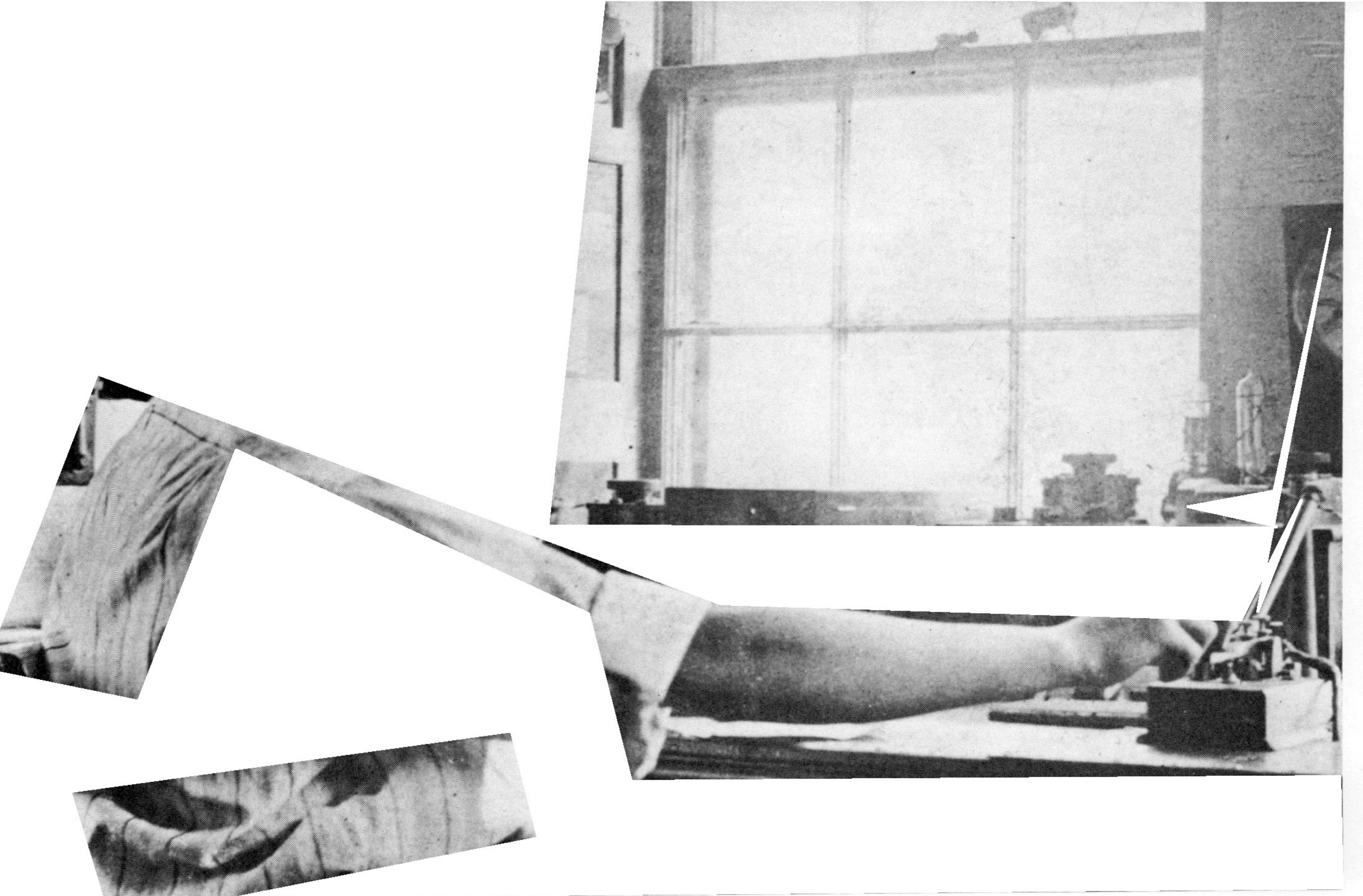

the *Carpathia* found her. The Marconi company planned to erect radio "lighthouses" to which ships could "tune" and pinpoint their positions.

Most survivors had been saved by lifeboats. Marconi designed a hand-operated wireless set that would soon become standard equipment in the lifeboats of many maritime lines.

One ship's operator had gone to bed at the end of his watch and missed the call. Marconi engineers designed a receiver, which, whether attended or not, would respond to a distress signal with a rousing blast on a klaxon.

Still another consequence was a gigantic surge of interest among young people. Inspired by the example of Marconi and Sarnoff, thousands took up set-building and short-range telegraphy as a hobby. Soon every large city had its Radio Row, with stores handling all kinds of electrical gadgetry. Suddenly boys who had wanted to be cowboys or aviators decided to become wireless operators. Do-it-yourself clubs sprang up in high schools and colleges. Physics classes turned themselves into wireless labs. Dialing for distance became an obsession. Even with a cat's-whisker set, almost anyone could listen to the daily time signals from the U.S. Navy transmitter in Arlington, Virginia, by which battleships all over the world set their chronometers.

A famous shot of a famous man—David Sarnoff, who taught himself Morse telegraphy, worked as office boy and radio operator for Guglielmo Marconi, became the Horatio Alger of electronics and eventually gave the world network radio and color TV.

Most of these experimenters were in their teens and twenties. Their purchases supported radio supply houses and their passion for wireless communicated itself gradually to the general public. One long-distance fan from New Jersey, seeking new worlds to conquer, took his equipment to Scotland and was able to tune in the signals of twenty-seven separate U.S. "hams"—amateur radio station operators.

Many of today's broadcasters are alumni of that great band of adventurers. Today some of them meet annually to swap reminiscences as members of a distinguished organization called the Broadcast Pioneers. In 1950 they established a Broadcasters Hall of Fame to which they have since elected such immortals as Marconi and Fessenden, Frank Conrad and Commander Eugene F. McDonald, Jr., H. V. Kaltenborn and Franklin D. Roosevelt.

Equally important, the Broadcast Pioneers have assembled an Industry Reference Center, an impressive documentation of the growth of broadcasting from a peanut tube enterprise to a vast cultural and industrial complex. Under the guidance of William S. Hedges, former vice president of NBC, this center has become a vital source of anecdotage, photographs, speeches and policies that trace the upward spiral of today's preeminent news, entertainment and advertising medium. Housed at the headquarters of the National Association of Broadcasters in Washington, D.C., it is invaluable to scholars and students.

By 1912, several giants of commerce began to stir, perhaps stimulated by the dominant position achieved by the American Marconi company. Fortune had not favored most American enterprises. Professor Fessenden's company, after ten years, gave up the ghost. Alexander White's financial sins could no longer keep his United Wireless Company afloat. He had built several shore stations and was offering a line of good equipment to all comers, but when American Marconi sued him for patent infringement, he and his fellow officers admitted their guilt and went into bankruptcy. Their assets went to American Marconi.

Even America's most optimistic scientist, Lee De Forest, was in trouble. Disgruntled stockholders, tired of waiting for a profit, hailed him into court, charging fraudulent promotion. Their attorneys said he knew that his Audion tube patents were invalid. An indictment described it as "a strange device like an incandescent lamp, which he called an Audion, and which device was proved to be worthless." Painful hearings followed and though he was discharged as guiltless, the judge gave some advice: "Get into a common garden variety of job," he told the inventor, "and stick with it."

Decades earlier, Western Union and the American Telephone & Telegraph Company had fought a similar technological war. Samuel Morse's invention of the telegraph had blossomed into a multimillion-dollar monopoly by the time Alexander Graham Bell's newfangled phone had attracted backers. Inevitably, the latter's underfinanced concern had run short of cash and offered its assets, the telephone patents, to Western Union. Bell's asking price was $100,000. The offer was contemptuously rejected.

Within a year, WU recognized its mistake but by now the Bell Company had recovered. Telephone exchanges were springing up all over America. Hastily, WU bought up whatever patents it could find and moved into the phone business on its own. Its violent anti-Bell crusade was a model of economic pressures, of Goliath and little David, but with the same results. Patent suits charging infringement were filed by both sides, but Bell was impregnable and WU knew it. They settled out of court. Bell's stock rose from $50 a share to almost $1,000. It was a preview of what would happen later in radio.

By the turn of the century, the Bell Company was one of the giants of commerce. With its vast electrical know-how, it was attracted to the field of wireless transmission. Bell executives were determined not to make the mistake of indifference. As they had learned, a technical product had to be built on a jigsaw puzzle of patents. The wireless patent they wanted was the De Forest Audion. It would serve two purposes: its power might increase the efficiency of their long lines operation and they would have a foot in the door of the expanding radio industry. To further this enterprise, they set aside $500,000.

Late in 1912, De Forest was invited to demonstrate his Audion for AT&T. The record says that the Bell people were "amazed."

Inserted in a land line circuit, the Audion multiplied clarity many times. After other tests, all satisfactory, an intermediary offered De Forest $50,000. He held off, hoping for more. His need for cash became so great that he pawned his watch and his wife's rings. Eventually, in 1913, he capitulated. The settlement enabled him to return to his real enthusiasm of "projecting sweet music into the air." AT&T would soon buy other rights. They wanted his Audion for a projected "radio telephone." He charged them $90,000. Later, they wanted all his remaining patents and he was glad to accommodate. Price: $250,000.

The Marconi company was not unaware that a powerful American rival was flexing its muscles. The AT&T subsidiary, Western Electric, had begun to make radio telephone tests. Simultaneously, lawyers everywhere seemed to be filing patent suits. But the most important suit of all was between Marconi and AT&T over De Forest's Audion.

In 1916 the issue was settled by the U.S. District Court in New York City. The verdict was a bomb. Its double-barreled ruling said that:

a. De Forest's Audion infringed patents previously granted to John Ambrose Fleming for his lamp-like detector, now licensed to the Marconi Company of America.

b. However, the grid with which inventor De Forest had converted Fleming's weak diode tube into a midget powerhouse was wholly protected by De Forest's patents.

What did it mean? Attorneys who unraveled the decision found that it meant chaos. Marconi could not use his tubes without the consent of AT&T. AT&T could not use its tubes without the consent of the Marconi company.

This stew was further seasoned by patents for more recent improvements held by a new crop of U.S. inventors. The most prominent of these was Edwin H. Armstrong, soon to be famous for his work with shortwaves, but now claiming incredible accomplishments for his far-out circuitry. He was still attending Columbia University when he put together a circuit which utilized De Forest's Audion, not as a transmitter, but as a hypersensitive detector. His 1914 patent on this idea elevated him to the magic circle of those with a vested interest in the Audion. Other experimenters were quick to note that there was more to the Audion than had even been patented. They discovered within its glass-caged vacuum an uncanny ability to generate radio waves. Their rush to the patent office, along with De Forest and Armstrong, created a patent jam, and frustration reigned in a dozen laboratories.

But the mind of one young man remained clear. He had received several promotions within the Marconi company since his spectacular stint as a wireless operator.

Looking backward, one can compare the career of David Sarnoff with that of an advancing glacier. A question asked often during the next half century was: What makes David run? And, equally pertinent: What makes David *win?*

Certain findings seem relevant. He was only ten years old when he assumed a major role in the support of his family. Decision-making and leadership were ways of insuring survival in his ghetto neighborhood. By good luck, he had been born into a family steeped in the tradition of scholarship and hard work. The hamlet of Uzlian in the Russian province of Ninsk was his birthplace. Its several hundred families performed good deeds day after day, and the supreme good deed, they had been taught, was to become learned. With no luxuries, living from hand to mouth, they learned to endure hardship with no bitterness and without accepting defeat. Young David absorbed these qualities. At a time when most children were learning their alphabet, he could recite entire pages from the Pentateuch. When his father went to America to seek his fortune, the boy was dispatched for further training to a relative who was a rabbi.

After four years, Father Sarnoff, a struggling paperhanger in New York, sent for his family. They arrived during the summer of 1900. Three months later, David enrolled in a class for immigrant children. Within a year, he was reading and speaking English.

Even then, the urge for self-improvement possessed him. He borrowed books from a nearby library and read them while walking to and from school. He joined a debating society to gain speaking experience. To fortify the family budget, he became a newsboy and then a newsstand owner.

Horatio Alger could have scripted the remainder of his life. Newsboy, office boy, telegrapher, inspector, chief inspector, department manager, general manager, president. The year was 1914 when he became a department manager.

In January, he and two Marconi engineers sat with Columbia University undergraduate Edwin Armstrong in the latter's laboratory and watched a demonstration of the newly invented "feedback" circuit. A locked black box the size of a breadbasket secreted Armstrong's latest circuitry. Rumor said that he had a way of "feeding back" a fraction of the electrical charge passing through the tube's grid, creating a kind of merry-go-round current which, with each revolution, multiplied itself a thousandfold.

"Put on the earphones," Armstrong invited. "Tell me what you hear."

Sarnoff heard code messages from far beyond the usual range. Some came from Europe. One, unbelievably, came from Hawaii. "Phenomenal," he said.

Step-by-step, an evolution of ideas was erasing the impediment of space. To Armstrong, the demonstration was a victory for science. To Sarnoff, it opened a vista of global communications which, with proper organization and industry, could render unprecedented services to men and nations. These must have been heady thoughts even for such brilliant young minds. Each youth was just twenty-three years old.

3

The Admirals and Generals Take Over

An assassin's bullet, fired into the body of an Archduke, started radio's next period of growth.

In Europe, an anarchist killed Archduke Francis Ferdinand of Austria, igniting long-suppressed racial and commercial conflicts. Huge armies mobilized and manned frontier stations. Germany, Austria and Turkey were on one side, England, France and Russia on the other. Later, many nations, including the U.S.A., would be engulfed by World War I.

In America, business continued as usual for some time. The Atlantic Ocean was her frontier and it could not be crossed by an enemy. The Panama Canal opened and the first ships sailed through. Henry Ford designed a new production line and raised the wages of his workers from $2.40 to $5 per day.

The American Telephone & Telegraph Company was stringing wires westward and installing their new vacuum tubes in circuits that stretched across the Rockies. Telephone service from coast to coast would be available in 1916. A few industries began to convert to the manufacture of military supplies for the Allies, England, France and Russia. Makers of radio parts received special encouragement. In the event of our being drawn into the war, there would be a need for endless quantities of vacuum tubes, those Marconi-owned diodes with their De Forest grids, and all of them using the Armstrong feedback circuit. Their supply would depend on a miracle of cooperation. Hugging their patents, the jealous patent-holders glared at each

other, each one unable to move without permission from the others.

Onrushing events plus a series of aerial traffic jams dissolved the impasse. Preparing to go on a war footing, the U.S. government placed orders for undreamed-of quantities of parts and sets. General Electric, the nation's largest supplier of electric lamps, was asked to convert its glassblowing machinery to war work. The Signal Corps placed a trial order for eighty thousand tubes.

"We don't own the rights. We're not permitted to make them," a GE executive explained.

"You produce the tubes. We'll take care of the rights," said the government.

David Sarnoff was in the midst of every development. He knew the instrumentation and personnel needed for all levels of communication, whether transoceanic or for battalion commanders. As he saw units pouring off production lines, each using the patents of dozens of inventors, an idea crystallized. Only a peacetime pool of patents would ever permit the art of radio communications to reach its utmost potential, a consortium bringing together all the ideas of Marconi, Fessenden, De Forest, Fleming and hundreds of others, perhaps even those of Alexander Popov, the Russian genius, and Adolphus Slaby of Germany's Telefunken. Cross-licensing could do it, giving everybody, for a fee, the right to use whatever was needed.

Meanwhile, the U.S. Navy had a new idea.

Of all government agencies, it alone had broad experience with radio operations. Besides, various brass hats had been irked on occasion by the inability of their transmissions to pierce the mounting bedlam of amateur chatter. Clearly, someone had to take charge. They regarded the law passed by Congress back in 1912 as a pussyfooting failure. They were right. It said every wireless station must have a license from the government, and that every transmitter had to be served by a licensed operator, but it mentioned nothing about hours of operation, amount of power, or wavelength assignments that would reduce interference. In Washington, admirals leaked their unhappiness to friends in Congress. Sooner or later, they said, national defense would force some agency to bring order out of the current chaos.

"Why not let the Navy do it now?" they asked.

The idea was reasonable. The admirals were interested in radio as a device for transmitting messages between ships; it was much more efficient than their recently abandoned carrier pigeons. But their arguments were contested by civilians who held a different vision. Young Sarnoff was one of them, his restless mind ranging ahead to postwar possibilities. One day he expressed his thoughts in a precise

David Sarnoff, young and ambitious, proposed a "Radio Music Box"—and proposed it and proposed it. One result—years later— was this handy gadget.

memorandum to his superiors. He also filed a carbon copy. Thus, we can read in 1970 the same remarkable sentences that appeared in 1916 on the desk of his boss, Edward J. Nally, general manager of the Marconi Company of America:

"I have in mind a plan of development which would make radio a 'household utility' in the same sense as the piano or phonograph . . .

"The receiver can be designed in the form of a simple 'Radio Music Box' and arranged for several different wavelengths, which would be changeable with the throwing of a single switch . . .

"The 'Radio Music Box' can be supplied with amplifying tubes and a loudspeaking telephone, all of which can be neatly mounted in one box. The box can be placed in the parlor or living room . . .

"The principle can be extended to other fields—as, for example, receiving lectures at home . . . This proposition would be especially interesting to farmers and others living in outlying districts removed from cities. By the purchase of a 'Radio Music Box' they could enjoy concerts, lectures, music, recitals, etc. . . ."

What was an aging telegraph executive to think? The recom-

World War I recruits like these used radios to lick the Kaiser, to pick up late news, and for entertainment. When they came home, they made their own sets out of coffee cans and doorbell batteries. Result? The $3 billion a year broadcast business of 1970.

mendation involved broadcasting entertainment rather than dispatches. It seemed heretical, even a bit disloyal. Surely there were already enough Victrolas and other record-playing music boxes to satisfy the demand. Though the memo suffered a pocket veto, Sarnoff, conditioned by a thousand encounters with adversity, swallowed his disappointment and resolved to try again some other day.

In the meantime, changes were occurring throughout the industry. The Marconi Company of America reorganized itself, creating a commercial department with more than seven hundred employees serving Marconi installations on more than five hundred ocean liners and freighters, negotiating new contracts, hiring and training operating personnel and regulating traffic. Its manager? David Sarnoff.

In Washington, an Inter-department Committee on Radio Legislation delivered a plan to Congress that would subordinate private enterprise to Navy control. High level sources said that the administration favored a system under which the Navy would build and operate tax-supported stations in competition with private concerns, both in war and peace. Industry spokesmen, backing up the cause of free enterprise, fought the take-over. Who was their spokesman before the Congressional committee? David Sarnoff. At his initial appearance, he embarked upon what his biographer, Eugene Lyons, called a "lifetime assignment" to maintain the independence of broadcasting.

Months earlier U.S. citizens had been shocked by the callous sinking without warning of the British liner *Lusitania* by a German submarine. Among the 1198 passengers who drowned, sixty-three were babies. One hundred and twenty-four of the dead were Americans. The German government promised to stop unlimited warfare, offered to pay reparations, but continued to sink ships regardless.

On February 3, 1917, President Wilson broke off diplomatic relations, and said to the U.S. Senate, "I think you will agree with me that this government has no alternative consistent with the dignity and honor of the United States." That same day, a submarine sank the U.S.S. *Housatonic*. The United States was at war.

For America, the subsequent upheaval was without precedent. For months a part of its army had been chasing Pancho Villa through Mexico. Troops were brought home in a hurry. A conscription act was passed. In April President Wilson signed an executive order placing all radio facilities under government jurisdiction, with the admirals in charge, officers who were in deadly earnest about pooling patents in order to produce the most efficient transmitters and receivers that could be designed.

Above, left: Amateurs and experimenters had a field day. This lad used the frame of an umbrella for his aerial. Above: Learned lecturers spoke to distant listeners. Left: The kiddies, helmeted and wired for sound, posed prettily through the bedtime story.

Many amateurs were shocked by an order directing them to take down their antennas and seal their instruments for the duration. In the East, detectives had already apprehended German hirelings operating illicit stations. Dutifully, the hams obeyed.

As an American Expeditionary Force took shape under General John J. Pershing, wireless equipment was allotted to infantry, artillery cavalry and the budding air force—then a branch of the Signal Corps. Pleas went out for volunteers to man the newfangled sets. Countless amateurs found a mission for which they had been preparing without knowing it.

Radio schools were established by the Armed Forces at Mare Island, California, and at Harvard, Loyola, Ohio and other universities. Many recruits were already radio experts but many others were teen-age enthusiasts enrolling in a glamorous vocation.

Within the year, they would be at sea or in a trench in France, helping to expand radio's services. Their routine missions were transmitting orders or establishing contact with missing units, such as the Army's famous "Lost Battalion." The delivery of regular news dispatches to battleships and infantrymen on patrol was an unprecedented, morale-boosting exercise.

In a score of factories, suppliers were turning out amazing sets and standard parts, each representing a goulash of patent rights. Nobody worried. For the first time, many manufacturers were producing in sufficient volume to show a profit. Marconi, largest of the suppliers for 1917, sold the government equipment worth $5 million. Everybody said the Navy was doing a great job, and so was radio.

One reason was a mighty monster called the Alexanderson alternator. Seeking a source of superpower at the turn of the century, Professor Fessenden had sketched out a difficult new concept and turned it over to the General Electric Company for development. A young engineer, E. F. W. Alexanderson, who had studied with some of the best scientists in Europe, took it from there. In due course, he delivered a machine that could revolve an "impossible" twenty thousand times a *second*, and produce a thundering kilowatt of power. By 1917 GE was manufacturing and selling alternators that were fifty times more powerful.

Guglielmo Marconi was a man who also knew their value. Before the war, he had piloted his floating lab, the yacht *Elettra*, up to Albany to visit GE's House of Magic at nearby Schenectady and to talk business. Eventually, he had talked very big business, seeking to buy all the alternators that GE could produce. Multimillions were involved. By controlling the only known source of superpower, he would have made more millions.

To implement that dream, the Marconi Company of Americas was pouring its brains and capital into the world's largest transmitter at New Brunswick, New Jersey. A 50 kilowatt Alexanderson alternator would be its centerpiece. According to plans, its signals could easily cross the ocean both night and day. When war was declared in 1917, the Navy smoothly assumed control. It finished building and equipping Marconi's dream station and installed the giant alternator. Later, it would add a more powerful 200 kilowatt machine. From the first, results were fantastic. Unprecedented clarity was achieved over improbable distances. The station's call letters, NNF, soon became famous around the world.

Philosophers have frequently observed that wars and other calamities accelerate man's ingenuity. It happened again in 1917–1918. Inventors examined many old ideas seeking new uses. The Navy encouraged research as the only way to stay ahead of German scientists. Back in 1915, Navy engineers had banked scores of vacuum tubes into a single device, hoping to develop enough power to broadcast the human voice. Incredibly, their words were picked up on the West Coast and even in the Hawaiian Islands. One exuberant songwriter memorialized the occasion with a new hit tune, "Hello, Hawaii, How Are You?"

In Pittsburgh, the Westinghouse Electric and Manufacturing

Company received Navy permission to experiment with two stations. The assistant chief engineer, Dr. Frank Conrad, had been a radio buff for years and now the state of war provided fresh impetus to his persistent and scientific thoughts. His garage at Wilkinsburg, Pennsylvania, contained one transmitter. The Westinghouse plant in nearby East Pittsburgh held the other. His assignment? To field-test some of the thousands of radio units being turned out by Westinghouse.

Early military sets were telegraphic. Later, interest veered to telephony. Conrad worked with both, trying to defeat the gremlin that bugged all early telephony, lack of distance. Eventually his success would introduce a new era in communications, one that would have its fiftieth birthday in 1970.

In Washington, an event took place that can be counted as an electronic milestone. It was the broadcasting of President Wilson's Fourteen Points.

After years of warfare, the vast military confrontation had degenerated into a muddy, bloody stalemate, leaving millions dead or maimed. Leaders and nations seemed to be paralyzed by hopelessness. Wilson's Fourteen Points were a fresh breeze from the New World. Within hours of his appearance before the Congress, code and voice radio telegraphy had hurled his words across the miles. That same night, they were the chief topic of discussion in chancelleries around the world. And in trenches and submarines, soldiers and sailors, huddled around their sets, felt a flicker of hope for the first time in months. In dozens of cities, stimulated by the newspaper headlines, millions of mothers and fathers rejoiced at this humane peace proposal addressed to the people themselves. Broadcasting had given hope to a war-weary world, stepping over walls and gunfire as if they were curbstones.

America's best radio weapon was the super-station NNF. Later her naval operators would deliver another vital message. The sender was President Wilson. Addressing enemy citizens man to man, he said, "Your cause is lost. Depose your kaiser, accept my Fourteen Points, and you will be treated fairly."

This was a new kind of warfare, talking across the trenches, talking across the ocean. Nobody knew what effect it might have until more than a million U.S. troops charged forward on September 26. Their objective was a German rail line beyond the Argonne Forest. If the Allies could control it, the Kaiser's divisions would have to withdraw.

In that offensive, each American unit had its own radio cart or carrier. Served by men or mules, it gave the generals unprecedented control of their forces. By day, U.S. airplanes circled the battlefield, sending back radio messages that corrected the fire of artillery batteries. Slowly, troops that had been dug into German caves were forced to retreat. When the German nation heard the news, it lost heart. Suddenly, everyone in the Fatherland was talking about Wilson's points. At the other end of the front, the Austrian army abruptly surrendered to Italy.

On November 6, an unprecedented wireless message was placed in the hands of the Supreme Allied Commander, General Ferdinand Foch of the French Army. German officials were asking him to name a place to which they could come to sign an armistice. His reply named a railway siding near the northern village of Compiègne.

Within days, other radio transmissions told of civilians and sailors rebelling in Kiel and Hamburg. The Province of Bavaria renounced the German state and declared herself a republic. In Central Europe, the armies of Bulgaria and Turkey gave up. November 9 brought the best news of all. Kaiser Wilhelm II had abdicated and fled to Holland. Forty-eight hours later, German army commanders walked into General Foch's railway car and signed a document of surrender.

Thus ended the first international conflict in which the tamed electron saw combat service. Now its use for peaceful purpose could be planned, to better man's lot instead of destroying him.

Certain of our nation's leaders had other ideas.

57

4

Patent, Patent, Who's Got the Patent?

The reaction to victory was swift and wild. The killing was over. The boys were coming home. Now, a new goal—get back to business.

"How can we do business without merchandise?" asked store proprietors along Radio Row. "We've got no parts. We've got no sets."

"Make them yourselves."

"We don't have patents," they answered. "So we make a few sets and right away get sued."

Acquiring patents permitting the manufacture of radio receivers soon became the principal obsession of powerful corporations and ambitious men. For the moment, their intentions were obscured by a general lassitude that enveloped the nation. The slaughter was over; the nation had mobilized 4.5 million men, sent most of them abroad and brought them home. Now America wanted to relax.

Gradually, as the nation's bloodstream cleansed itself of war work, men began to plan and design and execute. They fell into three general groups: manufacturers, financiers and amateur radio enthusiasts. Eventually their interests would coalesce in a giant technological breakthrough. But at the moment they had to survive a powerful challenge.

Even while Johnnie was marching home again, a bill was dropped unobtrusively into the hopper of the U.S. House of Representatives. It proposed that radio be made a peacetime responsibility of the U.S. Navy, just as the Army had its year-in-year-out assignments

of building dams and dredging waterways. The bill was supported by a formidable covey of politicians who testified for it.

Secretary of the Navy Josephus Daniels led off with a candid demand for a military monopoly. "We would lose much by opening up the use of radio communications again to rival companies," he asserted. "The passage of this bill will secure for all time the control of radio in the United States."

Reaction was prompt and forceful, some visible and some behind the scenes. The president of the Marconi Company of America put it this way: "We planted the seed, plowed the ground, and kept out the weeds. Now, when we are ready to harvest, the government comes in and says, 'We want that crop.'"

Radio amateurs hastily wrote letters to their congressmen. Their leader, Dr. Hiram Maxim, a famous inventor of firearms, spoke up in their behalf: "They're the best scientific brains in this nation. If you give this thing to the Navy, and block these boys out, you'll lose much more than you'll gain."

The bill died in committee. The development of radio would not be threatened by military control for another generation.

At this juncture, the American Marconi company proposed a transaction which—though they did not suspect it—would result in their suicide. They returned to the General Electric Company with their prewar proposal to gain control of GE's Alexanderson alternator, the only known device that could be counted on to pump messages across the oceans. The chairman of the board of General Electric was Owen D. Young, an ex-farm boy whose interests now encompassed the globe. A creator of power, he perceived the value of controlling its distribution. One form of power was intelligence and information. Beyond our Atlantic and Pacific coasts, information was transmitted almost exclusively over cable or wireless circuits controlled by our British cousins. He had an idea that would keep this power in American hands. He resolved to make some changes.

Word reached Young that Marconi and his own GE negotiators had agreed upon a price of more than $4 million for two dozen giant alternators. With them in operation, the British could girdle the earth and dominate the communications industry. Young wrote a quick letter stating his alarm to a friend, a young Acting Secretary of the Navy named Franklin D. Roosevelt.

In swift succession, giant steps were taken to protect American interests—and Owen D. Young's ambitions. Roosevelt sent Young's letter to Commander S. C. Cooper, in charge of naval radio activities, who got in touch with Secretary Daniels in Paris, who got back to

Roosevelt. The latter fired off a letter to Young, half request and half command, asking him not to sign any concordat with any foreign corporation until GE had conferred with Washington. Young was delighted to oblige.

Soon meetings were held, and the result was that Young was officially encouraged to create the communications empire he had visualized from the beginning. The new corporation would own all the patents it would ever need. It would buy out the American Marconi company and thus liberate U.S. communications from a foreign monopoly and at the same time acquire valuable licenses. As a partner, Young chose AT&T. General Electric had money, some key patents and international contacts, but AT&T had the De Forest patents plus others and vast operating experience.

Was the phone company interested in radio? The AT&T had extended its long lines to California by adapting De Forest's radio invention. Some of its executives were talking about setting up their own broadcasting station and renting it to all comers, like a public pay booth. In Deal, New Jersey, their engineers were erecting a brand-new ship-to-shore station. Interested? They were already in radio up to their earphones. Still, there was the patent problem. Their De Forest tube infringed the Fleming tube patent which was owned by Marconi. But the De Forest grid, without which the tube was worthless, belonged to AT&T. A patent pool would solve everything.

Considerable encouragement came from Washington. Agreements were drawn, and on June 30, 1921, documents were signed in the interests of patriotism and profits. The new corporation charter limited its board of directors to U.S. citizens. Only one-fifth of its stock could be held by foreign citizens. Its patriotic founders called it the Radio Corporation of America.

American Marconi knew they were licked. The Navy department still held most of their land stations and was not likely to return them to any company controlled in London. After a month of hard negotiating, all their operations and assets were transferred to RCA. The Marconi ex-president, Edward J. Nally, became RCA's first president, and Owen D. Young became its chairman. Within hours, RCA was a success, absorbing all the Marconi employees, running all its old services, and transmitting messages to England at the bargain rate of seventeen cents per word.

One new RCA employee, by way of the Marconi take-over, was young, restless David Sarnoff, strategically placed as the manager of the RCA commercial department. Now he recalled his 1915 memo, once vainly submitted to the old Marconi management. It discussed

World War I ideas were incorporated in this first-of-all mass production Westinghouse receiver of 1921. Months would pass before somebody would suggest adding a loudspeaker.

62

the future of radio in terms that as yet almost no one visualized. He retrieved it from his files, and marked it for the attention of his new boss, Owen D. Young.

The sales price of a music box, he estimated, would be about $75. Information on future broadcasts would reach the public through the RCA magazine to be called *The Wireless Age,* a forerunner of *TV Guide,* which could become self-supporting through advertising revenue. The profits gained from the sale of music boxes, Sarnoff said, would enable RCA to build and operate broadcasting stations.

"What profits are you talking about?" a query from the GE president asked. Sarnoff's estimates were ready. "In our first year," he wrote, "I think we can sell 100,000 music boxes. In our second year, at least 300,000. In our third year, 600,000 more. That's one million music boxes at $75 each. A gross revenue of $75 million. There'll be a profit, all right!"

Large bodies move slowly. RCA tossed young Sarnoff a bone: $2,000 with which to build one experimental music box. The notion of entertainment was still slightly abhorrent to those starchy communicators and lawyers.

It is hard to realize that the building of a new electronic empire took place against a background of much industrial distress. One sufferer was a Pittsburgh company named after George Westinghouse, who made his first fortune from inventing and manufacturing air brakes for railway cars. During the war, Westinghouse had converted much of its manufacturing facilities to electronic equipment for the armed forces. In 1919 its contracts were canceled, its factories idle and its management desperately seeking an escape from the dilemma of readjustment. Nor were its officers heartened by reports of a marriage of convenience between their bitter rival, GE, and AT&T.

RCA's patent round-up had swept in most everything except those issued to Professor Fessenden. These were controlled by the heir of one of his backers, who lived just down the street from the Westinghouse plant. He eagerly agreed to the financial arrangements that Westinghouse offered.

Westinghouse men next scoured the labs of Europe, but Owen D. Young had already been there. Then they heard that Major Edwin A. Armstrong, honorably discharged from the Army Signal Corps, had returned from France with a new circuit idea patented while he was abroad. Rumor claimed that it was many times more powerful than his earlier feedback.

"I call it," said Armstrong, "a superheterodyne circuit."

They offered him $335,000 to be paid over a period of ten

years. His acceptance of the contract gave Westinghouse an ace to tuck up its sleeve.

Step two in the Westinghouse renaissance was the conversion of a point-to-point experimental station into one designed to serve the entire community. Their efforts were aided by two talented engineers, Frank Conrad and D. G. Little. Conrad had been a radio buff for years and knew most of the prewar operators in his area. Little was a ham from Kalamazoo, Michigan.

When the war in Europe ended and the United States took the wraps off domestic radio, Conrad was one of the first to put his old transmitter back on the air. Other experimenters across the nation were doing the same thing. Conrad did it best, got the biggest press, and soon he and Westinghouse and KDKA were famous.

But early in 1919 he was concerned almost entirely with the quality of his signal and the distance it would travel. Ben Gross tells about it in *I Looked and I Listened.*

"Night after night, he would enter his garage, turn on the mysterious machine, and read from newspapers into the microphone. Men stationed at listening posts in nearby areas listened and reported on the quality of reception."

These men grew tired of Dr. Conrad's voice and the news they had already read in their papers. "How about playing some phonograph records?" one of them suggested. Dr. Conrad did so. Shortly letters began to pour into the Westinghouse headquarters. The "hams"—the checkers—had turned into critics.

" 'Give us some new records,' wrote one. 'I'd appreciate it if you would let me hear "Silver Threads Among The Gold," ' said another. Soon most of the mail was made up of requests . . ."

Without realizing it, Dr. Conrad, had become the world's first disc jockey.

A department manager in the Joseph Horne Department Store in Pittsburgh, alert to a potential profit, realized that people who might want to listen to Conrad might also be willing to buy ready-made radios. His advertisement appeared in the Pittsburgh *Sun* of September 29, 1920. Actually, it was more a news story than an ad.

It read: "Victrola music played into the air over a wireless telephone was 'picked up' on the wireless receiving station recently installed here for patrons interested in wireless experiments." It mentioned a soprano solo "which rang particularly high and clear." It said Mr. Conrad, a wireless enthusiast, "puts on" the wireless concerts periodically for the entertainment of persons with wireless sets.

The ad concluded with a modest sales pitch: "Amateur Wire-

less Sets, made by the maker of the Set which is in operation in our store, are on sale here, $10.00 up."

That same day engineer Conrad and a Westinghouse vice president, H. P. Davis, held a fateful conversation. Both had read the ad. What was dawning on them had nothing to do with telephony. Instead, it was the existence of a potential market for small parlor wireless receivers—like Sarnoff's music box—which Westinghouse could manufacture in its idle factories. "We've already got the design," Davis said. "It's that SCR-70 we made for the armed forces. It's light and all in one piece and anybody can operate it. Conceivably it could sell a million."

Was he right about the opportunity? Did people really want to turn a switch and listen to music? Time would tell. An official decision was made to install a new transmitter of greater power and to establish a station designed for public entertainment and service. Opening day was set to coincide with the biggest news story of the year, the Presidential election of 1920.

Conrad and Little now had a fresh objective: to get the biggest possible audience. Just before the election, tension mounted unbearably. The new station was not ready. No license had arrived from Washington giving Westinghouse authority to go on the air with a hopped-up signal.

Campaigners for publisher James M. Cox and Senator Warren G. Harding came and went singing the blues. Never was any nation more bedeviled than in 1919 and 1920.

The Ku Klux Klan had 4 million members and was growing. Communists were organizing some of the labor unions and taking control. To some, the country was teetering on the verge of anarchy.

Steelworkers, tired of working twelve-hour days, seven days a week, struck at every U.S. steel plant—343,000 men walked out.

In Boston, police went on strike and permitted criminals to roam the Commons. Belatedly, a governor named Calvin Coolidge sent in the Massachusetts National Guard.

Bombs were discovered in U.S. post offices addressed to prominent citizens, leading to the rumor of a Communist plot to murder every leader who was not sympathetic to trade unions.

Whites and blacks in Chicago argued about bathing-beach rights on the lakefront, began to fight and the riot spread throughout the city. White gangs invaded Negro districts, beating up people and destroying property. The fighting raged for four days, and left twenty-three whites and fifteen Negroes dead, plus five hundred injured. That year, twenty-five other cities were hit by race riots.

Did the nation want more of the same? Vote for Cox! Did the nation want a change? Vote for Harding! At the last minute, a license arrived from Washington naming the new station KDKA. Workmen took so long to hook up the equipment that Conrad and Little made their inaugural broadcast without a signal test.

The Pittsburgh *Post* had agreed to telephone wire service reports as they came over the ticker. A Westinghouse publicity man copied down the figures and read them over the air. Between reports, he played phonograph records. By midnight everyone knew that Senator Harding had won a landslide victory. But KDKA listeners knew it first, and they heard the news while sitting in their warm, dry homes while other citizens stood in the rain reading newspaper bulletin boards. Harding got 16,000,000 votes. Cox got 9,150,000. Since then KDKA Pittsburgh, WWJ Detroit, KCBS San Francisco and WHA Madison, Wisconsin, have laid claim to being first on the air. A further complication was added in 1969, when The Netherlands' government announced that one of its radio stations was the world's first. No claim has been entered thus far by the USSR. Orrin E. Dunlop, Jr., veteran radio columnist for *The New York Times* and later an RCA vice president, tried to unravel the problem, but he only went back to 1921.

Opposite: Radio sold itself. Dealers carried battery-powered miracles from house to house and gave front-porch demonstrations. Above: Probably the first retail ad to offer a "wireless telephone" to the public was this notice in a Pittsburgh newspaper. The price was $10—and up. By 1925, the first "portable" appeared. RCA's Radiola was a lineal ancestor to the midget transistor that now covers the earth.

He found that the first *and regular* broadcast license was issued to WBZ, Springfield, Massachusetts, September 15, 1921. WWJ, Detroit, was issued its first regular license October 13, 1921. KDKA was issued its first regular license October 13, 1921. However, Pittsburgh had held an experimental license dated October 27, 1920; that license arrived just before the Harding-Cox election.

For reasons lost in time, newspapers all over America gave the KDKA election broadcast the full story-and-picture treatment. WWJ in Detroit had done the same thing but its effort was scarcely mentioned. Letters poured into the Westinghouse headquarters from listeners, even from ships at sea, asking for more. KDKA obliged with a program schedule that they printed and mailed, eventually to a list of two thousand newspapers.

At first there was no studio; many broadcasts came from a tent. Since remote pickups got public attention, a church service, a prizefight, a baseball game and a Davis Cup tennis match went over the airwaves. When Herbert Hoover visited Pittsburgh to raise funds for European relief, he made his plea via the new medium. And William Jennings Bryan and Teddy Roosevelt were initiated into the tiny brotherhood of broadcasters.

Soon farmers asked for a program of their own. Conrad and Little served them bulletins, approved by Washington, giving prices for livestock, hay and grain, as well as weather reports.

As the publicity spread, other stations opened elsewhere, with many types of programs. From coast to coast, cities began to develop their own electronic enclaves, based usually on some enthusiastic amateur with a pile of phonograph records and a transmitter surrounded by a peppering of individual owners of receivers.

David Sarnoff, busy with many new duties, did not fail to note the connection between transmitter growth and the expanding market for receivers. His earlier memos had anticipated it. That a rival company was doing what he had proposed was bitter medicine.

Disquieting rumors told of other Westinghouse forays into the field he had marked out as his own. Already, their 100-watt transmitter had been abandoned in favor of equipment five times as powerful. The result was new listeners, new enthusiasm and an expanding market for sets. The Westinghouse management, reports said, was very high on this new notion of programmed broadcasting. So high, in fact, that it was secretly preparing duplicate transmitting stations which would be unveiled presently in such cities as Newark, Chicago and Springfield, Massachusetts.

WBZ opened in Springfield in September of 1921.

WJZ Newark opened in October.

KYW opened in Chicago thirty days later.

But already Owen D. Young had moved another pawn on the radio chessboard. Why not take Westinghouse into the GE-AT&T-RCA pool? Its patents were valuable. Its broadcasting know-how was unique. Young made the proposal to his board of directors and heard their approval, including that of the observer representing the U.S. government. Nobody mentioned that RCA might be breaking the law.

Two or three months earlier, a minor agreement with the United Fruit Company had provided a precedent. The company's patents had been added to the RCA pool and its shore stations (some in Central America) had been taken over for RCA communications in exchange for value received. Now, giant Westinghouse, GE's bitterest rival, accepted RCA's hegemony in the worldwide radio empire.

The line-up of stockholders in the Radio Corporation of America finally looked like this:

General Electric owned	*30.1% of RCA stock*
Westinghouse	*20.6%*
AT&T	*10.3%*
United Fruit	*4.1%*
Other investors	*34.9%*

Below: A man, a typewriter, a phonograph and some records was the program department of WJZ Newark, New Jersey operation in 1921.
Bottom: Radio's most famous election broadcast—the Harding-Cox returns that made KDKA Pittsburgh famous—was achieved without computers, anchormen or forecasters, but by a crew of four pioneers.

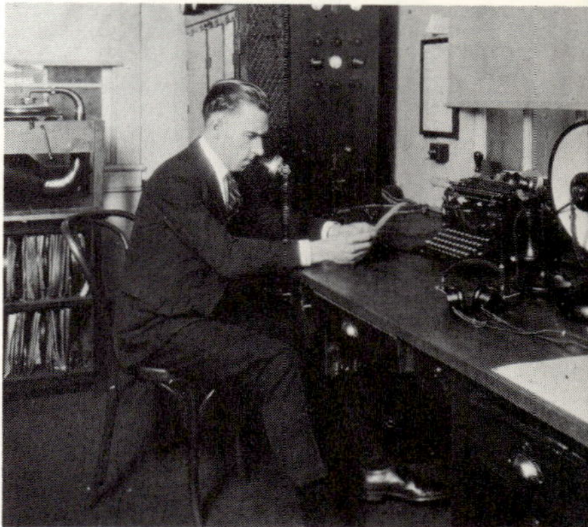

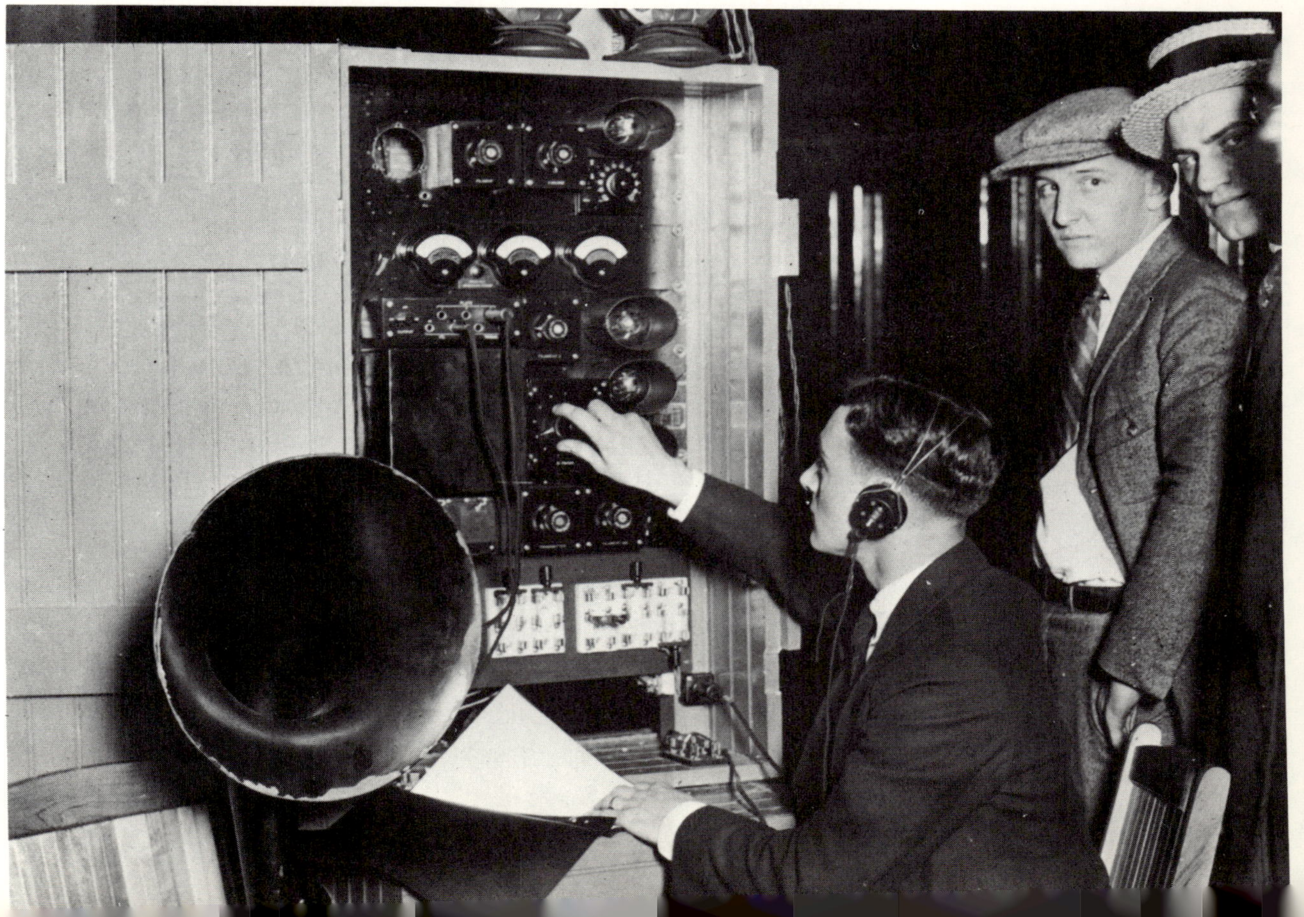

William Jennings Bryan spoke from the Point Breeze Presbyterian Church in Pittsburgh in 1922. It was his first broadcast and one of the first "remotes" in history. KDKA carried it.

Westinghouse agreed to contribute its patents to the patent pool and received, in turn, the right to use all RCA patents. Westinghouse was assigned the task of manufacturing 40 percent of all the sets RCA could sell, at a guaranteed profit of 20 percent. RCA would manufacture the remainder.

In Manhattan, thirty-year-old David Sarnoff was not impressed by this affiliation; rather, he anticipated more trouble than ever in meeting the competition of smaller, fast-moving rivals whose marketing footwork was speedier than his own. As a counterbalance, he was determined to make a new name, RCA, the most significant trademark in the nation. Restlessly, he searched for some event that would rivet the public's attention on RCA and on his product. He wanted a real earthshaker, a genuine grabber. He found it in a match for the world's heavyweight boxing championship between Jack Dempsey and the French champion Georges Carpentier.

"That's it," Sarnoff told his people. "We'll broadcast it from ringside, blow-by-blow and round-by-round."

Two obstacles intervened. He had no radio station. He had no audience. Obviously, his project was insane.

But GE had just completed a powerful transmitter for the Navy that was ready for delivery. With the assistance of his friend Franklin D. Roosevelt, Sarnoff got the Navy to cooperate. He filed for a broadcasting license and ordered the transmitter shipped to the Hoboken railway yards in New Jersey, 2½ miles from the fight arena at Boyle's Thirty Acres.

Swiftly an aerial was draped between two railway towers. The phone company grudgingly provided a wire connecting the ringside with the transmitter. A shack, used by Pullman porters as a dressing room, housed all the equipment. Sarnoff had his station.

Now he wanted listeners, enthusiastic listeners—listeners who would later be called "influentials." Four phone calls provided them. One call went to Roosevelt, who provided the sponsorship of the Navy League. Another went to Anne Morgan, daughter of J. P. Morgan and head of the American Committee for Devastated France, who promised support by her group. A third went to Marcus Loew, owner of a chain of motion-picture houses, who agreed to contribute his auditoriums for the night of the fight and carry the broadcast "live" on loudspeakers playing for paying customers. Miss Morgan's committee and the Navy League would get a share of the receipts. Loew's theaters would get a surefire box-office hit. RCA would get publicity. That was only the beginning. Where theaters were not available, groups of people rented their own halls, school auditoriums and clubs.

On fight night, July 2, 1921, Major Andrew White, editor of the radio magazine *Wireless Age*, turned fight announcer, with Sarnoff sitting apprehensively at his side. The signal went out over WJZ and WJY. The action was fast, but was it too fast for the untrained ears of captive listeners? Nobody would know until morning.

It was perfect! Aided by White's description of blows struck and countered, each listener filled in the blanks, creating his own contest. Approximately 200,000 patrons of clubs and theaters, not to mention uncounted amateur set-owners, were thrilled by their first boxing broadcast. Since Jack Dempsey had defeated the French challenger, Georges Carpentier, perhaps a glow of patriotic pleasure increased their satisfaction.

When it was over, everyone in broadcasting could feel the dawning of a new age. Deep in their bones, they knew that the '20s would be a time of progress and perdition, of winning and losing. Most of all, the members of the patent pool, GE, AT&T, Westinghouse, et al, saw their places of power as unassailable.

So let the boom come! RCA was poised to claim the lion's share. It seemed impossible that so happy a dream could turn into a nightmare.

5
Growing Pains

In 1922 broadcasting was an infant—the brawlingest, noisiest toddler this nation had ever seen. It had parents and godparents aplenty, but no two of them could agree as their child fattened on the heady pablum of jazz, bathtub gin and laissez-faire.

Earlier technological breakthroughs had crept gradually into the nation's daily life. Electric lights and telephone services had spread slowly from cities to small towns as poles were erected and wires strung. Automobiles had stalled on hills and stuck in the mud for years. But broadcasting exploded across the U.S.A. like a series of Fourth of July pinwheels spraying the sky with sparks that talked.

Warren G. Harding was President, Herbert Hoover was Secretary of Commerce and Andrew Mellon was Secretary of the Treasury. They agreed that the government's business was to help business, and their policies caused stock prices to rise and the money supply to swell. But something also was happening to the people. An impatient and indecorous spirit possessed both young and old. F. Scott Fitzgerald, idol of the jazz age, described what he saw happening to the older generation, the parents of flappers and tea-hoppers. They acted, he said, as if "tired of watching the carnival with ill-conceived envy, [they] had discovered that young liquor will take the place of young blood, and with a whoop, the orgy began . . . A whole society going hedonistic, deciding on pleasure."

Within a year, licensed radio stations zoomed from a sprin-

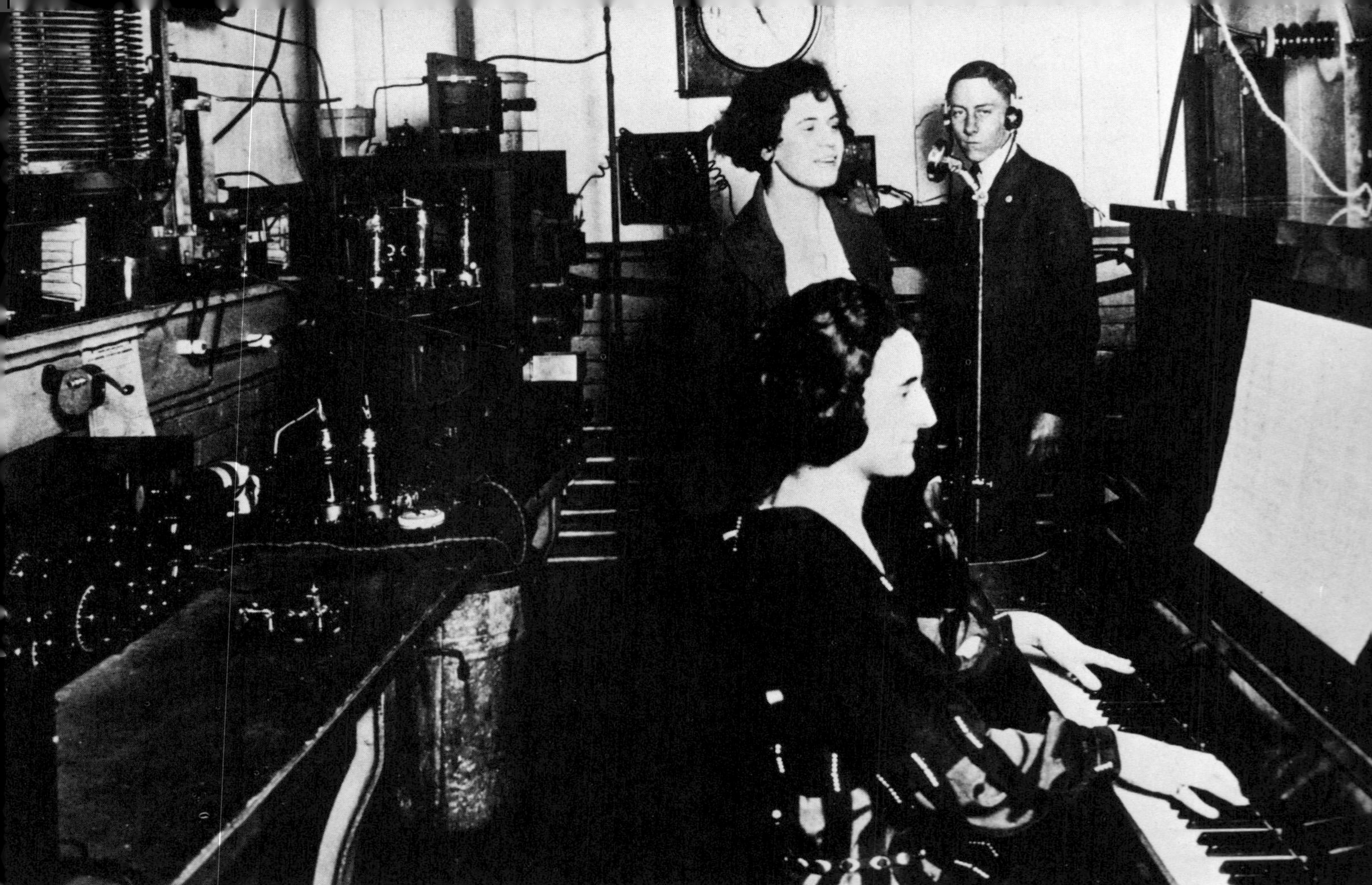

kling of sixty to applications for more than five hundred. The frenzy to own and operate a transmitter spread to all kinds of men and institutions. Church steeples sprouted aerials, and colleges applied by the score. That spring, the young man in the Department of Commerce who allocated call letters to applicants announced that he had run out of three-letter combinations and licensing was at a standstill. When permission was granted for four-letter combinations, the crisis ended.

Some people called it a gold rush, but precious little gold would be mined any time soon. The rush included newspapers in Detroit, Chicago, Rochester, Atlanta, St. Louis, Des Moines, Fort Worth, Spokane, Los Angeles, New Orleans, Richmond—with a dozen other publications readying their applications.

Erik Barnouw, in *A Tower in Babel*, documents the almost senseless variety of business concerns who joined the club: "Radio was a crowd-maker, and the stores loved it. . . . Stations were also started by a stockyard (WAAF Chicago), a marble company (KHD Colorado Springs), a laundry (KUS Los Angeles), a poultry farm (WPG New Lebanon). Several were started by rich men as hobbies."

An enginering oddity of the day was the wavelength assignment. Regulations said that a place on the spectrum at 360 meters (618 kilocycles) was available for entertainment, talks and news; every station was ordered to broadcast on that same frequency. An exception was required when transmitting weather information; in that case, the transmitter switched to 485 meters. It was a mindless regulation and it was applied relentlessly during radio's early days. Finally, overlapping signals churned the air into chaos and forced official revision.

About that time, the Bamberger department store in Newark, New Jersey, wanted a place on the radio bandwagon. The government gave it the call letters WOR. New Jersey had been WJZ territory. Surely a conflict impended. The Department of Commerce said that no law or regulation applied. It was up to the stations to work it out between themselves.

The manager of WOR called the manager of WJZ. "We'd like to have our premiere program on next Washington's Birthday," he explained. "Would you mind staying off the air?"

"Happy to oblige," said the WJZ manager. Afterward, they

The WBAY New York studio (later WEAF) was the epitome of plush carpeting, elegant draperies and stiff-collared AT&T efficiency. But its signals got lost among skyscraper skeletons.

In her time, no star was bigger than Marian Davies, and no studio was more determined that her image should not be corrupted by appearing on radio than her studio. Eventually, Hollywood's anti-radio front broke wide open, and pop entertainment took a giant step forward.

worked out a division of hours. The same thing happened in every city.

The American Telephone & Telegraph Company built a station called WBAY in downtown Manhattan. Its signal sounded like an asthmatic midget whispering through a pipe. The building's steel frame was soaking up the transmitter's energy. A second try from another building boomed out to the suburbs in Connecticut and Pennsylvania. WBAY departed from the scene and WEAF was born.

The AT&T policy is worth special comment. Its service to customers was called "toll telephony." The wording was no accident.

Telephony on a commercial basis was the exclusive province of AT&T. The new venture, AT&T was saying through its choice words, was a form of commercial telephony—reserved for AT&T and not open to GE, Westinghouse and RCA. Those companies could engage in radio telephony for their own purposes or to equip amateurs, but could not provide the general public with such a service. At stake was the revenue to be earned during all the future years of broadcasting.

Under its policy, the telephone company assumed no programming responsibility. Instead, it would rent its facilities (like a phone booth) to any passerby with a message for the world. The blueprint for tomorrow foretold a network of thirty-odd identical stations laced together by AT&T long lines One or all could be rented for a fee.

"Frankly, it's an experiment," AT&T admitted. "But if this experiment succeeds, a commercial basis for broadcasting will have been established."

The light dawned gradually. First, it became obvious that a station without regular listeners was no bargain at any price—in order for the station to survive, programming was required. Second, performers were reluctant to travel to the factory building that housed the studio. The sleazy neighborhood was spooky and badly illuminated. The discouragement of WEAF executives was somewhat dispelled when the station got its first "commercial" customer.

On August 28, 1922, a real-estate pitchman for the Queensboro Corporation rented the station for a ten-minute talk that went something like this: "The cry of the heart is for more living room, more opportunity to get near the Mother Earth, to play, to romp, to plant, to dig . . . Get away from the solid masses of brick where children grow up starved for a run over a patch of grass and sight of a tree. Apartments in congested parts of the city have proven failures . . . but imagine a city apartment lifted bodily to the middle of a large garden within twenty minutes' travel of the city's business center . . ." The final, easy step was a visit to the Queensboro apartments in Jackson Heights, New York, to "see for yourself."

Legend reports that several apartments were rented. The program cost the sponsor $50; it was the first commercial ever broadcast. Its example encouraged too few others, and the total income for the following month was only $500. Commercially, from the AT&T viewpoint, the experiment was a disaster.

Soon, the company tried another tack. Building an elaborate studio at its plush headquarters building, it hired a fine staff of salesmen and program personnel. Ad agencies took notice and so did their clients. Three of New York's leading department stores rented the refurbished "toll booth" studio and put on programs. So did the maker of Mineralava, a mudpack facial, who hired movie star Marian Davies to plug the product in a talk titled "How I Make Up for the Movies." Her program ended with an offer of an autographed portrait. Fan letters and orders arrived by the hundreds. At last, WEAF knew it had an audience.

In Newark, WJZ executives were listening to entertainers who objected to the trip from New York to New Jersey; they decided to move their studios closer to Broadway. Their Manhattan outpost was in Aeolian Hall, a cultural citadel second to none, where they installed waiting rooms and enough overstuffed furniture to comfort the most artistic ego. Soon Ted Husing and Norman Brokenshire, announcers, would be working there and making history of a sort.

But history was being made every day somewhere in America as producers tried out new ideas and personalities. WJZ broadcast the first World Series ball game on October 5, 1921. The Yanks played the Giants (four straight wins for the Yanks) and an announcer sat at a phone rigged to a last-row seat at the Polo Grounds. As he reported each play to Tom Cowan, WJZ manager and jack-of-all-trades, Cowan repeated him word-for-word into the WJZ mike. The fans at home were delighted.

VIP's were constantly solicited to make studio appearances. Nobody got paid, so why not ask the biggest names? Public events interested listeners and were easy to cover. The first formal address by an American President was broadcast in 1922 by President Harding when he dedicated the Francis Scott Key monument at Fort McHenry, in Baltimore, Maryland. Al Smith, soon to be a Presidential hopeful, was heard during his inauguration as governor of New York over WGY, Schenectady.

Some producers ad-libbed, looking for novelty. On an un-

usually hot day, a half-dozen stations could be counted on to broadcast the sound of an egg frying on some hot sidewalk. When Gar Wood, the speedboat driver, undertook to beat the Twentieth Century Limited on its run down the shore of the Hudson River, WGY put it on the air.

In Pittsburgh, KDKA equipped a touring car with a half ton of gadgets and reporters and sent it in pursuit of fires, robberies and riots. The opening of Congress, full of pomp and dullness, was first broadcast in 1923. Both political conventions of 1924 offered some bright moments, but nearly ended the career of announcer Graham McNamee who had to work from an airless booth through the longest Democratic session in history.

As stations multiplied, one-shot programs gave way to weekly presentations that would hold an audience. Suddenly, popularity became important. Fortunately, exposure of talent via the airwaves quickly built an unknown into a celebrity. First it happened to announcers. At one point, station management insisted that announcers remain anonymous, permitting only the mention of their initials. But qualities of voice and personality made such an impact on listeners that front offices soon reconsidered. Milton Cross, once a so-so tenor, rose to a distinguished role as a commentator on the world of music, first at WJZ and then on many network shows.

Song-and-patter teams, long standard fare on vaudeville bills, moved into radio. One of the first was Billy Jones and Ernie Hare, better known as the Happiness Boys. Their sponsor, the Happiness Candy Company, got its advertising plug with every mention of their name; this was the result of a management policy which frowned on direct selling but permitted the entertainers to bear the name of the sponsor. Listeners heard "The Cliquot Club Eskimos," "The Eveready Hour," "The Atwater Kent Hour," and "The Goodrich Silver Masked Tenor," among a score of similarly tagged acts.

In the South and West, talent was often programmed into a variety-type show that included home talent—comics, singers and actors. It filled an evening and everybody had fun. Broadcasting was still a glorious experience and the performer's fee was the heady feeling that maybe his words were being heard, perhaps even as far away as the next state.

But along Broadway in Manhattan, a new attitude was stiffening the necks of stage and concert veterans. They asked a telling question: Is the publicity to be gleaned from a ride on the kilocycles all that valuable? Their new attiude was that a workman was worthy of his hire. When actors asked for a wage, some stations paid them

$3 a performance. The Atwater Kent Hour, seeking the best, gave a hint of what radio might become when it hired two of the nation's greatest soloists, John McCormack and Lucrezia Bori. Formerly scornful of the new medium, they were persuaded to sing into a mike with the same beauty they had lavished on the audience in the Met's Diamond Horseshoe. Their price was $1,000 each.

It was a period of learning by doing. Ed Wynn, called the funniest man in the world, brought his Broadway hit "The Perfect Fool" to the WJZ studio one night. Spinning his best joke into the mike, he discovered that it neither applauded nor laughed. In agony, he finally turned to the announcer, saying, "I can't continue."

The show-wise announcer raced into the hall and collected an audience of scrubwomen, telephone girls and visitors and hastily shoved them into the studio. Excited and delighted, they listened to Wynn's jokes and their roars rippled the roof hangings. Ed came alive as if before a first-night audience and the performance was a triumph. Later, when Texaco hired him as its Fire Chief, his contract guaran-

Honey-throated Norman Brokenshire, one of Big Radio's most effective salesmen, played himself in a movie, "The Big Broadcast."

teed a studio audience, as indeed it should have—he was its inventor.

Another learning experience was Vincent Lopez' first live broadcast from the Hotel Pennsylvania. He and his band had broadcast before from a studio but this "remote" was something new. Listeners would be able to hear the same music to which diners were dancing. WJZ asked AT&T for a land line connection. They were told that no circuits were available. It was a well-understood dodge; any station competing with WEAF invariably had trouble renting a telephone line. Western Union studied the situation and gladly installed one.

That afternoon, WJZ made an announcement of the up-coming remote from Lopez at the Hotel Pennsylvania. Within an hour, the Grill room at the hotel began to fill. By broadcast time, the room was jammed. The bandsman said, "Hello, everybody! Lopez speaking," and the program was under way. It all sounds commonplace today, but in the early '20s that idea for a remote was as bright as a new-minted penny.

Lopez was so carried away that he offered a free photograph of himself to radio listeners. The deluge descended. Ben Gross says that the mail, according to Lopez, filled ten big clothes hampers. "I just couldn't take care of it," Lopez told him. "I apologized on the air and changed my offer so that anyone telephoning the hotel would get a picture. The incoming calls actually knocked out one of the mid-Manhattan telephone exchanges and jammed the hotel's switchboard."

As stations multiplied, so did the audience. In two years, 1922 and 1923, the government issued more than 1,440 transmitter construction permits. Most stations operated on less than 50 watts and were on the air only two or three hours a day.

The sale of receiving sets zoomed: 100,000 in 1922; 550,000 in 1923; 1,500,000 in 1924; 2,000,000 in 1925.

Who made them? Everybody and his brother! Scores of set manufacturers sprang up in every city. Tubes were patented so most sets were made without tubes. The customer bought a chassis, bought RCA vacuum tubes as specified, often in the same shop, and plugged them in himself. RCA fought the infringers—mostly in vain.

The year 1924 was especially interesting. Calvin Coolidge, who became President after the death of President Harding in 1923, was running for his first full term. The times were not good. You could buy a new Ford without a self-starter for $290. The posters urged, "Keep Cool With Coolidge." Set sales were stimulated by radio coverage of the two political conventions and by a new circuit designed by a genius, Major Edwin Armstrong. Its super-regenerative

trick of multiplying an incoming signal permitted even the elimination of an outside aerial and gave birth to the truly portable radio set.

The Radio Corporation of America bought Armstrong's patent and built the circuit into its 1924 models. Sales jumped to new heights and RCA led the field thereafter until a federal re-shuffle of patent rights made the super-circuit available to all. According to the authoritative *Broadcasting Yearbook*, radio buffs in that year invested $358 million in sets, tubes and other parts.

And what sets they were! Only a few models sported loud-speakers. The majority were equipped with earphones. Power was supplied either by two dry cells the size of milk bottles or by awkward storage batteries. Accurate tuning required three hands because three dials were involved.

But no matter, the wireless set was still a miracle and the public wanted more. A radio magazine guessed that the fad would probably last until at least 5 million homes had been equipped. Nobody dreamed that the year 1965 would see 24 million radio sets sent to market. Or that total sales in the United States from 1950 to 1969 would reach a half-billion sets.

In the early '20s almost nobody asked how a radio station

PENNSYLVANIA
VERMONT
NEW JERSEY
OKLAHOMA
OHIO
KA
MAINE
ORK
N

could be supported. Perhaps it was because the "plaything" concept still obsessed many minds. Others permitted themselves to think that public-spirited citizens might come forward with endowments, a notion that is still entertained in 1970. Another group proposed that the grateful listener, after a week of amusement, should write a check and mail it off. But commercial advertising? The idea was—for the moment—unthinkable.

When station owners met at Secretary Hoover's invitation, he made a suggestion that would soon gain the name of "the Hoover method." It permitted a mention of the sponsor's name. at the beginning and end of each broadcast. No middle commercial. In fact, no commercial of any kind. Few applauded.

Perhaps taxes could be found to sustain a station, some suggested. Several towns had founded stations, and each lumped its operating costs in with the city's annual budgets. Several universities did the same thing. But their budgets were low and presently both operators and listeners learned that cheap budgets guarantee cheap entertainment.

In England, a fund-raising device was under study that involved the licensing of each set. Just as a citizen needed an auto license in order to run a car, so he would need a license to own a receiving set. This method is functioning today in many countries, including Great Britain.

By 1925 the cost of operating a station had risen so high that owners were ready for almost any solution that would provide revenue. A bright salesman bought an hour of time on one station and peddled it, minute by minute, to a score of small-business men. His profit was the difference between what he paid per minute and what he got. He made a small fortune.

In New York, WEAF put all its bets on the phone-booth idea and moved steadily toward solvency. Rules were strict. No price could be mentioned. No specific retail store could be mentioned by street address. Regardless, sponsors bought time to talk about their products. Toward the middle of the decade, WEAF was in the black.

Watching the unfolding drama and anticipating its next development, David Sarnoff of RCA donned the mantle of a prophet: "Very soon, every household radio will draw its power from a lamp or wall socket," he told the National Electric Light Association. "The day of the awkward radio battery is over."

He promised a new market. "Automobiles will soon have radios as standard equipment. The time is coming when the driver of any car or truck, speeding down a highway, can listen to the programs

Opposite, above: Milton Cross, tenor turned announcer, became famous as the Voice of Opera. His throne room was Box 44 in the Met's Diamond Horseshoe, from which he made fine music come alive for millions.
Below: Graham McNamee, another former singer, took up announcing and became an overnight celebrity.

Right: Handsome, ambitious and talented, Vincent Lopez was one of the first of the "big band" leaders to utilize the power of radio. Below: Billy Jones and Ernie Hare, the original Happiness Boys, worked under different names for a handful of stations.

of nearby stations." This last raised many eyebrows; who could drive and listen at the same time?

He sketched a tiny pocket-size receiver that he called a Radiolette and asked his research department to "invent" it. His mind was afire with a hundred ideas. One was television. He told a 1924 student audience at the University of Missouri: "The greatest day of all will be when not only the human voice but the human image of the speaker will be flashed through space in every direction."

Less of a prophet but more of an administrator, Herbert Hoover believed in sitting down and talking things out. Working under a hazy mandate dealing with ships at sea, he tried to cope with the chaotic chorus that was filling the land. As stations became more powerful, their signals thrust farther and farther until they interlaced with the signals of other hopped-up transmitters. The result was bedlam. Broadcasters adopted their own methods, some riding one side of the broadcasting band while a competing station rode the other side. The improvement was minuscule. Some operators jumped brazenly to clear channels under a personal policy of "let the devil take the hindmost."

Ed Wynn, one of the greatest clowns of all time, tried to start a network of his own. Its resounding failure drove him back to show biz, sadder and wiser—but funnier than ever.

Poised for action or passion, these thespians await the signal that they are on the air. A sound effects man stands at the far left, then big Charles Coburn, straight from Broadway, and David Ross (second from right), called the world's smoothest announcer.

A beautiful evangelist, Aimee Semple McPherson, operated her California station so carelessly that a radio inspector took her off the air and sealed up her equipment. Her telegram of protest to Herbert Hoover smelled of brimstone: "Order your minions of Satan to leave my station alone. You cannot expect the Almighty to abide by your wavelength nonsense. When I offer my prayers to him, I must fit into his wavelength. Open this station at once."

Four radio conferences were held in Washington from 1922 to 1925. They all concluded that soon Congress would have to act. When Congress refused to act, Herbert Hoover did. Some say he loved bossing things; some say he took charge of the radio mess in fear and trembling, knowing that something had to be done. His most significant ruling divided stations into three groups. Group one included high power stations on exclusive channels that served large areas. Group two, less powerful, served smaller areas and were spaced

King of Jazz Paul Whiteman, who made modern music respectable with his symphonic arrangements, equipped his first radio orchestras with earphones, one per man, so they could hear themselves as others heard them.

so they would not interfere with each other. His third group included the ragtag remainder, low in power and often serving a small religious or educational audience. The setup is similar today.

Opposition to Hoover's plan first developed in Chicago. A rugged American, Commander Eugene McDonald, who was both a radio set maker and a broadcaster, was dissatisfied with the channel given his station. He re-tuned his transmitter and put it squarely on top of a channel that had been ceded to the government of Canada. "Sue me!" he challenged. When the federal government did, it lost. No existing law authorized Hoover's housekeeping. Now Congress felt the pressure and set about studying the booming industry's needs. It was about time.

In this same period, the government threw another haymaker, this time at the Radio Corporation of America. The attack came un-expectedly from the Federal Trade Commission. The complaint de-

History in the making: David Sarnoff, at the mike, delivers a speech called "Birth of an Industry" as he opens the RCA Pavilion at the 1939 World's Fair. Among his predictions delivered to an infinitesimal TV audience: television would become a great medium of entertainment, culture and education.

clared that members of the RCA alliance had "conspired for the purpose of, and with the effect of, restraining competition and creating a monopoly." RCA had been shaped under the government's eye and even had a military representative on its board of directors. Surely, the charge was a mistake.

On the contrary, the FTC lawyers were grimly serious. A shift in Republican politics, it seemed, had turned the regulatory lapdog into a bloodhound. A date would be set for public hearings, the intent of which would be to take the Radio Corporation of America apart subsidiary by subsidiary.

But there was more. The ultimate blow came from within the corporate brotherhood, from the American Telephone & Telegraph Company itself. It had begun as a feud between WEAF, the AT&T station, and WJZ, the Westinghouse station. Their guerrilla warfare involved fees for artists, musicians and so forth. Each claimed that the other was operating in violation of the cross-licensing pact that had brought them together.

Then the rumor mill produced news that AT&T's Western Electric Company was readying its own radio receiver for the market. This hanky-panky could not be tolerated and RCA reacted with threats of legal action. Secret hearings were held behind locked doors. Evidence piled high that the AT&T-GE-Westinghouse-RCA agreement had been widely violated—but who was the transgressor? An arbitrator was named to study the matter.

No simple explanation can be given of the controversy or the bad blood it generated. Let us say that all parties were probably sincere and honorable. Perhaps the trouble was that the alliance, which had been created largely to conduct a business involving overseas wireless communications, now suddenly found itself in an entirely new business—much richer, with even greater riches in prospect. One fact stood out above all other arguments: both AT&T and RCA wanted to control the lion's share of the broadcasting business. Both wanted to market its own sets to the millions who were thronging the radio stores.

The arbitrator, when he made up his mind, decided in favor of RCA. He said that AT&T, under the agreement, had no right to run a broadcasting station. Moreover, RCA had exclusive sales rights to all sets manufactured under the joint patent pool.

The telephone colossus was down but not out. In the face of what appeared to be total victory for RCA, AT&T rallied and attacked again with a brand-new study of the pact that bound the principals together in the cross-licensing pool. It was written by John W. Davis, one of America's most distinguished lawyers, a former solicitor general of the United States and a 1924 candidate for the U.S. Presidency.

With words as weighty as if they had come from the Supreme Court, he asserted that the pact itself was illegal. He said that all concerned had broken the law. All were guilty of conspiring to act in restraint of trade. The new charge turned the tables on RCA.

Owen D. Young, who had masterminded the creation of RCA, took steps to prop up his confederation. His astute judgment dictated a settlement instead of a fight. With that in view, both sides settled down to hard bargaining, not to punish each other but to preserve that which was almost within their grasp. A public hearing must be avoided.

The burning question was: Could they reach agreement in time to forestall the Federal Trade Commission in Washington? Its executioners, rumor said, were whetting their axes. It was a race, and it would be close.

6

That's How Networks Were Born

In the late '20s and early '30s many critics wondered if broadcasting would ever grow up.

Maybe it was the boom-and-bust spirit of 1928–1929 that fogged so many minds. Or was it the small boy in every man who insisted that radio was his personal toy? At any rate, an incredible amount of time was devoted to stunts of one sort or another.

"If it's new, we'll try it," many stations admitted. Some of them packed jazz bands and transmitting equipment into airplanes and flew them around while boasting of "our studios in the sky." Everyone seemed to enjoy it except the musicians.

FM made news through stunts designed to show off its seven-league boots. At the GE plant in Schenectady, New York, a group of radio engineers won headlines by broadcasting a song called "I Love You Truly" after it had hurtled around the world. Using a complicated series of relays, the much-loved melody was delivered to startled American listeners via Europe, Java, Australia, and finally Schenectady. "The music you are hearing," WGY announced, slightly out of breath, "has come to you after completely circling the earth." As they say on Broadway, "it was a big nothing."

Their next stunt was better. It was genuine "first." In Australia, a dog. In Schenectady, a cat. Both animals were installed in small studios before mikes and speakers. At the moment of truth, an American engineer pinched the cat's tail, eliciting a howl. In Australia, the dog's hackles rose and he barked. The cat, taking no chances, spat

KNX
1050 KILOCYCLES
CBS RADIO PLAYHOUSE
THE · VINE · STREET · THEATRE

noisily at the loudspeaker. It was the first electronic cat and dog fight.

Today overseas broadcasts and telecasts pour in on us like spring rain. In the '30s they possessed a special magic. Many old-timers still recall the procession of famous writers and statesmen whose voices brought the foreign world into American parlors. They included such giants as George Bernard Shaw (who called us boobs), Mahatma Gandhi, John Masefield, Benito Mussolini, Leon Trotsky and the Prince of Wales. Every guest was a lion and the lion tamer was a dynamic little newsman named Caesar Searchinger, whose specialty was wooing and winning their consent to visit his studio at the BBC in London.

One of the first of the new breed of radio correspondents, Searchinger thoughtfully appointed himself CBS's European Director (the title lent dignity to negotiations) and set a course record that even Ed Murrow, at a later date, would not surpass.

Every historical event starts with a notion in some person's brain. David Sarnoff's notion involved building a market for radio sets manufactured and sold by the Radio Corporation of America. In 1922 he had written to the General Electric president:

"It seems to me that in seeking a solution to broadcasting, we must recognize that the answer must be along national lines . . . for the problem is a national one. Let us organize a separate and distinct company to be known as the Public Broadcasting Company or some such . . ."

Already, the rival American Telephone & Telegraph Company had taken several purposeful steps. After various tentative hook-ups, testing transmission quality, they connected WEAF New York and WNAC Boston in what has come to be recognized as the first regular chain broadcast. Growth was rapid and, within a few years, their network embraced twenty cities. By mid-1923 they were ready for the first coast-to-coast hookup of a Presidential address. San Francisco was the proposed site until President Harding's illness and death canceled it.

A seven-station network broadcast the convening of Congress that fall. When Calvin Coolidge was inaugurated for his first full term, twenty-six stations carried his words. The announcer was young Norman Brokenshire, working for $65 a week.

By the mid-twenties, a number of broadcasters had organized their stations on a strictly business basis. WEAF's success in attracting advertisers showed the way the industry had to go if it was to survive. Officially, neither government nor industry was ready to endorse advertising, but the handwriting was on the wall.

92

Opposite, top: Philosopher-Comedian Will Rogers, who abandoned the "Ziegfeld Follies" for a radio fling, with Movie Czar Will Hayes, former U. S. Postmaster and hired protector of the public morality. Below: Mammy Singer Al Jolson and his bride, tap-dancing Ruby Keeler, who became a cinema star.

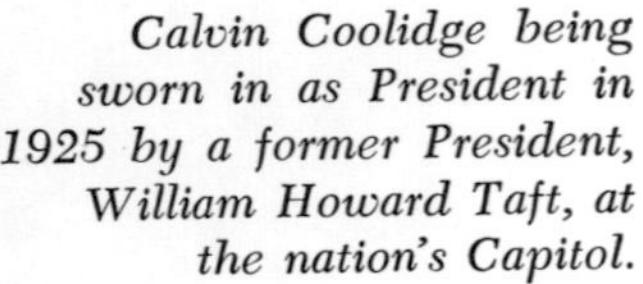

Calvin Coolidge being sworn in as President in 1925 by a former President, William Howard Taft, at the nation's Capitol.

Most of the action at that time was in favor of powerful AT&T. They owned the long lines necessary for a network, and they usually refused to rent them to rivals. RCA resorted to Western Union wires but with disappointing results. One consequence was a decision by Westinghouse to try to substitute shortwave transmissions for the phone company's long lines. Shortwaves introduced a new element in the tug of war within the RCA giant; shortwaves were temperamental but they could cover fantastic distances. Guglielmo Marconi on his yacht in the English Channel spoke with Australia. Arctic explorer Donald B. MacMillan talked from near the North Pole with friends in New York and Chicago. An English editor declared: "Who now has the temerity to say that prayers are not heard in heaven?"

In other sectors of the industry, ear-splitting confusion prevailed. One city had twenty-five stations, all on the same channel.

College and university stations were struggling to stay alive. In 1924, forty-nine of them threw in the towel; but the lesson was lost on 151 others who obtained new licenses.

"Dialing for distance" was an "in" pastime among most listeners, and community stations helped it along by making a pact to stay off the air one night a week. For a while, almost every city in America had its own "silent night" but it was too good to last. A maverick station would violate the silent night pact, then all the others would return to the air and chaos reigned.

To solve the problem of interference for RCA-owned stations, David Sarnoff and several others hit upon the idea of superpower. Most stations operated on a few hundred watts of electricity. Why not a station so powerful that it would blast through rival signals? In 1924, Secretary Hoover considered the idea and rejected it. But again, Sarnoff blazed a trail. He went on the air over RCA stations and asked for letters from anyone who thought a few powerful stations around the country might provide better service. Thousands of listeners answered, approving the idea. When their letters were delivered to the Secretary of Commerce, he reversed himself and authorized WJZ and WGY to increase their power to an unheard-of 50,000 watts. It was the beginning of big-time radio.

Another major problem was patent infringement. Whereas the Radio Corporation had no end of trouble with competing set makers, the American Tel & Tel people battled radio station owners. For a long time telephone company executives had felt that almost every station on the air was using tubes and parts that were covered by AT&T patents. Now it was time to take a stand. Their solution was to offer the right of continuing use in exchange for a licensing fee. For a sum, to be paid annually, any station could stay on the air by renting the right to use the "infringing" equipment. Broadcasters were stunned, and many responded with such epithets as "octopus" and "monopoly."

When no one came forward with the prescribed fee, AT&T made a test case of their neighbor, WHN New York. The public and the press favored the station, but the lawyers favored the "octopus." An out-of-court settlement resulted in WHN agreeing to pay an annual fee of $1,500. Other stations followed suit.

Suddenly another quake struck. Broadcasters had played musical recordings for years without a thought of payment. Their attitude was that exposure on the air helped to popularize a tune. The copyright law said that music, when used for profit, called for remuneration of the copyright owners. So the American Society of Composers, Authors and Publishers (ASCAP) decided that radio should pay.

Again a disdainful industry shrugged off their claims. All except WEAF New York. Owned by AT&T, whose power play was still fresh in everyone's memory, it was a sitting duck for ASCAP. It signed an agreement to pay an annual fee of $500. Still the industry resisted. ASCAP began to monitor stations, seeking a test case. They found it when they heard someone singing a copyrighted old "standard," "Mother Machree." Station WOR Newark was the offender. The case went to court and a judge held that the ASCAP claim was just.

Two consequences emerged from that decision. First, the fee system produced revenues that have turned many threadbare composers and authors into near-millionaires. Second, concerned broadcasters formed their own group to combat future forays by covetous outsiders and called it the National Association of Broad-

Ray Kelley, high priest of sound effects, with some of the NBC gadgets he used for reproducing the howling wind, beating surf, charging cavalry and demonic lightning—not to mention the sighs of young love.

Morton Downey, CBS star, parlayed a clear Irish tenor into a fortune and friendships with the great of his day.
Below: On NBC's 30th anniversary the network collected these stars for a nostalgic laugh-in (from left to right): Bob Burns and his bazooka, Tommy Riggs, Edgar Bergen and Charlie McCarthy, Rudy Vallee and Joe "Wanna buy a duck?" Penner.

Paul White (left), head of CBS News, and H. V. Kaltenborn, ace commentator, whose teamwork during the Munich Crisis established radio as the news medium of the future. Opposite: Columnist Walter Winchell, in his cubbyhole office, from which he extended his uninhibited flashes and "lotions of love" to America's four corners.

casters, with headquarters in Washington, D.C. Their initial battle—against ASCAP's demands for higher and higher fees—is still not over.

But surely the supreme consequence to most Americans was the agreement that divorced AT&T from RCA and provided the skeleton for what is now known as the American system of broadcasting.

Months of haggling finally produced a recipe for peace between the giants. A separate company would be established, owned jointly by RCA, GE and Westinghouse. It would own, operate and contract with stations to offer a nationwide toll service to advertisers. At long last, the advertiser's dollar was recognized as the only practical means of support.

AT&T would supply the telephone lines needed to tie the networks together, with the new company paying standard fees. A payment of at least $1 million per year would be handed to AT&T for the next ten years. RCA would also buy WEAF New York from AT&T for another $1 million.

Everybody was happy. At last David Sarnoff had his network, the National Broadcasting Company. A full page ad in *The New York Times* announced the good news. "The purpose of the new company," it said, "will be to provide the best programs available for broadcast

When vaudeville stars turned to radio, they brought their wives with them. Above: Fred Allen with Portland Hoffa. Right: Jack Benny and Mary Livingston. These were 1933 publicity stills. Opposite, top: Erno Rapee, dynamic maestro of the Roxy Music Hall programs. Below: An early Red Skelton in an early funny hat, broadcasting over KNX in Hollywood.

in the United States . . . The National Broadcasting Company will not only broadcast these programs through station WEAF but will make them available to other broadcasting stations throughout the country . . . It is hoped that every event of national importance may be broadcast widely throughout the United States."

For some station operators, the times were full of optimism. Set sales were booming, spurred by the elimination of bulky, messy batteries. "Just plug it in and turn the switch," salesmen advised pop-eyed customers. Wall Street stocks that year were up by about 50 percent. A new metal called aluminum was the source of several new fortunes, and a New York newspaper reported that the family of Andrew Mellon, Secretary of the Treasury, had profited by over $100 million. Nobody got excited; this was still the American dream.

Within the industry, only a few twinges of unease disturbed a generally placid surface. In 1925 Secretary Hoover had begun to tell new station applicants: "All the wavelengths are used up," and refused to issue more licenses. There was little else to be done. Chicago was typical: already the home of more than forty stations, twenty additional applicants clamored for broadcast rights. Some corporations, unable to get a license, passed the word that they were willing to buy. Overnight, a rising market developed for the outright sale of stations.

Many churches and colleges unloaded at a giddy profit. Some unhappy applicants, outbid by rivals, took their peeves to Congress. "There ought to be a law," they said.

In the meantime, the new National Broadcasting Company threw a wingding at New York's Waldorf-Astoria that made history. Advance notice called it "the inauguration of a new epoch of American life." The cream of society and business attended, wearing ermine and swallowtails. Merlin H. Aylesworth, the first NBC president, welcomed the socialites and celebrities. "Twenty-six stations will be carrying tonight's broadcast," he said. "The same program that we hear will also be heard by as many as ten or twelve million persons. Think of that!" The audience gasped.

The entertainment came from all over, including the stage of the Waldorf's magnificent ballroom. Will Rogers wisecracked in Kansas. Mary Garden, most glamorous of opera stars, sang in Chicago.

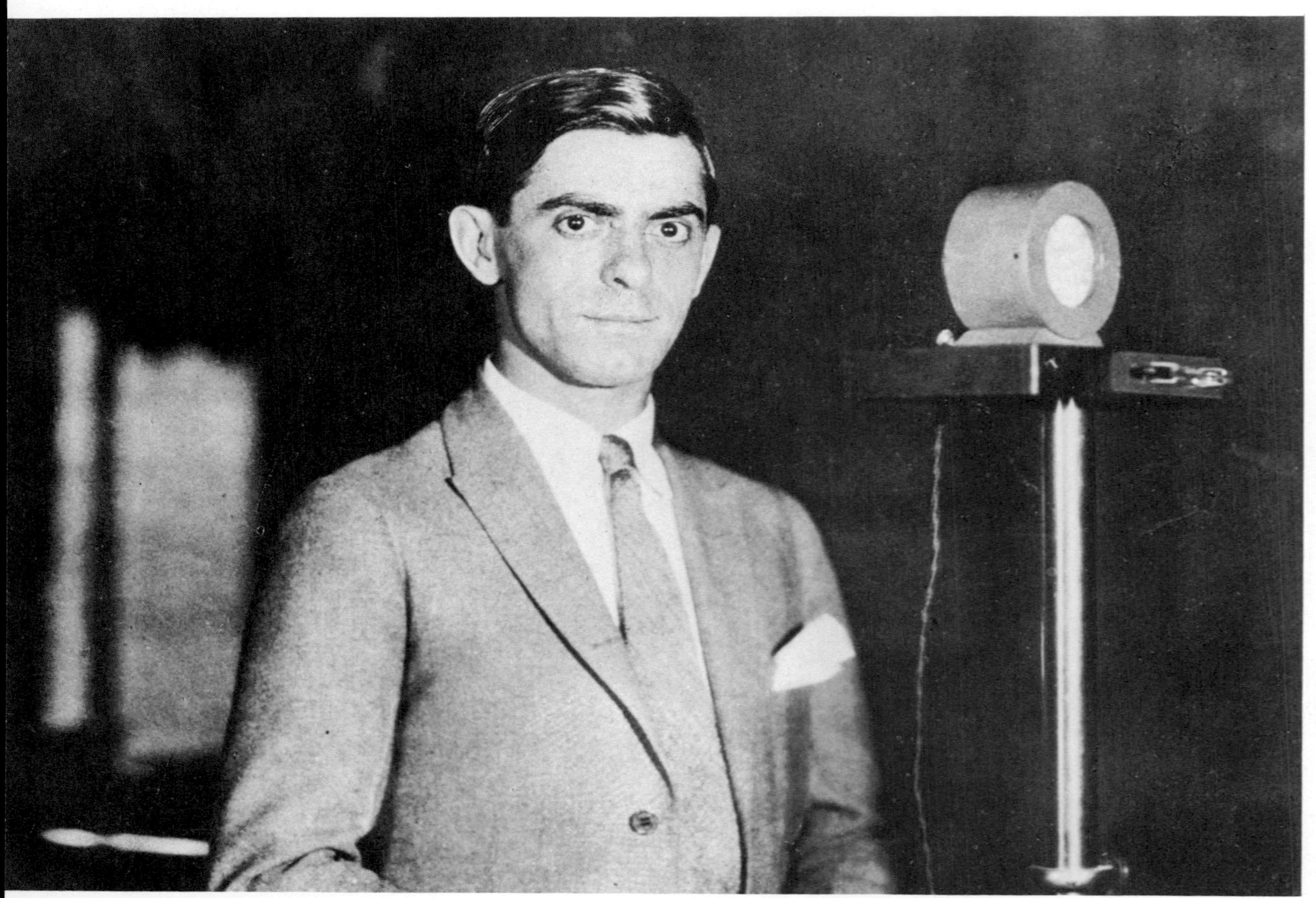

COLUMBIA
C.10173-4.

Dr. Walter Damrosch conducted the New York Symphony. The program included pianist Harold Bauer, the Oratorio Society, Titta Ruffo of the Met and—a change of pace—comedians Weber and Fields, with dance music by Ben Bernie, Vincent Lopez, George Olsen and B. A. Rolfe. The gala lasted for four hours and every weary guest agreed that the new broadcasting company was well launched.

By 1927 NBC had two networks, called the Red and the Blue. Why name a network for a color? Because connections were made on a switchboard (push buttons were not yet installed) with a myriad of plugs and holes. To prevent mistakes, all plugs leading to one network's stations were painted red, and those for the other network were painted blue.

That same year workmen began to fashion luxurious new studios at 711 Fifth Avenue in New York. Every studio was a free-floating chamber with its own control room, poised on springs to assure freedom from vibration and noise. A "Farm and Home Hour" was introduced. Walter Damrosch, hired to advise on high culture, created the "Music Appreciation Hour," which was addressed to classrooms in grade schools but actually listened to by the entire nation.

Most important, advertisers responded, not for a single broadcast but for increasingly longer periods of time, even a year. So, on calm seas, the new NBC frigate sailed into the unknown, oblivious both to shoals ahead and the jury-rigged privateer that was coming up from astern.

At long last Congress began to pay attention to the tattered communications law of 1912. Court decisions made it clear that the Secretary of Commerce possessed no real authority. The result was a bill expressing a compromise between the many pressures of the time. Three of these pressures got into the law that was finally passed in 1927—ownership of the airwaves, censorship and monopoly.

The act specified that its purpose was to "maintain control of the United States over all channels. . . ." Further, it was to allow the use of those channels by licensees "but not the ownership thereof." By default of contrary opinion, federal ownership of the airwaves was asserted and written into the law of the land.

Freedom-of-speech exponents added a clause saying: "Nothing in this Act shall be understood or construed to give the licensing authority the power of censorship over the radio communications or signals transmitted." Battles would be fought—and are still being fought—over that.

Anti-monopoly legislators had their say in a section asserting that a license would be denied any person or corporation which was adjudged "guilty of unlawfully monopolizing or attempting unlawfully to monopolize, after this act takes effect, radio communications. . . ."

The act also established a Federal Radio Commission of seven commissioners, with the pressing assignment: "Bring order out of this terrible chaos." They were to do it in one year. President Coolidge signed the bill on February 3, 1927. Then Congress adjourned on the heels of a filibuster that prevented its appropriating money for salaries or supplies. Secretary Hoover cleared a space in his Department of Commerce and scraped together emergency funds. "We started with a chair, a desk and a filing cabinet," one commissioner recalls. It was an unpromising beginning for one of the most complex and significant regulatory chores in the history of government.

Congress expected results, and one of the first was RCA's sensitivity to the threat of the new law's monopoly clause. In every operation, big business provides an easy target for the "outs." RCA was a giant; relatively, its competitors were pygmies. But they were two hundred strong, and they had access—which they used—to a battalion of congressmen. The Federal Trade Commission's earlier charge against RCA of "practices in restraint of trade" was soon to be aired. Eagerly, the pygmies awaited their chance to testify against Goliath.

RCA lawyers huddled and concluded that unfriendly testimony in a public hearing might destroy confidence and jeopardize license renewal for their stations WEAF and WCY. The bone of contention was RCA's untouchable patents. Perhaps they could serve another purpose.

That purpose was embodied in a royalty agreement by which RCA ended its monopoly of its huge patent pool. Through it, other manufacturers could now dip into its treasury of goodies, provided they paid a reasonable percentage of their gross. Twenty eager setmakers signed up at once, each one contracting to pay at least $100,000 per year, or 7.5 percent of their sales. The deal pleased everyone, the heat on RCA diminished, and the first year's take was $3 million. Within a year, the mollified Federal Trade Commission canceled its hearings, and the Radio Corporation was home free.

Basically, the new law solved almost nothing, because it assumed that stations controlled their own programming, as had once been the case. Recent network policy had changed that for most of the nation's largest stations. All the big broadcasts now came from NBC. Local stations re-broadcast what was fed to them, and were paid for the service. Programs—the big, prime-time programs—were controlled by the networks, which were almost wholly disregarded by the act. The FTC tried to influence network management, not by direct dealing, but through their power to deny new licenses to all of the net's owned-and-operated stations. The result, in 1928, was not entirely happy.

But FTC perplexities and NBC frustrations were as nothing compared to those which presently beset a quartet of starry-eyed adventurers in New York City. These gentlemen, reading the signs of boom ahead, decided to start their own network. In the face of NBC's Blue and NBC's Red, they talked themselves into the naive belief that their company—the United Independent Broadcasters—could succeed. It was David and Goliath all over again. The two big names involved were Arthur Judson, a super-successful talent manager, and Major J. Andrew White, whose fame rested on his broadcast of the Dempsey-Carpentier brawl. Their partners were businessmen dreaming of profits.

In summary, they had very little money. NBC had already tied up most of the best stations. NBC's payment to AT&T had rented practically all the cross-country telephone lines in existence. When news of their suicidal project reached the ears of David Sarnoff, it is

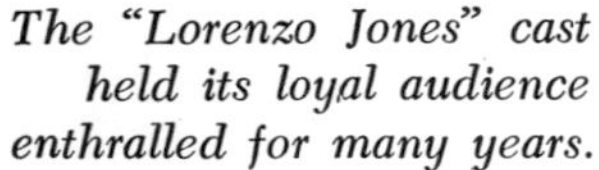

The "Lorenzo Jones" cast held its loyal audience enthralled for many years.

Lucile Wall starred as the heroine of "Portia Faces Life," NBC's popular daytime serial.

related that he threw back his head and laughed uproariously. He would not laugh last.

This dark horse of a network, this upstart and usurper, is now the Columbia Broadcasting System, the world's largest advertising medium.

Its first steps were ungainly and stumbling. AT&T refused to rent wires to United Independent. Western Union and Postal Telegraph wires were incapable of high-fidelity transmissions. A partner, George A. Coats, uncovered a "fixer" in Washington, and presently long lines became available. On a trip to sign up stations, Coats met the Levy brothers, owners of WCAU in Philadelphia. They joined up and brought in other stations. One of them was WOR Newark, which would become the United Independent flagship.

The partners announced opening ceremonies—nothing to compete with the regal display of NBC at the Waldorf-Astoria—using excellent artists from Judson's stable and a brand-new opera. Having spent their ready cash, they allowed Mrs. Christian Holmes, an opera buff, to buy several thousand dollars' worth of stock. It paid for the train tickets that allowed the budding broadcasters to beat the bushes for sponsors. But every solicitation was a failure. They then heard that the Columbia Recording Company had extra cash and was looking for

an investment; they pitched an idea at Columbia's executives: "We'll sell you stock. We'll put your stars on the air and millions will hear them and buy their records. You'll make it two ways."

Those executives agreed and wrote a check for $163,000. The reorganized company changed its name to the Columbia Phonograph Broadcasting System. That took them through their opening, for which they had found only a single commercial sponsor. Symphony conductor Howard Barlow had been hired out of the orchestra pit of New York's Neighborhood Playhouse. His assistant was a youth called "Kosty"—Andre Kostelanetz. The inaugural program was produced in a studio that WOR was still building. It had neither wall clock nor control room. Engineers monitored the premier performance from a men's room. The opera was a new American work by relative unknowns, Deems Taylor and Edna St. Vincent Millay. *The King's Henchman* failed to stampede the critics but it did set a lofty standard. Thunderstorms jarred the transmissions, the program overran its time and critical reviews were very mixed. Worst of all, the treasury was empty again. For three weeks nobody got a paycheck. The company owed AT&T $45,000 for line rental. The Columbia Recording people announced that they wanted out.

Judson remembered Mrs. Holmes and her overflowing heart

Opposite: When Amos 'n' Andy—Charles Correll and Freeman Gosden (right)—began to advertise a toothpaste on NBC, its sales tripled. Below: Fred Waring's band and the Lane Sisters.

and hand. Unfortunately, she was aboard a ship in mid-Atlantic. He composed a poignant radiogram that explained his plight. The answer came through her bankers who delivered a check for the sum he had mentioned—$45,000. She had given the faltering company breathing space, and obtained in return another seemingly worthless bundle of stock certificates. But her loyalty was rewarded. According to CBS legend, she eventually sold her holdings for $3 million.

Two other men of great faith were Isaac and Leon Levy of WCAU Philadelphia. Their optimism persuaded Jerome H. Loucheim, a subway builder, to contribute $135,000. The company's third name was achieved by dropping the word "Recording." As the Columbia Broadcasting System staggered into 1928, their new angel broke his hip and lost his interest. "Besides, it's a crazy business, I never know what's going on," he said.

What was going on was the extraordinary experience of a brand-new CBS sponsor whose program was called "La Palina Smoker." A young assistant advertising manager had placed the business with CBS while his boss, Samuel Paley, of the Congress Cigar Company of Philadelphia, was in Europe. The adman was Paley's twenty-six-year-old son, William. Papa ordered the radio contract canceled, convinced that show business was no way to sell cigars. But

Opposite: By 1935, the Mills Brothers were so popular that the movies hired them to support Dick Powell in "Broadway Gondolier."
Above: Bing Crosby, complete with mustache, in 1934. Left: Rudy Vallee with the megaphone that made his crooning famous.

La Palina sales were jumping from 400,000 to one million a day. "La Palina Smoker" continued.

Broadcasting fascinated young Bill Paley. His friends, the Levys, knew this. Introducing him to the bedfast Loucheim, they painted a brilliant future for a dynamic new company spurred by a dynamic young executive. Would he like to go up to New York, look over the books, meet the people and see some broadcasts?

Twenty-four hours later, Paley, Loucheim and assorted lawyers made a deal. For approximately $400,000, William Paley bought control of the bedraggled Columbia Broadcasting System. In September of 1928, business was booming from coast to coast, and the sign on young Paley's door read "President." At last, CBS had the right man and the right financial backing.

Network competition became a cat-and-mouse game as the webs enlarged their staffs and extended their long lines. A roll call of 1931 showed NBC's two networks with 1,931 employees. Columbia, in second place, had only 408. Yet, CBS had produced 415 special events against NBC's 456. Each net announced a profit of a bit over $2 million.

One day in 1930 an unprecedented order went out from Paley's headquarters to all affiliates. "Clear all stations!" it said, announcing an emergency program. As affiliates canceled local shows and tuned in to the CBS master cable, their listeners suddenly heard sobbing and screaming, crackling flames and ambulance bells. CBS had decided to bring into millions of parlors the bitter sounds of human agony. It was a fragment of the scene of the catastrophic Ohio State Penitentiary fire. Via radio, Americans were finally learning about the real world.

The program was a daring harbinger of a Paley concept— that eyewitness reporting was a basic function of broadcasting. The notion would come to full bloom, first with Ed Murrow and his talented tribe, and ultimately with a TV camera recording mankind's first giant step on the surface of the moon.

The early Paley achievements, all the more remarkable because of his youth, are now radio history. But then, everybody was young. Sarnoff, a top executive at RCA, was only thirty-seven.

One item that had caught Paley's ear was the fact that Adolph Zukor, founder of Paramount Pictures, had once expressed interest in the new network. An interview confirmed the fact and set up a deal. Paramount bought 49 percent of CBS in exchange for a bundle of Paramount stock. The arrangement gave Paley a good image at the bank, and access to Hollywood stars.

Right: Brace Beemer, the
Lone Ranger, with his
sidekick Tonto, was a hero
to adults and kids.
Below: Pop orchestra leader
Ozzie Nelson and vocalist
Harriet Hilliard after
their marriage in 1935,
looking not too different
from the way they appeared
on the Johnny Carson
show in 1970.

Next, Paley bought his own flagship station. WOR was for sale but so was smaller, cheaper WABC. Paley bought it, made it famous and it became the current WCBS.

Instinct told him that listeners like to listen to other people, so he set out to get very special people before CBS microphones. He borrowed stars from Paramount; they publicized their films and everyone was happy. With the embargo against radio broken, other studios soon offered their celebrities.

But Paley wanted still more stars. Working through Arthur Judson, he bought and consolidated a half dozen concert organizations to form the world's largest concert bureau, named for Columbia, of course. This gave him control of so many personalities that the federal government would one day demand divorcement, alleging restraint of trade. Meanwhile, they attracted new listeners by the millions.

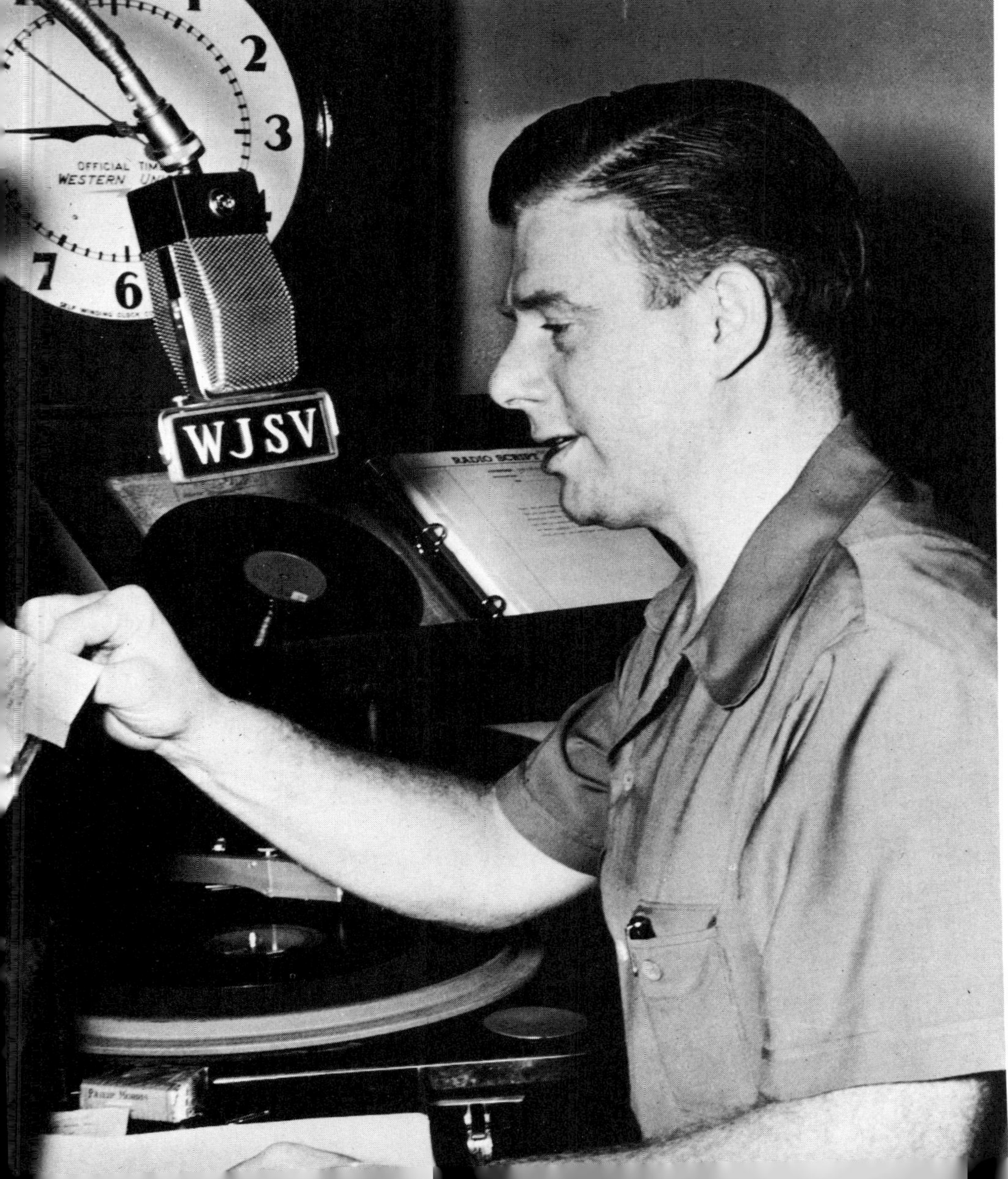

Arthur Godfrey first built a solid reputation in Washington, and then moved up to network stardom on CBS.

Next, Paley resolved to make stars out of nobodies, a project that would continue through the years. He took a kid named Bing Crosby out of a trio of rhythm singers and gave him a fifteen-minute program, anchoring him to the same hour day after day in order to build listener loyalty. He took Kate Smith, an unknown singing and hoofing performer, and featured her on a full hour every week. Tenor Morton Downey became a regular. And presently, the singular Arthur Godfrey.

Rivalry became a frenzy, enticing both audiences and sponsors. Two imitation blacks, Amos 'n' Andy, had won an audience for themselves as "Sam 'n' Henry" over WGN Chicago. When NBC put them on their network they became America's premiere source of entertainment. The program was broadcast at seven o'clock each night in the East, and the nation adjusted its activities in order to listen. Movie theaters installed loudspeakers and switched off their films every night. Factories in the Midwest, where the program went on the air an hour earlier, advanced their closing time so employees could drive home in time to tune in. Many restaurants refused to take orders during the broadcast. President Coolidge told his staff, "Don't bother me when I'm listening to Amos 'n' Andy."

Later, Chicago's studios would produce many other radio favorites. One of the greatest, a forerunner of subsequent Disney-type programs for children, was "The Singing Lady." She was Ireene Wicker, a talented actress who combined song, biography and drama to attract a Pied Piper's following of children that has never been equaled.

In many cities other young executives were also making decisions that would shape the future. At WSM Nashville, Edwin Craig, the son of the principal owner of the National Life and Accident Insurance Company, had been a ham enthusiast. He particularly enjoyed a late-night show called "The Coon-Sanders Night Hawks," out of Kansas City. After a visit to Missouri, he sold his father and the board of directors on starting their own company station.

Encouraging the talents of local rustics, WSM soon created the "Grand Ole Opry," discovered Roy Acuff and a host of "country music" stars and made Nashville a great musical production center. Dinah Shore first found her voice on WSM. Executive alumni include announcer Jack Harris, who joined the Army, served in the Pentagon and as PRO to General Douglas MacArthur in Japan; he is now presi-

The Quiz Kids came out of Chicago to amaze the nation with their erudition. Here they visit with Mayor LaGuardia of New York City.

dent and general manager of KPRC Houston. Engineer Jack De Witt entered the Army Signal Corps during World War II and became the first man to bounce a radio signal off the moon.

In Chicago, WGN, owned by the Chicago *Tribune*, was "remote" conscious. In 1924, their sports announcer, the golden-throated Quin Ryan, covered the Cubs-White Sox city series and the Illinois-Michigan football game in which a lad named Red Grange scored four touchdowns in the first twelve minutes of play. WGN's early coverage of a Kentucky Derby has never been surpassed; Ryan's blistering account of the race was prefaced by songs from a harmony duo named Freeman Gosden and Charles Correll, soon to become Amos 'n' Andy. A few days later, Ryan announced the Indianapolis Speedway races.

Another WGN "first" was a pickup from the village of Dayton, Tennessee, during the notorious Scopes "monkey" trial, in which William Jennings Bryan and Clarence Darrow locked horns and philosophies. Bryan won, and died five days later of apoplexy. The ten days of the trial cost the *Tribune* $10,000 daily.

Heroics in time of catastrophe became routine for broadcasters. In 1937 a flood washed down the Ohio and Mississippi rivers to inundate Louisville, Kentucky. Station WHAS, founded in 1922, became a lifeline. Mayor Neville Miller, besieged by water and tragedy, went on the air for endless hours to direct people to evacuation routes. When the flood drowned out WHAS's power supply, stilling its voice, engineers spliced its mikes to a fire alarm circuit, then to a high, dry line that ran over the hills to Nashville, where WSM amplified its signal and broadcast it back to Louisville.

Ed Kirby recalls, "We dropped all commercial and sustaining programs and gave WHAS the first five minutes of every half hour for service messages. Such things as 'Ten thousand units of vaccine en route by air. Where shall we drop or land?' Or 'Five ambulances are on the way. What roads are open . . . ?' "

Another WSM-WHAS service was a people locator. WSM devised a missing persons bureau. Families had been evacuated by boats going in every direction, ending up in three states. Frantic parents searched for lost children. Orphaned babies were sought by relatives. Mayor Miller and station personnel gradually untangled the skein of disaster. After a few days, WHAS got back on the air to complete its task. "With God's help," Kirby remembers, "200,000 families had been taken to safety, thanks to the instantaneous use of radio, of battery and auto sets; and then, when the flood subsided, they were reunited."

Opposite: Clarence Darrow (left) and William Jennings Bryan in the courthouse during their famous confrontation at the Scopes "monkey trial." A few days later, Bryan died.

At WLW Cincinnati business was brisk even throughout the Depression, and the management encouraged all kinds of creative writers to devise offbeat programs. In Cleveland WTAM developed a schedule of half-hours good enough to attract a waiting list of sponsors. Though affiliated with NBC, the station refused so often to clear time for network programs (local buyers had already bought it) that Messers. Sarnoff and Aylesworth in New York were able to solve the problem only by buying the station.

WWJ Detroit was also busy with whodunits, romances and adventures, hiring their actors from down-on-their-luck stock company veterans at $5 per performance. They needed only one scriptwriter, however; their man could turn out from ten to fifteen dramas each week. At KPO San Francisco, the management usually put on scripts sent from New York by the network office. One day a writer named Carlton Morse, who had read *The Forsyte Saga*, started his own dramatic series. "One Man's Family" became so popular that NBC put it on the network, turned it into a coast-to-coast favorite and watched it succeed for the next twenty-eight years.

Even so, progress was spotty. The Federal Radio Commission, undermanned and overworked, did not know for three years if they would be held over the following season. Their basic problem was what to do with 732 radio stations. Broadcasting got the space from 550 to 1500 kilocycles. That made room for 94 ten-kilocycle-wide channels. An engineering ruling, designed to relieve interference, had sorted broadcasters into three categories: clear channel, regionals and locals. But 732 channels were still too many.

The FRC decided on major surgery; it suspended all licenses and sent notices to 164 stations asking them why they should not be abolished. The nation's air vibrated with indignation. Owners begged their listeners to write attesting to their need of the radio fare provided by Station ZZZZ, or whatever. Then they shipped their mail in huge packing cases to the commission. Some stations sent as many as 500,000 letters. About half of those licenses were renewed, but mostly with lower power and curtailed hours. It was the beginning of order.

With station growth stabilizing, networks booming and people hearing the same programs and experiencing the same emotions from coast-to-coast, a singular mania developed throughout the country. Suddenly, all Americans shared an identical itch to get rich via the stock market. Many of them were partial to shares in the glamorous electronics field. An astounding performance by RCA shares on the New York Stock Exchange reflected this lunacy.

Below, left: Father Charles E. Coughlin became powerful enough, through his radio addresses, to found a new political party. Below: Huey Long came from the governorship of Louisiana to the U.S. Senate and might have gone farther but for an assassin's bullet.

A solid price for a share of RCA in 1928 was $85 or so. A month later, it rose to 91. A week later, it was at 138. Next day it jumped another 20 points. In May it spurted above 200. By November it hit 400. The sensational rise continued through winter, spring and summer. With Hoover elected, defeating the not-so-happy warrior, Al Smith, the July price per share was 500 and still it zoomed, even after being split five for one. In October 1929 it began to slide. The show biz journal *Variety* said it all in a headline that has become a classic: "Wall Street Lays an Egg."

The boom was over. The bust had begun. Soon the Depression would produce a new use for radio and a new radio star. His name was Franklin Delano Roosevelt, elected in 1932 in the midst of bank closings, sit-down strikes and farmers' revolts. A single stellar performance insured his place in history and perhaps saved the nation from revolution. It was called "A Fireside Chat."

Franklin Roosevelt was a man whose time had come. Radio as a political tool was an idea waiting for the right person. For the first time in history, every citizen who owned a radio receiver could sit in a front row seat at the 1932 Presidential Inauguration.

The average breadwinner of 1970, with his concerns about Vietnam, the drug explosion, crime on the streets and racial tension, is well off compared to his prototype during the Great Depression of the '30s. Millions lost their jobs, farmers lost their farms, families lost their homes. Hundreds of banks locked their doors, never to reopen. In most cities, desperate fathers sold apples on street corners.

In that radio audience awaiting F.D.R's inaugural address, people were numbed and hopeless. Their crisis was not in the ghetto or in Vietnam. It was in the pantry. On Saturday, March 4, 1933, a half-million spectators huddled against the raw wind that swept across bleachers erected along Pennsylvania Avenue in Washington. Millions more sat before their loudspeakers. As F.D.R. took the oath of office, his face was unusually serious. He confronted the crowd packed around the platform, leaned slightly toward the microphones atop his lectern, and addressed a waiting nation. In ringing tones, he summoned everyone to shake off despair. He demanded that they face the future with a brave heart. And then he offered a challenge and gave a promise.

"This great nation will endure as it has endured, will revive and will prosper," he said. "So first of all, let me assert my firm belief that the only thing we have to fear is fear itself—nameless, unreasoning, unjustified terror which paralyzes needed effort to convert retreat into advance . . ."

Many historians believe that those words, pouring into millions of homes, were the cement that held this fractured land together.

The first "Fireside Chat" came on March 12, 1933, in the midst of a banking crisis. The President's role was that of a family friend sitting down after dinner to discuss mutual problems. Here was no politician pounding a podium, shouting out trite panaceas. Here was true communication. During his first year in office, F.D.R. sat down with America four times.

Meanwhile, NBC went ahead with its plans for a gigantic building project in mid-Manhattan. The undertaking would cost $250 million. It would rise eighty stories high and would cover three blocks. Its name was Radio City and its central tower would house network offices, dozens of studios and a movie theater to be called Radio City Music Hall. Rockefeller interests were supplying the money, boom or bust, and they ordered the work to begin.

Other cities were desperate for jobs. Everywhere the rate of unemployment rose, and so did pied pipers who took to the airwaves to argue in behalf of their special nostrums. The most persuasive was Father Coughlin, Catholic priest of Royal Oak, Michigan, who gradually turned into a national nightmare. The runner-up was Huey P. Long, ex-governor and at that time a freshman senator from Louisiana.

Their story represents yet another facet of American inexperience in dealing with mass communications. Hitherto a blessing, radio suddenly became a threat. Father Charles E. Coughlin had been a priest with a tiny parish of twenty-five families when he began broadcasting to children over WJR Detroit. At his peak, his income from contributions was $500,000 a year. He built a plush office for himself atop a 150-foot marble column next to his tiny church, and created a radical political party with a million members.

Such power was possible only because so many things had gone wrong that wild remedies, sanctified by priestly garb, made sense to many ill-informed listeners. For a time, CBS became Coughlin's pulpit, at regular commercial rates. When overtones of anti-Semitism and frank attacks on certain groups and races emerged from his Sunday "sermons," CBS acted. First they asked to review his scripts. "My next talk will be on an entirely different subject," he promised.

It was! It asked his CBS audience if they thought CBS had the right to muzzle him. The network was inundated by 1,250,000 pro-Coughlin letters.

Retreating for the moment, Paley and Company invented a program and a policy. It was called "The CBS Church of the Air," with a rotating roster of pastors from all major faiths, filling air time contributed by the network. Henceforth, no time would ever be sold by the network for religious broadcasting. This ruling eased Coughlin off the CBS kilocycles and into organizing his own web. In the beginning he had supported Roosevelt and even attended his inauguration. Later he damned the President and helped arouse the general discontent that was being stirred up by a senator from Louisiana, Huey Long.

Long had a simple remedy for the nation's ills. His theme was Share-the-Wealth. Take from the rich and give to the poor. His popularity grew by leaps and bounds. His oratory was sprinkled with biblical excerpts and hillbilly philosophy. He called himself the Kingfish after the fraternal potentate of the same name in the "Amos 'n' Andy" show. Soon Share-the-Wealth clubs spread into eight thousand cities and towns.

A bullet from an assassin's gun ended Long's life in 1935. In 1936 Coughlin ranged the country campaigning against Roosevelt's reelection. Some of his talks referred to Franco's revolution in Spain, suggesting that America might do the same. "Democracy is doomed," he proclaimed. "This is our last election."

Better sense prevailed. Though his party gained only a few victories, F.D.R. won by a landslide, and Coughlin retired to lick his wounds. By the time they had healed, broadcasting had got its house in order; Coughlin's comeback efforts never got off the ground.

Another offshoot of the Depression was a general relaxing of advertising standards. Earlier, both network presidents had protested that they were opposed to "direct selling," a euphemism for mentioning prices or making extravagant claims. Hard times fractured their good intentions. George Washington Hill, president of the American Tobacco Company, even got his way on CBS when his announcer was permitted to tell the world, in support of Hill's sanitized cigars, that "spit is a nasty word."

The sale of spot announcements soared. Odd sponsors appeared on the air, including fortune-tellers, astrologers and bookmakers. Out-of-work salesmen solicited business for stations, asking only a commission.

In 1930 David Sarnoff became the president of the Radio Corporation of America. Already his company had bought and assimilated the Victor Talking Machine Company. He was anticipating other acquisitions when the U.S. Department of Justice filed an antitrust suit, demanding that the alliance between RCA, Westinghouse and General Electric be dissolved. Many felt it was a low blow engineered by the competition.

Day and night meetings ensued. Top officials were determined that the trial should not get into court where an adverse decision could be fatal. Deals were made, papers signed and a proposal delivered to the Department of Justice. With federal approval, all concerned accepted a consent decree, and the antitrust trial was canceled. At last RCA was its own boss—and the boss of RCA was ambitious David Sarnoff. Now he could move without interference from jealous partners. One such direction would be television.

In 1934 an advertiser wanted to talk to buyers in only New York and Chicago. He brought representatives of WOR and WGN together and arranged a two-station hookup for his program. Smelling an untapped market, WOR and WGN called themselves the Mutual network and began to offer their joint facilities to others. The idea caught on. WLW Cincinnati joined, and Detroit, and then an army of regionals and locals until a full Mutual buy included four hundred stations.

One day in July 1937, radio listeners were startled to hear the air go silent. Spinning the dial did no good. The ether was as empty and lifeless as it had been before the taming of the electron. The silence continued for two long minutes and then gave way to the normal transmissions of a busy day. Guglielmo Marconi, the father of radio, had died. All over America, Europe and England, radio stations had left the air so that girls at switchboards and operators at sea could pay their silent tribute.

An epoch had ended. The small black box Marconi had carried to London had grown into thousands of stations and millions of receivers. Broadcasting had spawned satellite activities employing countless workers of every kind. There were advertising agencies, station sales representatives, libraries of recorded music, independent producers for the networks, independent producers of transcribed programs, music licensing organizations, research companies, psychological testing outfits, commercial producers and employee unions. All this was in addition to the industry's manufacturing and technological activities, its engineers, its battalions of lawyers and, in Washington, its lobbyists.

The king was dead. Long live the king! But who would he be? Or was it time for some new invention?

7

Broadcasting Goes to War

All Europe is a tinderbox!" That phrase was heard frequently during the late '30s.

The man of the year, most years, was Adolf Hitler, a former army corporal who had become the maniacal chancellor of Germany. Radio brought news of his successive power plays into millions of American homes. Step by step, U.S. citizens heard him rant as he moved toward the cannibalizing of his neighbors. In an early move, he repudiated the war guilt clause of the Versailles Treaty, which held that the German nation had started World War I and was therefore responsible for the payment of reparations. He signed a treaty guaranteeing the borders of Austria, and then invaded the country. An unknown correspondent named Edward Murrow described the takeover of Vienna to CBS audiences.

When Hitler claimed a portion of Czechoslovakia called the Sudetenland, England's Neville Chamberlain and France's Edouard Daladier sought to talk him out of it. After two conferences, they signed an agreement with him and his partner in aggression, Benito Mussolini, dictator of Italy, dismembering the Czech Republic, and giving him whatever he wanted in exchange for peace.

CBS followed every move, with Murrow and William Shirer in Europe, and H. V. Kaltenborn in New York. Their reports during the next months of tension established radio as worthy of the protection of the First Amendment and deserving of the preference of the mass hunger for news.

Gradually, America's nerves tightened to concert pitch. Human ears had never been so constantly bombarded with such evil intelligence. Let a book drop, let a tire blow, and every human within earshot jumped. Then came a Sunday night when the national tension was released in a twanging orgy.

The trigger was a radio broadcast presenting an earnest group of actors and actresses headed by Orson Welles. From the very beginning, they had no idea of the national (or international) havoc they would wreak. Their instrument was an innocent radio dramatization presented on a quiet Sunday evening.

It happened during "The Mercury Theater of the Air" production of H. G. Wells' *The War of the Worlds*. A news flash interrupted "dance music from the Park Plaza Hotel in downtown New York." Strange activity was being observed on the planet Mars. More dance music. Another interruption. More news flashes. First an announcer said that a meteor had crashed near Grover's Mills, New Jersey. Next, an on-the-spot "remote" pickup from New Jersey explained that a thousand persons had been killed, not by a meteor as supposed, but by death-ray guns brandished by an army of invaders from outer space. An eyewitness described the scene: weird creatures

Adolf Hitler used his hypnotic voice to become dictator of the German nation—and to lead it into a ruinous era of conquest by force of arms.

streaming from a huge silver cylinder and burning everything that lay in their path. Martians, it seemed, had landed on earth.

This terrifying report was cut suddenly . . . "due to circumstances beyond our control." Now other parts of the country began to report. Staccato news bulletins said that the National Guard had been called out. The Secretary of War was mobilizing the Army. The White House had declared a state of national emergency. "Keep calm! Keep calm!" voices urged the public, the same voices that told of men from Mars burning their way toward New York.

Before the broadcast, several CBS people had feared that a few late tuners-in might be upset by the broadcast. "Make it clear that this is only a broadcast," they ordered. "Make it clear this is only make-believe." The writers and cast followed these orders. The words they spoke offering caution and reassurance were as futile as spitting into a gale. A multitude of neurotics simply failed to listen. Once the hysteria set in, reason went by the board.

Switchboards were swamped. Some people donned gas masks. Sailors on shore leave were called back to their ships. Crowds mobbed churches, seeking confession before the end. Highways were jammed in many areas with cars speeding between relatives in city

Benito Mussolini, dictator of Italy, made the trains run on time but his invasion of Ethiopia was the precurser of World War II.

130

and town or heading for the Martian "landing spot" in New Jersey.

In a little town in the state of Washington, a power failure was the convincing last straw to its horror-stricken citizens. Police stations everywhere were visited by frenzied refugees who claimed they had seen the Martians with their own eyes.

The dramatization in CBS's New York studio was a brilliant technical performance, perhaps too brilliant. It gave rise to thousands of learned discussions in nearly every field of endeavor affecting modern man. How could such an obvious studio enactment, announced as such, seem so real to so many persons? It was another "first" for CBS. No broadcast has since gone on the air without a doubling of precautions to make clear that the program is merely playacting.

In 1940 Hitler's Panzers struck across the Low Countries, skirted the Maginot Line and routed both French and English armies. The British evacuated their beaten battalions at Dunkirk and the French surrendered at Compiègne in the same ancient wagon-lits in which Marshal Foch had received the German capitulation of 1918. The scene reached American ears in the words of war correspondents William L. Shirer of CBS and William Kierker of NBC.

The Nazi bombing of Britain began during the summer and mounted in ferocity, preparing the way for a cross-Channel invasion. Amid falling bombs war correspondent Ed Murrow sent the sound of doomsday winging across the Atlantic night after night with the words: "This—is London!" Only in the year's final week did it become clear that young British fliers had beaten back the bombers, and

Winston Churchill said: "Never in the field of human conflict was so much owed by so many to so few."

The mounting tide of conflict impinged on every plan made by an American broadcaster or set manufacturer. Most authorities agreed that we would certainly become involved as combatants soon. In the meantime, Congress had passed laws designed to turn the nation into what the papers called "an arsenal for Democracy."

RCA in particular had to decide what to do about presenting its new million-dollar baby, television, to the public. David Sarnoff had been hinting that it was almost ready. "We have passed the point of conjecture," he said in the '20s. "It is an accomplished fact. Not only by wire but by radio, the image can be flashed from point to point."

In the '30s he added, "We may also dream of television in faithful colors."

A half-dozen corporations were busy with differing systems. CBS had come into the homestretch using a mechanical scanning device. Their first program in 1931 presented a welcoming speech by Mayor Jimmy Walker, songs by Kate Smith, a piano solo by George Gershwin and announcements by Ted Husing. Don Lee on the West Coast began to experiment. So did Chicago. So did Philo Farnsworth and Philco in Philadelphia. Some manufacturers built receiving sets and passed them out to radio critics and advertising executives.

As they jockeyed for position, as tension tightened around the world, RCA and NBC decided to take the plunge in 1939. Their stage was, ironically, the Court of Peace in the just-opened New York

The greatest "scare" broadcast ever came from a studio like this, with Orson Welles directing the cast of a "Mercury Theater of the Air" show.

World's Fair. Franklin Delano Roosevelt made a congratulatory speech, and thus became the first American President ever to appear on the tube. A handful of friends and company executives had sets with five-inch tubes; later, a reflecting mirror increased the picture size to twelve inches.

A mobile unit of two huge buses lumbered around the city transmitting programs: a baseball game, a sidewalk interview, a skating party at Rockefeller Plaza. In the Radio City studio, blazing lights turned the place into a sweatbox. Actors took salt pills to survive. Also in New York, CBS and the Dumont Company were telecasting modestly. Elsewhere, another score of TV pioneers were going through the same motions. Hardly anyone watched. Sets cost from $600 to $1,000.

Within a year, metals became so scarce that mass production was impossible. TV programs were cut from fifteen to four hours per week. Factories reeled under emergency orders for electronic equipment of all sorts, especially for a new thing called radar. The need was obvious. Overseas, Japan's armies were rampaging through Indo-China and the South Pacific. German Panzers were advancing across Russia toward Leningrad. In Africa, the British were digging in for a last stand outside Alexandria.

All at once, television seemed very unimportant; free world survival was at stake. In 1940 the Presidential election returned F.D.R. to the White House. A draft law provided for conscripting healthy Americans between the ages of twenty and thirty-six. Other laws permitted the sale of arms to belligerents for payment in goods or services. The United States was less than a year away from the sneak Japanese attack on Pearl Harbor.

Another prewar casualty was Frequency Modulation—FM— invented by Edwin Armstrong. Sarnoff had once told him: "I wish someone would come up with a little black box to eliminate static." After years of research, Armstrong came up with it.

He had expected RCA to buy his patents, but the radio giant was already committed to popularizing television. Furious at what he called "sabotage," the inventor gave a series of demonstrations so successful that critics marveled and General Electric decided to go into mass production of FM receivers.

With FM stations being designed, many set manufacturers sought licenses. So did RCA. Armstrong saw that his invention was about to turn to gold. But the White House ended the dream, declaring a state of emergency. War priorities stopped all set manufacturing except for the Armed Forces. Armstrong had been a Signal Corps major in World War I. Now he gave the use of his patents, royalty free, to the government. Static-free FM promptly became the standard method of battlefield communications. Every radio-equipped vehicle that went to war carried an Armstrong set, for which he would never receive a penny.

The prospect of war presented the broadcast industry with a question of survival. In World War I, radio had been taken over by the Navy. That it could happen was ominously indicated in Section 606 of the Communications Act of 1934. "Upon proclamation by the President," it said, "should there exist war or threat of war or public peril or disaster or any national emergency, or in order to preserve the neutrality or the United States, the President may suspend or amend for such time as he may see fit, the rules and regulations applicable to any or all stations within the jurisdiction of the United States as prescribed by the Federal Communications Commission, and cause the closing of any radio communication and the removal therefrom of its apparatus and equipment, or he may authorize the use or control of any such station and or its apparatus and equipment by any department of the government under such regulations as he may prescribe, upon just compensation to the owners."

The Washington office of the National Association of Broadcasters had been energized recently by the appointment of Neville Miller, former mayor of Louisville, Kentucky, as association president, and an unusually competent staff, including Ed Kirby, formerly of WSM Nashville. A Virginia Military Institute graduate and a reserve officer, he was directed to discover if there was an Armed Forces plan for broadcasting in wartime.

Simultaneously, pressures for air time mounted as government agencies demanded plugs for special projects. "At one time," an observer remembers, "we counted fifty-one demands, from 'Eat more fish; save meat for defense' to 'Buy coal now to relieve the railroad's overburdened winter traffic.' "

Two facts became apparent. The government had no plan. Radio had grown so lustily that it was now an entirely different creature. And it gave the President instant access to the nation. He had used it often for "Fireside Chats" since 1933. Now he could continue to use it as a wartime weapon. To curtail broadcasting was out of the question. The industry's problem—instead of a fight for survival—was how to help win the war.

Learning by doing, the White House established an information agency called the Office of Facts and Figures under Archibald MacLeish. His second in command for radio was William B. Lewis,

134

vice president for programs at CBS. The War Department organized a new Public Relations Department.

Very soon, a radio branch in the Army's Bureau of Public Relations was organized. Its staff came from station operations, networks, ad agencies and production companies. With millions of Americans in training, a need arose to tell the folks at home about their sons and brothers. Fortunately, those broadcasters-turned-soldiers had almost a year in which to learn their new business.

Some of them solved the problems of censorship. Others resolved the difficulties of accrediting reporters from press and radio organizations. Later they took those untried correspondents, such men as Eric Severeid and George Fielding Elliott, on maneuvers in Louisiana where they were briefed by a lieutenant colonel named Dwight

Eisenhower. There they learned the rugged truth that modern combat would not settle down into trench warfare as it had in 1917–1918 but would be a series of feints and thrusts, requiring correspondents to use their legs and brains to get their stories out. (The tape recorder had not yet been invented.)

Broadcasting would also serve as a weapon for psychological warfare. False broadcasts could deceive a listening enemy. On the other hand, truthful accounts could instill confidence and undo propaganda. This was a whole new field.

On Sunday, December 7, 1941, Bob Colson, administrative chief of the Radio Branch of the War Department, started for the Munitions building to make a routine check. He turned on the car radio. The broadcast was suddenly interrupted:

"'Flash!—Washington: The White House announces the Japanese have attacked Pearl Harbor!'"

Colson sped to his office. There, he telephoned the Adjutant General for instructions. "Have all stations in Washington recall officers and civilians on duty back to the War Department immediately," he was told. "Officers will report in uniform."

The Army radio staff came in and handled the battery of

William L. Shirer of CBS watched Hitler and his panzers occupy Vienna— and told the world that disaster lay ahead.

telephones, already jammed with calls, asking for confirmation and advice from networks and radio stations all over the country.

Their questions would not stop for half a decade. The variety of problems that broadcasting was asked to solve over the next few months was astonishing.

At distant bases where green soldiers were lonely, commanders tried to prop up morale with homemade radio programs. One of the first was at Kodiak, Alaska, where radio hams built a mouse-powered transmitter and concocted home talent skits for several thousand troops. In 1942 they wrote to various Hollywood stars, begging for transcriptions. The stars called the War Department asking how to ship the stuff. Soon other GI stations were heard from. Their development made it clear that men in training camps needed a network of their own. By the war's end, one was operating with hundreds of stations. It was called the Armed Forces Radio Service.

Washington leaders feared there might be a morale problem with Negro soldiers. The Army's radio branch enlisted the interest of Mr. and Mrs. Frank Hummert, who wrote a dozen daytime radio serials each week. One of the best was "Our Gal Sunday." In 1942 its lily-white cast gained a young black GI. In this and in other programs, the Hummerts planted messages which dealt with race a quarter of a century before the networks opened their arms to similar subjects.

To reassure worried mothers and grandmothers, they also wrote a series called "Chaplain Jim." Each episode revealed some facet of military life and explained that every lonely GI had a friend at hand to whom he could talk.

Training camps sprang up all over America, bringing thousands of men into confused, uprooted groups. Commanders knew the necessity of off-duty entertainment and begged Washington for radio programs and live shows. Sponsors offered to originate their broadcasts from camps. The War Department had never before faced such a situation. Hours were spent with lawyers in the Adjutant General's office and a formula was worked out. The result was a brief announcement at the beginning and end of each program: "The origination of this commercially sponsored program from an Army installation in no way implies endorsement of the product by the Army or the War Department."

That broke the dam and delivered the entertainment. Three of the earliest programs were Kay Kyser's "College of Musical Knowledge," for Lucky Strike, Bob Hope for Pepsodent and Bing Crosby for Kraft. Many others followed.

One government role was to inform the American public of its activities. Erik Barnouw says: "Many agencies became involved. . . . Edward Kirby, Public Relations Director of the National Association of Broadcasters, transferred to the public relations division of the War Department in 1941. . . . It was his demand for a troop morale idea that generated 'Command Performance' and he set it in motion. In the early stages of the war . . . Kirby's office branched in many directions."

One direction was the "Army Hour." It would bring to every American home reports from all the services, sharing with every family the bravery and fortitude of their sons and—remember the first WACS?—their daughters. Behind it, the War Department would place its worldwide resources. When the idea was presented to the networks, one by one they turned it down until only NBC-Red was left. Frank Mullen, NBC executive, saw in it a greater opportunity for service than anything else his company could do. He said, "We'll carry it."

It cost NBC $500,000 a year but no stockholder ever complained, for it gave to Americans the truest, brightest, most intimate picture possible of what was happening overseas. General Claire Chennault reported on his "Flying Tigers" in China. General Jimmy

In 1939, curious crowds gathered at the New York World's Fair to look at their first television set— a demonstration RCA model in a clear glass cabinet.

Color TV—and some early tuning problems—came on the market when RCA introduced receivers like these, made at their plant in Bloomington, Indiana, in 1954.

Doolittle described his bombing raid on Tokyo. More than any other medium, it taught Americans about war. Secretary of War Henry Stimson called it "not a radio program but a military operation of the United States." Eventually, there was a "Navy Hour," as well, but the pioneer and bellwether was Kirby's baby.

Soldiers, no matter where they served, had their own show called "Command Performance," made in Hollywood. The idea was simple: what a soldier wanted, he got. Requests were solicited, and they came in by the bale. Some wanted stars, and they got them. Some wanted to hear the wail of a son born after Dad had shipped out. They got it. Produced in the movie capital, it was created by writers and directors whose studio stipends ran to thousands of dollars per week. With the biggest stars in America living down the road, it was easy to summon them to rehearsals. One 1945 program made history, jamming eleven super-stars into a single program: Frank Sinatra, Bing Crosby, Judy Garland, Dinah Shore, Bob Hope, Harry Von Zell, Jerry Colonna, Frank Morgan, the Andrews Sisters, Jimmy Durante, Cass Daly.

The normal values of domestic broadcasting were turned topsy-turvy by the war. Having converted to military production, many sponsors had no product to sell. Gasoline, automobile tires and certain foods were rationed. New cars were nonexistent. But the game of advertising continued as if every showroom were fully stocked. The reason was a government decision which permitted war contractors to count advertising as a cost of manufacturing their military products. Inasmuch as most contracts were on a cost-plus basis, it was clearly to the advertiser's advantage to spend and spend and spend, and to have Uncle Sam foot the bill. Despite voices of discontent in Congress, the ruling held and the number of sponsored programs increased. It was a weird and wonderful system and many radio stations fattened on it.

The quality of broadcasting improved, too. Corporation executives, instead of building sales, tried to improve the company "image." Traditionally, the best image builder is culture. So General Motors sponsored broadcasts by Arturo Toscanini and the NBC Symphony, and U.S. Rubber backed the classical offerings of the New York Philharmonic.

A hint of the growing dependence of the citizenry on radio came when government sociologists polled a cross-section of the public, asking: "Do you have more confidence in the war news on the radio or the war news in newspapers?" Radio won, 46 percent to 18.

A listener, hearing interminable spot announcements urging

the saving of tin cans and the planting of victory gardens, must have
thought that a love affair existed between the radio industry and the
government. The truth was otherwise. In a strange, underground way,
broadcasting was fighting for its life. The struggle began when the
Federal Communications Commission started to investigate chain
broadcasting in 1938. By 1941, they had reached an unfriendly conclusion, and their report was a shocker.

The energy behind it came from a new New Deal FCC
chairman, James Lawrence Fly, a tough Texan.

"A wrecking operation," asserted William Paley in behalf of
the entire industry.

The FCC had decided that no corporation could operate two
networks; either the NBC Red or the NBC Blue would have to go.

The FCC said that a network could not own its artists
bureau. To do so represented a conflict of interest in that the net's
interest required it to hire performers at the lowest possible price,
while the artist's interest sought the highest possible remuneration.
Under single ownership, the artists were unfairly squeezed. "Sell your
artist bureaus," the FCC directed, hoping to give talent greater
independence.

Another reform challenged the relationship between a network and its affiliates. Both sides had friends in Congress, who joined
the increasingly violent fray. In the meantime, the air was full of
examples of harmony between broadcasting and many branches of
government. The industry wanted to help win the war, so the air
hummed with an incredible clutter of spots, Armed Forces reports,
and even a hometown service that transcribed the publishable military
adventures of local heroes and dispatched them to hundreds of local
stations. Broadcasters were also united in feeling that an attitude
of cooperation would win more Brownie points than stiff-necked
defiance.

Nevertheless, the commission had its way. NBC Blue was
sold for $8 million to Eward J. Noble, the entrepreneur who had built
Lifesavers into a national compulsion. The networks sold their artist
bureaus. An effort to restore control of program content to local stations was less successful, but that struggle would continue inter-
mittently even into the '70s.

On the other side of the Atlantic, Allied armies stormed the
beaches of North Africa, and Lieutenant André Baruch, recently a
network announcer, set up a doughboy station by using a French
transmitter that he and his men "liberated" in Casablanca.

Hundreds of thousands of U.S. troops in England were roam-

Right: The Armed Forces network became a potent morale factor for soldiers overseas. Below: Bob Hope in New Caledonia in 1944, at the beginning of his long-running, worldwide mission to bring laughter to our troops.

Top: A dynamic Mickey Rooney was another of the stars who toured the world's battlefronts to entertain the troops. Above: America's "Town Meeting of the Air" pioneered after World War II with a dual program, one studio in Berlin and another in New York, with a discussion of the problems of occupation.

ing the countryside, looking for something to do. Two ex-CBS executives decided that good radio programs might keep them off the street. Teakettle transmitters, each with a range of two or three miles, were installed at American camps. Disc jockey type shows used phonograph records, lively patter and homemade offerings. Within a few months, millions of Britons were tuned in, preferring the Yankee stations to their own.

In the Pacific, an almost identical growth produced a "Mosquito" network with stations on most of the big islands that General Douglas MacArthur had occupied. An enemy, to be defeated, was the malaria-carrying mosquito. Regular broadcasts told how to fight it, using a Harry James rendering of "The Flight of the Bumblebee" for its theme. GI's called it "the Atabrine Hour" after the prophylactic pills they were required to take.

At home the Air Force asked radio to help recruit pilots, bombardiers and technicians. A production center at Santa Ana, California, turned out one hit show after another, using the top stars of Hollywood and Broadway. "Soldiers with Wings" became a favorite report to the public. "Hello, Mom" spoke to the home. "Wings over America" made the heart beat faster.

Nobody contributed more, however, than the big bandleader Glenn Miller. At the height of his fame, he chucked it all and joined the U.S. Air Force, where he formed what was probably the world's greatest jazz band. When General Eisenhower ordered him to Europe, his appearance at a training base was as heartening as a night at home. Later, while on a mission to expand his activities, the plane he was traveling in vanished at sea. Major Miller's body was never recovered.

At the war's start, Secretary of the Navy Frank Knox, a Chicago newspaperman, had a low opinion of radio. In consequence, the U.S. sailor was not well represented. Eventually, however, policy changed and the Navy permitted programs to originate at their training centers and offered support to program packagers. "The First Line" resulted, a report sponsored by the Wrigley chewing gum company, and "Meet Your Navy," presented by Hallmark and Raytheon. Finally, the "Army Hour" was matched by a "Navy Hour," which featured such web-footed guests as Lieutenant Tyrone Power, a Marine pilot, Seaman Gene Kelly and a ninety-piece symphonic navy band.

Finally, on D-Day—June 6—the long military buildup was over and broadcasting became the nation's number one news medium. One thousand planes and gliders crossed the Channel to drop paratroopers in Normandy and 1,000 Royal Air Force and 1,400 U.S. bombers attacked German installations from the coast to the Rhine; thousands of water craft began the task of delivering almost 3 million soldiers to the European Continent.

After the first news flash, Ed Murrow read General Eisenhower's initial Order of the Day. It said in part:

"Soldiers, sailors, and airmen of the Allied Expeditionary Forces, you are about to embark on a great crusade . . . you will bring about the destruction of the German war machine, elimination of Nazi tyranny over the oppressed people of Europe, and security for ourselves. . . .

"Your task will not be an easy one . . .

"The tide has turned . . .

"Good luck and let us all beseech the blessing of the Almighty God upon this great and noble undertaking."

Radio correspondents rode gliders, landing barges and escort vessels. Scholarly George Hix, representing the new American Broadcasting Company—lately NBC's Blue—was aboard a Navy ship. His report set a standard for all that followed.

"It is now twenty minutes to six and the landing craft have been disembarked from their mother ships and are moving in. . . . Our bombardment fleet lying out beyond us has begun to blast the shoreline, and we can see the vivid yellow burst of flames. . . .

"We can hear the thud of shells or bombs landing on the French coastline, and the steel bridge on which we stand vibrates from the concussion of heavy guns. . . .

"The first Allied forces are reaching the beaches."

(Pause—filled by roaring of an airplane motor.)

"That baby was plenty low, the first German plane we've seen so far. Just cleared our stacks. Let go a stream of tracers that did no harm. . . ."

(Sound of a crash.)

"That was a bomb hit. . . . Very heavy firing now off our stern. Fiery bursts, and the flack and streams of fire going out . . .

"Flares are coming down, down. You can hear the machine-gunning. The whole seaside is covered with tracer fire. Planes come over, closer . . . and there's brilliant fire down low toward the French coast. I don't know whether it's on the shore . . . or is a ship on fire . . .

"Here's very heavy ack-ack, right close. The plane seems to be directly overhead [sound of plane, machine guns, and ack-ack]. Well, that's the first time we've shot our guns . . . directly over our heads, as we pick up the German bomber . . .

"If you'll excuse me, I'll just take a deep breath for a moment and stop speaking. . . .

"Here we go again. . . another plane has come over our portside. Looks like we're going to have a night tonight. Give it to her, boys! Another one is coming over. . . . A cruiser is pouring it out! Something burning is falling through the sky and hurtling down. It may be a hit plane. [Loud noise nearby.] There he goes! They got one. Great splotches of fire came down and are smoldering now just off our portside in the sea. . . ."

So the awful day began in the English Channel, with pain and bloodshed. Broadcasting reached its finest hour. That evening, President Roosevelt told America:

"In this poignant hour, I ask you to join with me in a prayer. Almighty God, our sons, pride of our nation, this day have set upon a mighty endeavor, a struggle to preserve our Republic, our religion, and our civilization, and to set free a suffering humanity.

"Lead them straight and true; give strength to their arms, stoutness to their hearts, and steadfastness to their faith. They will need Thy blessings. . . . For these men are lately drawn from the ways of peace. They fight not for the lust of conquest. They fight to end conquest . . .

"Some will never return. Embrace these, Father, and receive them, Thy heroic servants, into Thy Kingdom."

The prayer was long and eloquent, and it ended. "Thy will be done, Almighty God. Amen."

Every network carried it. On that night, America was united as never before.

First newscasting found its sea legs through ship-to-shore battlecasts. Then as the Allied armies drove across France and Germany they established press camps with portable transmitters to send the day-by-day story back home. Reporters rode with front-line units, capturing interviews on spools of wire and tape. Technology was changing journalism, eliminating the reporter-middleman and taking the listener right into the heart of action. German scientists were the first to develop and manufacture portable recorders. They used a fine wire for capturing the sounds of struggle and conflict. When American troops captured the first machines they were rushed to Washington, where Signal Corps technicians quickly handcrafted a GI version. Before the war ended paper and then plastic tape had succeeded wire—eliminating the horrendous task of splicing a broken hair-thin wire—and electronic journalism was firmly established. At last people could say, "I know it's true. I heard it with my own ears."

Later pictures in color would be captured and stored, the quality of reproduction faultless. Commercially it would mean that programs could be automated, that "spots" could be duplicated ad infinitum—and more economically. Ultimately it would make possible not only the instant playback of a sports event but the electronic video recorder, promised for 1971, with its library of instant entertainment and ideas.

The election that autumn presented the unprecedented spectacle of an American President asking the people to elect him to a fourth term. F.D.R.'s opponent was Thomas E. Dewey, governor of New York State. Radio carried most of the political campaign. One program, written by Norman Corwin of CBS, used a Greek chorus of Citizens for Roosevelt chanting their support. It sounded like an irresistible juggernaught chugging across the nation. Its cast included Irving Berlin, Lucille Ball and dozens of stars, plus a cross section of unknowns, ranging from farmers to fiddlers. "It was worth a million votes," politicians said. Roosevelt won, delivered a five-minute Inauguration Address, and left at once for Yalta to meet with Joseph Stalin and Winston Churchill.

Reporting to Congress on his return, Roosevelt's face was lined and drawn. To his associates he mentioned his constant tiredness.

Within a few weeks, he was dead. The "Fireside Chats" were over. He had made more broadcasts than any nonprofessional in history, just under three hundred. With the help of broadcasting, he had reshaped America.

When Douglas Coulter, program chief of CBS, felt that victory was near, he commissioned his star writer-director, Norman Corwin, to prepare a program of solemn celebration. As Corwin wrote, radio brought reports of the enemy's collapse. Mussolini was captured and murdered by his own people. As Russian troops swept into Berlin, Hitler committed suicide.

Corwin started rehearsals. The German surrender came on May 8, at the red schoolhouse in Reims, France, and Corwin's program went on the air that night.

It said many important things, matching the liberated emotions of millions of people. It was tender and harsh, it was arty and gutsy. It looked backward fleetingly—and ahead longingly:

"Lord God of test tube and blueprint, appear now among the parliaments of conquerors . . . ," Corwin wrote. "Measure out new liberties so none shall suffer for his father's color or the credo of his choice. Post proofs that brotherhood is not so wild a dream as those who profit by postponing it pretend. . . ."

8

The Agony and the Ecstasy in Living Color

he American giant was bursting with suppressed voltage when the war ended in 1945. Its industrial muscles had developed unprecedented strength. Its nervous system quivered from the eyeball-to-eyeball confrontation its citizens had experienced.

Inevitably, some of that pent-up power and passion flowed into the mainstream of broadcasting, manifesting itself in titanic struggles among the networks for stars, for program popularity and for prestige. Longer, more bitter and more costly than any other contention, however, was the dispute over television. Station owners lined up against networks, networks lined up against each other and the industry lined up against the Federal Communications Commission in a maze of conflicts as scrambled as a barrel of worms.

No electronics scientist was surprised when David Sarnoff announced, in 1939, that television was no longer "around the corner." Instead, it was ready, willing and able to take its place as an American industry. Its mentor, everyone understood, would be the Radio Corporation of America. Telecasts in the RCA Exhibit Building at the New York World's Fair aroused great public enthusiasm, but powerful broadcasters soon began to see ghosts in every shadow. As the automobile had ruined the buggy business, as the telephone had superseded the telegraph, so television might annihilate the radio business, writing finis to stations that some people were already calling "money machines."

Above, right: In the last century, inspired dreamers drew their concept of this TV heaven—and missed by a mile. Above: By the 1920s, everybody was experimenting, even the Bell Telephone Labs. Here AT&T president Walter S. Gifford speaks to Herbert Hoover in a public demonstration of inter-city TV. Right: This odd contraption is a "prehistoric" TV camera. Photos of astronauts walking on the moon were produced by the same principle.

"Sarnoff is a madman. We must stop him," became the cry.

Since much of their criticism was technical, an understanding of how TV works will be useful. Reproduction of a moving picture depends on a characteristic of the eye called "persistence of vision." A scene is retained in the brain for about one-tenth of a second after the scene itself has disappeared. Without persistence of vision, motion picture film would be impossible. For example, the movie camera takes a series of "still" pictures at the rate of sixteen per second. When these "still" pictures, or frames, are projected successively at the same speed, the persistence of vision creates a bridge from one still picture to the next and the impression that movement is continuous is created.

In the case of television, instead of photographing the entire scene that fills the frame, racing electrons "scan" it. Someone has said that the method can be understood by imagining that the camera's eye "looks" at a scene through a clear glass checkerboard. The electron beam starts at an upper corner and proceeds along that top row of squares to the opposite end, then it drops to the next lower line and returns looking through one square at a time—but with incredible swiftness—along that level, and on and on, back and forth across the lower and lower levels of squares, until the beam has swept the entire checkerboard. All this is done at a speed of hundreds of sweeps per second.

Visualize one of those paintings that one paints by the numbers. Its picture is broken into hundreds of tiny segments, each of which is to be colored according to a numbered code. In the end, when a thousand or so dabs have been painted, you have a perfect reproduction.

The purpose of this scanning action is to modify the amount of electricity flowing from each square of the checkerboard, an arrangement modeled after the working of the human eye. The retina of the eye is composed of thousands of rods and cones, each of which is a separate nerve cell subject to stimulation by light. Each is connected to the brain by its own tiny strand of nerve fiber. Light that is focused by the eye's lens falls on each rod or cone in relation to the brightness of the scene being observed. Inventors of the last century understood all that but could not apply it to picture transmission until the discovery of a mineral called selenium.

By chance, a telegrapher in Europe inserted a section of selenium in his electric circuit and discovered that the current stopped flowing when the room went dark, but when he turned on a light the current flowed again. The brighter the light, the stronger the current, and vice versa. Scientists decided to imitate the eye's retina with its rods and cones by breaking up the photographic image, as concentrated by the lens of the camera, into a matrix of innumerable separate electric circuits, each with an "eye" coated with selenium, each feeding its segment of the whole picture into an appropriate converter. In practice today, that converter is the television set.

The first successful method of scanning a scene was achieved by a mechanical, spinning disc perforated with a spiral of holes. Paul Nipkow, of Germany, invented it in 1884. His sketches had gaps in them, awaiting later inventions, but his theorizing was sound and provided the basis of a workable system. It was a remarkable achievement.

One of the first to conceive of painting a scene with electrons was a Russian professor, Boris Rosing. As described by Lee De Forest in *Television, Today and Tomorrow*, "He proposed to shoot a stream of . . . electrons at a screen coated with a fluorescent material . . . to bombard the screen and to follow the corresponding path across the picture as did the light beam through the scanning disc, which he proposed to use at the transmitter."

Early American experiments looked toward the same application. In 1923 a scientist named Charles F. Jenkins created a clumsy camera before which he held a picture of President Harding. His device converted the image into radio waves which were broadcast by the Washington, D.C., Naval Radio Station. In Philadelphia, 130 miles away, a receiver picked the likeness out of the air and assembled it on a tiny screen.

AT&T assigned its Bell Laboratories to develop a color camera. Twelve months later, Bell experts sent color pictures from one lab room to another. Unfortunately, they were about the size of postage stamps.

By 1927, the AT&T president, Walter S. Gifford, talked to Secretary of Commerce Hoover in Washington as the latter sat before the latest camera, and an audience in Manhattan heard his voice and saw his image on a screen.

The General Electric Company's House of Magic in Schenectady learned how to create king-size pictures in 1930, and gave a demonstration using the screen in a Schenectady theater.

England, usually a little bit ahead of the U.S.A. in invention and application, achieved a breakthrough when John Baird used the Nipkow spinning disc to broadcast a picture of a British beauty and an associate on a steamship 1,000 miles away in the Atlantic picked it up.

It is interesting to note that in every other country experi-

Dr. Vladimir K. Zworykin demonstrates an early cabinet TV receiver, based on the cathode ray system that he invented and that laid the groundwork for all-electronic television.

mental work was supported by government grants. In America, TV was financed by private enterprise and, in the opinion of most authorities, was "unquestionably more advanced."

One reason was a remarkable refugee from Russia, Vladimir Kosma Zworykin. When studying in Leningrad, he had met Boris Rosing, the man who had pioneered in scanning a scene with electrons. That encounter turned him toward a productive scientific career. Arriving in the U.S.A. in 1919, a fugitive from Communism, he went to work in the laboratories of the Westinghouse Company in Pittsburgh. His passion was the development of a cathode-ray tube (some called it a "gun") that would shoot electrons, not like a blunderbuss, but like a rifle.

In 1923 Zworykin had what he wanted. To name his invention he used the Greek words *eikōn,* meaning "image," and *skopein,* meaning "to watch," to create the name "Iconoscope." That was his camera. To receive its signals, he invented a much larger tube with a flat end, like a king-size funnel closed across its mouth by a screen covered with a fluorescent substance. He named it for movement—the Greek word *kinēma,* meaning "movement"—and it became the Kinescope of modern broadcasting.

After Westinghouse became an RCA partner, Zworykin sought out David Sarnoff, also born in Russia, and laid his cards on the table. It was a fateful meeting. Sarnoff asked, "How much will it cost to make your Kinescope ready for sets that we can sell to the public?"

"About $100,000," said Zworykin.

RCA hired him and began to think in terms of manufacturing and sales, never dreaming that they had taken the first step toward a program that would ultimately cost them, out of pocket, at least $50 million.

Even then the American system of private enterprise was providing plenty of competition. Rivals included Farnsworth, General Electric, Dumont, Philco and Zenith. On July 1, 1941, RCA beat them to the punch with its first commercial program, a report giving the time, temperature and weather, and sponsored by Bulova Watch Company. Then, in fifteen-minute segments, came Lowell Thomas with a newscast, "Truth or Consequences" and "Uncle Jim's Question Bee." Both Thomas and "Truth or Consequences" are still broadcasting favorites.

By 1942, Lee De Forest wrote: "Nowhere in the history of engineering science can be found another field of industrial endeavor or line of inventive research into which has been poured, through a decade of years, such intensive effort or lavish sums of money with so little of economic return as that of television."

The invention of various necessary TV devices was probably something less than half the battle. Persuading the broadcasting industry to agree on standards and other manufacturers to produce their own TV receivers was now the major obstacle that confronted Sarnoff and RCA.

The sudden surge of publicity and the public's enthusiasm unsettled a number of powerful station owners. "We're doing fine," they argued. "Why bring out a product that might knock us off the Christmas tree?"

They were a minority but they had powerful political connections. At one point Sarnoff proposed to manufacture and distribute 25,000 sets and then to ask the public what they thought. Chairman Fly of the FCC denounced the idea, and had the commission issue a ruling which threw NBC's TV off the air. *The New York Times* called it "a bureaucratic blackout of television."

A majority of the industry, including RCA, fought back. A special committee convened and recommended minor improvements in standards, and presently Fly reversed himself, setting aside a part of the spectrum for television and permitting unrestricted commercial broadcasting. His decision was an RCA victory but it came too late. German submarines were beginning to sink American ships. Our troops were moving into Greenland and Iceland. In May President Roosevelt declared an unlimited national emergency.

So David Sarnoff put his expansion plans in mothballs "for the duration."

The war merely postponed the commercial conflict. At the war's end, in 1945, nine so-called commercial television stations were on the air serving about 7,500 sets distributed among New York City, Schenectady and Chicago. That fall the FCC suddenly flashed a green light. Commercial television could go ahead. Engineering standards were distributed, a dozen factories retooled to make TV receivers and sales organizations began to sign up dealers.

When RCA threw a birthday party for David Sarnoff in 1946, celebrating his forty years in broadcasting, congratulations poured in from all over the world. The industry seemed united, ready to drive ahead into the golden future of which Sarnoff so often spoke. But the harmony was all on the surface.

Again, the Hatfields and McCoys of broadcasting chose sides. On the right, RCA headed a go-go force that included GE, Dumont and Philco. On the left, CBS and Zenith—the brilliant William Paley

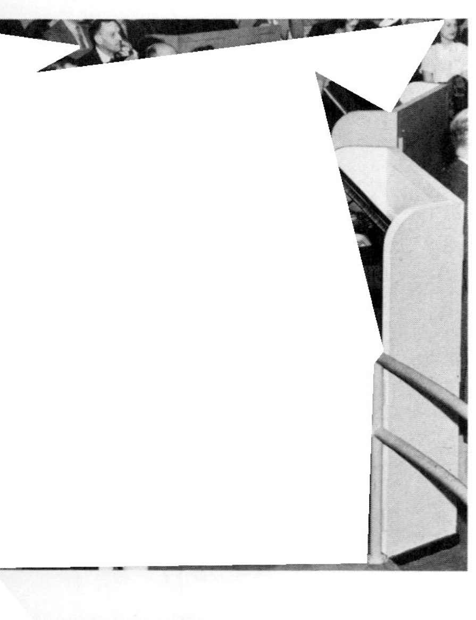

In 1939, TV was a miracle. RCA's first sets, demonstrated at the New York World's Fair, fascinated millions who watched "nothing" programs reflected from slanted mirrors. Opposite: In the first public telecast, David Sarnoff, TV prophet and industry statesman, talked mostly to himself. Almost nobody owned a receiver.

and the hot-tempered Commander McDonald—were the opposition. Their weapon was a demand for still higher engineering standards, using a wide band and a fine screen. The public refused to wait. They liked what they saw, demanding more of the same.

In particular, an audience in Washington in 1946 liked what they saw. In June, heavyweight champion Joe Louis fought Billy Conn in New York. In Washington, dozens of dignitaries were invited to the Statler Hotel where special screens had been installed. As cabinet members, congressmen and generals watched, the eye of the camera showed every detail of Joe Louis's mastery even better than a ringside seat.

One guest who watched was Harry Bannister, manager of WWJ Detroit, who returned home with a resolve to get into television. Less than one year later, WWJ-TV was on the air. Bannister learned quickly that he had an expensive toy. Even though he sold every TV program to a sponsor, his first two years of operation cost his owner, the Detroit *News,* losses of over $800,000. Other early birds were in the same predicament.

Another vexation was the appearance of a lattice-like shading that resembled a Venetian blind on the screens of many receivers. It was caused by interference. In the WWJ case, it came from a Cleveland station. By 1948, more than one hundred TV stations were on the air and Venetian blinds were rippling the screens and ruffling the tempers of thousands of viewers.

The FCC cried "Halt!" and declared a six-month freeze. They shuffled stations, devised all kinds of engineering tricks, unscrambled most of the interlocked radio beams and finally announced they were again open for business. The job had taken four years, and their waiting list of applicants for new stations was hundreds strong.

President Truman was inaugurated in January 1949 and TV cameras covered the ceremonies. Thirty-four stations located in sixteen cities composed that first inaugural network.

The growth of TV set production through the late '40s was phenomenal: 1946—about 5,000 sets; 1947—160,000; 1948—944,000; 1949—3,000,000; 1950—7,000,000.

By the end of 1948, 127 black-and-white TV transmitters were on the air. CBS remained aloof, engaging in experimental work and talking earnestly about the imminence of full color telecasting.

The success of RCA—and in England the BBC—must have galled CBS, but apparently the junior network never considered backing off. What lay behind such dogged resistance to the inevitable advance of television? An informed guess, made by some, is that the

CBS management knew that great prestige would accrue to the first network that could introduce *complete* television or *color television.* In the CBS lab, they were putting the finishing touches on just such a service, based on the spinning disc system. If they could postpone black-and-white TV, perhaps their own color system could be the first on the market.

At the same time, Zworykin of RCA was working hard to improve his still-imperfect electronic color scanner. When comparative screenings were held for the FCC in Washington, the CBS system far outstripped the fledgling RCA technique. The principal handicap of the CBS whirling disc—one that ultimately turned the tide toward RCA—was that its signals could not be received by any of the millions of black-and-white sets already in use. On the other hand, the RCA method would, when perfected, supply full color to color receivers and a black-and-white picture to existing receivers. Both companies utilized every ounce of one-upmanship in their assault on the emotions and intelligence of the FCC commissioners. The record of witnesses for both sides used up eight thousand pages. David Sarnoff alone spent two full days and one evening on the witness stand telling the commissioners in a dozen different ways: "You are being urged to build a highway to accommodate the horse and buggy when the self-propelled vehicle is in existence."

The decision was a hard one. Screenings had shown that CBS color pictures were consistently better. Sarnoff asserted that, given another six months, the RCA method would be perfected. Rival attorneys challenged him, asking: "How can you be sure your scientists can deliver in six months?"

"Because I told them to," said the unruffled Sarnoff.

True or not, it illustrates the spirit in the RCA camp. Finally, the FCC—Wayne Coy was now chairman—made up its collective mind. It approved the CBS system.

Immediately, RCA launched a crash program. Research labs at Princeton, New Jersey, hummed eighteen hours a day, seven days a week. A suit was filed in a Chicago court asking that the commission's order be set aside. The court ruled against RCA. An appeal was taken to the U.S. Supreme Court with the same result.

Sarnoff had promised a Washington demonstration as soon as progress in his laboratory would justify it. As the legal battle raged, RCA trucked its latest transmitter and receiver to the nation's capital. Government officials and the press attended, shepherded by anxious NBC and RCA press agents. Critic Jack Gould of *The New York Times* reported: "Last week's demonstration of the improved color

*Opposite, top:
Ex-vaudevillian
Fred Allen hated studio
audiences, treated the mike
like a listener and became
the thinking man's quipster.
Lower left: Fibber McGee
and Molly became prewar
bumblers and won
millions of hearts. George
Burns and Gracie Allen
(lower right) made mental
midgets feel like geniuses.*

154

system of the Radio Corporation of America materially changes the whole outlook on the dispute over video in natural hues. The success of the demonstration . . . puts the Federal Communications Commission on a spot which appears certain to become controversial and embarrassing."

In New York, CBS prepared a gala premiere for its FCC-approved color system. On a warm night in June they assembled small, select audiences in five cities—New York, Philadelphia, Baltimore, Washington and Boston—and gave them a beautiful sixty-minute color program. Compliments and congratulations were exchanged between broadcasters and politicians. The performance, however, was fatally flawed by a circumstance to which CBS remained insensitive. Not one of the 20 million owners of black-and-white TV sets in America could see it.

Actually, black-and-white TV was bursting its buttons. NBC had introduced an early morning catchall program, with Dave Garroway as anchor man, called "Today." It made such a hit that CBS tried to match it and failed; there was only one Dave Garroway. Then CBS presented Ed Murrow in a TV follow-up of his successful recording of wartime broadcasts. It was called "See It Now," and it was such a hit that NBC tried to match it, but there was only one Ed Murrow.

On the other hand, a private RCA color demonstration for two hundred members of the press, given a few days later, revealed that giant strides had been made. Now the RCA colors were true and the images crisp. Most important, while the twenty-minute color demonstration was being seen by newsmen and critics, NBC's New York transmitter was also sending it—in compatible black-and-white—to hundreds of thousands of viewers in their homes. The point was not lost on the public.

In 1953 the inevitable happened. The FCC reappraised the situation. Despite earlier approval of the CBS system, that network had made almost no progress toward providing either color sets or color programs. On the other hand, an industry-wide committee, led by RCA, had adopted color standards to which most manufacturers subscribed. The FCC reversed itself and gave approval to industry-RCA color specifications. In his biography of Sarnoff, Eugene Lyons wrote: "No prolonged hearings were now required. Time had done its job of education. On December 17, 1953—three years and one month after the previous decision—the FCC in a historic about-face approved the competing apparatus." At last, RCA was in the color television business.

That decision made compatible color television a fact. It also made the ownership of a color television set as much of a family necessity as an automobile.

The RCA victory seemed total, applaudable and profitable. It was not—not yet. The company would soon be forced to add to its expenditures until its total investment in the future of TV would amount to $160 million. For the moment, and for some years, RCA stood alone, bearing the whole load of creating a market. Its NBC stations broadcast color program after color program, gaining many plaudits along the way, but the majority of independent stations stuck by the status quo. Color was expensive. Why rush into it?

Most reluctant of all, understandably, were the rival networks, CBS and ABC.

The eye of the hurricane, now that color TV was out of the laboratory, moved to the Federal Communications Commission. The storm would hover over that hard-pressed body for the remainder of its days, veering to one side or another as the winds of politics changed. Almost monthly it faced some situation without precedent. Original thinking was required, research was needed, but neither was ever sufficiently available. Nevertheless, decisions were made, both wise and foolish, in the public interest.

Competition among the networks increased on many fronts, complicated by the fact that radio was changing its character. Networks were spending so much money on television programming that they were neglecting their radio affiliates.

By 1950, listeners to radio had settled comfortably into the habit of tuning in ABC's "Breakfast Club," CBS's "Helen Trent," "Our Gal Sunday," "Ma Perkins" and "Young Doctor Malone" and NBC's "Life Can Be Beautiful," "Pepper Young's Family," "Portia Faces Life."

Monday was the night for news and all-round entertainment. Ed Murrow, Gabriel Heatter, Lowell Thomas, or H. V. Kaltenborn were followed by "Inner Sanctum," "The Lux Radio Theatre," "My Friend Irma," "The Voice of Firestone," "The Telephone Hour," and "Kate Smith Calls."

Tuesday was for comedy, offering Bob Hope, Fanny Brice as Baby Snooks, and Fibber McGee and Molly.

The nets outdid themselves on Sunday, showing off their biggest stars: Jack Benny, Amos 'n' Andy, Fred Allen, Edgar Bergen with Charlie McCarthy, Red Skelton, and—coming up fast—a maverick idea with a big cash prize called "Stop the Music."

As one writer wrote about that year of 1950: "It's practically the same stuff we were hearing in 1930."

Though station owners worried that TV would soon make radio obsolete, the public entertained no such thoughts. More than 50 million radio sets were scattered across the land, served by 2,000 radio stations. The average listener, polltakers reported, wanted both radio and TV.

Nevertheless, the decay of radio entertainment had started and both time and technology hastened it. Sam J. Slate and Joe Cook describe it in "It Sounds Impossible." "The exodus began with 'Lux Radio Theatre.' It was followed by the Bob Hope Show, then others like Martin and Lewis, and Edgar Bergen. Old Jack Benny shows were edited and rebroadcast. . . . Amos and Andy became disc jockeys. . . . Television became the Pied Piper of media . . . sponsors became TV happy . . ."

Locally, disc jockeys were riding high. The trend had started before the war. A pile of records and an announcer with personality was about the cheapest program available. The practice spread like a plague and some jocks became near-millionaires. Martin Block with his famous "Make-Believe Ballroom" is an example.

Musical entertainment changed, too. As the popularity of the "big band" ebbed, young people opted for records with the "big sound." It was noisy, raucous and anathema to adults. Tin Pan Alley called it "rock 'n' roll." In turn, this brought a new kind of disc jockey; a jolly, jazzy parrot of a man who talked like a machine gun crossed with a laughing hyena.

How could such a thing happen to the medium that had presented symphonies and operas and "The Chicago Round Table" and H. V. Kaltenborn?

So, for a time, radio surrendered to teen madness. Hundreds of stations became no better than roadhouse jukeboxes.

Changes occurred also in high level executive positions. William Paley moved up to chairman of the board of directors of CBS, and elevated his right-hand man, Dr. Frank Stanton, to the presidency; Ed Murrow became a CBS vice president in charge of news and public affairs. Across town, a few years later, David Sarnoff assumed the title of chairman of his board of directors and placed Frank M. Folsom in the RCA presidency. Neither move diminished the authority of either network boss, but gave him greater help by increasing the scope of his principal assistants.

In any case, the internecine battle for network supremacy raged on. Its ebb and flow was indicated by the FCC's rejection of CBS's color system for TV, their subsequent approval, and finally their total rejection in favor of the "compatible" RCA system. Even in the

field of color research, Paley's gladiators were no pushovers. Nor was the relatively new American Broadcasting system without wiles of its own.

NBC had an ironclad rule that no recordings could be used on network shows. Popular Bing Crosby, tiring of the strain of weekly "live" broadcasts and "repeats" for the West Coast, asked permission to pre-record his program on magnetic tape. When NBC turned him down, ABC stepped forward to offer its facilities. Bing's show moved —and with it, a good many NBC viewers.

Twin blitzkriegs were launched by CBS in 1948. One involved unexpected competition for best-selling RCA-Victor recordings. Standard record speed was 78 revolutions per minute, which provided such a short playing time that many customers were abandoning phonographs for no-effort radios. RCA planned to offset the slump through a new kind of record that would turn at 45 rpm, giving nearly twice as much music for the same price. With pomp and circumstance, they announced a new day for phonograph records. Their product would be available for the Christmas season.

CBS was working on the same idea. Their records would revolve at 33⅓ revolutions per minute, giving even more value for the money. Their product, called LP's (for long-playing), reached the public before RCA knew what was happening. The resulting battle raged in ads, on the air and in the press. The big independents (Decca and some others) soon adopted the 33⅓ speed. When the National Association of Music Dealers also opted for the Columbia disc, the fight was over. Soon, LP's saturated the market, leaving RCA with millions of 45's nobody wanted.

Blitzkrieg No. 2 was a feat of legal and psychological legerdemain engineered by the personable Paley. For years, NBC's audiences had been the biggest, its rates the highest, its profits the juiciest. Experts attributed this to the NBC stable of super-stars: Jack Benny, Edgar Bergen, Amos 'n' Andy, among others. Programmer Paley heard of the formidable income tax these individuals were paying as top-bracket earners, and consulted his experts. The answers they gave him were just what he wanted to hear. In a tax sense, a star was not a person, but a program or a property. As such, he could be bought and sold in the same way as other merchandise, subject only to low business taxes. So why not buy Benny and the others? It might take millions, but their massive audience would put CBS ahead.

After much figuring and some finagling, deals were made. Millions of dollars changed hands. Radio favorites, no longer flesh and blood, became institutions subject to barter. Erik Barnouw de-

Above: Edward R. Murrow, who "slept too little and smoked too much," was an authentic giant of the "golden age of broadcasting." Below: "I Love Lucy," starring Lucille Ball and Desi Arnaz, proved that canned comedy (on film) could be a hit.

scribes what happened: "In 1948 Jack Benny stepped over to CBS, followed by Edgar Bergen and Charlie McCarthy, Amos 'n' Andy, Red Skelton, Burns and Allen. The move was a blockbuster. CBS had bought NBC's Sunday night and gained control of important talent for the television age."

Years would pass before NBC would recover from the coup.

Perhaps the sorriest chapter in broadcasting's history was the treatment it accorded many of its writers, directors and entertainers in its paranoid fear of Communist infiltration. In the late '40s, the disease afflicted millions of Americans. Senator Joseph R. McCarthy of Wisconsin had appointed himself Grand Inquisitor and used his senatorial immunity to make attacks on the loyalty of thousands of citizens. His venom spread a black cloud of suspicion.

Space is not available for even an outline of his iniquitous crusade, which continued until a brave and talented broadcaster, Edward R. Murrow, exposed his ruthless vanity over the Columbia Broadcasting System and laid him low. In the meantime, lesser inquisitors crawled from beneath rocks to do their mischief. A sheet called "Counterattack" and a book titled *Red Channels* were published listing thousands of radio entertainers who were alleged to be either "Communists" or fellow travelers.

Radio Row shuddered, pulled down its shades and made up blacklists. If a "listed" person performed on the air, letters poured in from "patriotic" organizations, and stores carrying the sponsor's products were picketed. Innocent persons whose names had somehow been listed along with the guilty went from agency to agency in a hopeless search for work. Many old friends vanished from the air. Many bright careers were shattered. Many hearts were broken.

On the plus side, listeners were tuning in a new kind of static-free, crystal-clear broadcasting called frequency modulation—FM, for short. Inventor Edwin Armstrong had patented it—although others had had similar ideas long before—and the Federal Communications Commission had authorized its use in 1941—just in time to be stopped by the World War II curtailment of scarce materials. After the war, it had been stymied by RCA's enthusiasm for television.

Presently, a grim battle of wills began between the inventor and RCA. The issue was complex, but one facet involved the payment of royalties. While most manufacturers paid Armstrong a small percentage of the price of each set, RCA policy decreed a lump sum settlement. They offered $1 million. Years passed with the issue unresolved. Another irritant was RCA's promotion of television to the exclusion of all else. Armstrong came to feel that RCA was conspiring

Lowell Thomas, peerless veteran of radio and television, succeeded Floyd Gibbons to establish a reputation in newscasting that has won every honor, including the Medal of Merit of the National Association of Broadcasters.

to keep his greatest invention from the public. He built a towering station across from New York in New Jersey and took his case to the people, determined to demonstrate FM's popularity. Working night and day, he became so obsessed that his family and friends feared for his sanity. The end came suddenly when he leaped or fell from the window of his Manhattan skyscraper apartment.

His widow settled for the $1 million payment that RCA had offered her husband. He had lost his life but, in a technological sense, he had won, for other FM stations were erected and their new sound attracted an ecstatic audience. RCA and other set-makers soon were forced to manufacture FM receivers by the thousands. Today the nation is served by two thousand FM stations, with more than six hundred broadcasting in multiplex stereo. Year after year the annual production of FM sets runs into the millions. And by order of the FCC, the sound that comes out of every TV set is produced by frequency modulation.

Broadcasting fads come and go, but none ever came faster or went higher—and then lower—than those giveaway quiz programs introduced by "Stop the Music." Orchestra leader Harry Salter originated the idea and took it to Lew Cowan, originator of the Chicago-born "Quiz Kids" program. They hired Bert Parks as a kind of barker-medicine man-announcer who, while Salter's orchestra belted out a pop tune, would shout, "Stop the Music." In the ensuing silence, Parks would place a phone call to a random number somewhere in the United States. "Are you listening? Can you identify the tune?" Parks asked. If the answer was affirmative—and correct—a cornucopia of gifts was awarded: cars, boats, glamour vacations, mink coats, washing machines—worth in toto thousands of dollars.

The American Broadcasting Company, with little to lose, booked the untried show into its prime time opposite NBC's top-rated comic Fred Allen. The result was traumatic for the comedian and hypnotic for viewers. Allen's NBC rating, hitherto one of the highest, gradually sank from 28.7 to 11.2; "Stop the Music" soared from zero to 20. The giveaway idea, once initiated, spawned "Hit the Jackpot," "Chance of a Lifetime," "Shoot the Moon," and others.

From 1949 to 1951, even indestructible Bob Hope lost half his radio listeners and half again over the next two years. By the time President Eisenhower was installed in the White House, in 1953, Hope's share of the audience had dwindled to five percent.

Now television was the "in" entertainment. The exodus of performers from radio into TV was massive. Comics had to invent visual styles. Hope perfected a poker face, an insinuating stare and leering eyes. Jack Benny exploited a shrug, an air of chronic suffering and a walk unlike any other on earth. The giveaway shows, transferred to television, waxed richer but not wiser, and managed to hypnotize half a nation with offerings of instant affluence.

The hit of that election year, 1952, was a series featuring Lucille Ball and Desi Arnaz called "I Love Lucy." Mr. Television, otherwise known as Milton Berle, was still a show-stopper, "Toast of the Town" was well established and so was Chicago's unpretentious "Kukla, Fran and Ollie."

This was also the year when television took two trail-breaking leaps into the arena of political science. The first was a "remote" pickup from hearings of the senatorial committee probing organized crime. Senator Estes Kefauver was chairman. Exercising a chairman's right to admit or reject TV cameras from committee chambers, he chose to show the public the kind of people he was fighting. For days and weeks, America saw and heard at firsthand many of the hoodlum bosses who were undermining U.S. law and order.

For weeks, high drama was played under the ruthless stare of the Iconoscope, particularly when chief mobster Frank Costello took the stand. When he refused to answer questions, an alert camera-man trained his lens on the witness's writhing, tortured fingers as he clenched and unclenched his fists. It was more exciting than Greek tragedy, and the eyes of millions were glued to the spectacle in one of TV's most effective services. When the hearings were over, Senator Kefauver was a folk hero and a Democratic candidate for the nation's highest office.

TV's second great adventure in partisan politics was the so-called "Checkers Speech." The Republican candidate for the Vice Presidential nomination, Senator Richard M. Nixon, delivered it. He was fighting for his political life.

Running on the ticket with General Eisenhower, he had been smeared by a New York newspaper that revealed the existence of a slush fund made available to him by well-heeled friends. The paper suggested that the money was a bribe for favors received. Nixon asserted that it was given and used exclusively for campaign expenses. Many voters were either critical or skeptical. Several Republican leaders came forward to say they had known about it for months, as did other newspapermen who had found nothing in it worthy of publication. In headlines, however, it raised a national rumpus that was made crucial by General Eisenhower's determination to seek office only in company of a candidate who was "as clean as a hound's tooth."

Was Nixon clean? Would war hero Eisenhower keep him on the ticket? In mid-campaign, with Ike stumping the Midwest and Nixon campaigning in California, the revelation made gossip from coast to coast.

Most Republican leaders thought the senator should withdraw. Others said, "Let him present his case. Let the people decide." General Eisenhower, who scarcely knew his fellow candidate, agreed. The party raised $75,000 and bought air time on the NBC and CBS television networks and hundreds of Mutual radio stations.

On Tuesday night, September 23, 1952, the critical program opened with a tight close-up of Nixon's calling card. As the scene widened, viewers saw the candidate at a modest desk in a simply-furnished office. Mrs. Nixon sat at one side, her eyes on her husband.

Immediately, the senator dealt with the charge. "Not one cent of the $18,000 or any other money of that type ever went to me for my personal use," he said. With little further mention of the fund, he turned to the story of his life, the poverty of early years, the religious conviction of his Quaker mother, his struggle to get through college, his romance with Pat and his zeal to serve his community. Talking slowly, he turned occasionally toward his wife, and the camera, following his glance, found her always composed, attentive and trusting.

In Cleveland, General and Mamie Eisenhower and about thirty guests clustered around a TV set in the manager's office of the Convention Hall. A crowd of fifteen thousand was waiting for Ike in the auditorium. As Nixon spoke, Mamie dabbed her eyes with a wisp of lace. The general's face was expressionless. Hardly anyone seemed to breathe.

Having exposed his family to public scrutiny, Richard Nixon ended his talk with a confession. With a glance at Pat, as if asking her indulgence, Nixon said: "One other thing I should probably tell you, because if I don't they'll probably be saying this about me, too. We did get something—a gift—after the election. A man down in Texas heard Pat on the radio mention the fact that our two daughters would like to have a dog. And believe it or not, the day before we left on this campaign trip we got a message from Union Station . . . saying they had a package for us. We went down to get it. You know what it was? It was a little cocker spaniel dog in a crate that he sent all the way from Texas. Black and white spotted. And our little girl—Tricia, the six-year-old, named it Checkers. And you know, the kids love that dog and I just want to say this right now, that regardless of what they say about it, we're going to keep it."

Observers say that a giant sigh followed that story, as if millions of Republicans were beginning to relax.

General Eisenhower is reported to have made two remarks. First, he told Mamie that he thought young Nixon was a completely honest man. Then, evaluating the benefit to the campaign of that $75,000 investment in TV time, he told an associate: "Arthur, you surely got your money's worth."

So Nixon was clean and Ike would keep him, complete with Checkers, on the Republican team. That his television talk saved him, there is no doubt. The final act of the drama had Ike meeting Nixon's plane in Wheeling, West Virginia, where the honest lens of a TV camera transmitted to millions of homes their fraternal handshake and the unabashed gesture of Dick Nixon wiping his eyes like a small boy.

In 1952, Richard Nixon was in deep trouble as he made a speech to explain expense fund his friends had placed at his disposal. These photos, made from a TV screen, reflect his moods. His explanation was accepted by the public and he went on to become Vice President and finally President of the U.S.A.

9
Money, Money

bservers have asked: "Why do so many broadcasters have ulcers?" An NBC president once told an assembly of affiliates: "Let's face it, men. We're in an ulcer-producing business."

First, to stay in business a broadcasting company must serve the public. Like a politician who cannot improve the lot of his constituents unless he is reelected, the broadcaster cannot serve his community unless his license is renewed.

Second, he must derive a financial gain from the sale of air time to advertisers.

These opposing conditions lock him into a contradictory programming commitment. To retain his license, he creates and broadcasts unprofitable informational, educational, cultural and community-oriented shows. To make a profit, he broadcasts programs designed to persuade the largest possible audience to buy the greatest possible amount of the sponsor's merchandise.

The result is a constant process of balancing license-assuring shows with profit-assuring shows. Men have been known to collapse under the strain.

Networks face the same dilemma. NBC's original solution was to have two nets, one for the money, the other for the image. The Red was the big profit maker. The Blue was the merit-award winner. The FCC decree that forced NBC to sell the Blue put each group of stations on its own.

NOEL

Competition is a wonderful characteristic of American broadcasting, providing benefits not sufficiently admitted. A fact of life little recognized by armchair critics is that any newcomer to a competitive situation has an advantage. For example, NBC's time was already sold out to advertisers when CBS entered the lists. Being sold out, the older net could rarely innovate or experiment for fear of losing an account or antagonizing faithful listeners. Starting from scratch, CBS pioneered in news and music, crooners and dramas. One consequence was a bouncy, relevant kind of entertainment that pleased millions, plus the crowning of William Paley as a "genius of programming."

But by 1953, the shoe was on the other foot. Now CBS was suffering from the rigidity of programming for profit whereas a newcomer network could tease the listeners with aural tricks that ranged from Merlin the Magician through the Pied Piper to P. T. Barnum. Its name was the American Broadcasting Company, née the Blue.

These next paragraphs briefly illustrate several points: the essentiality of creative thinking, the vigor of the broadcasting business, the merit of contentiousness and the blessings of serendipity.

From the beginning, the Blue network was handicapped by bobtailed budgets. Low man on the totem pole, their programs sold largely to sponsors who could not find a place on NBC or CBS. Splashing along in the wake of the giants, they nevertheless managed to make several valuable contributions. They were the first to put programs on tape, an innovation that persuaded Bing Crosby to jump networks. Using tape, they were the first to schedule an eight o'clock EST show at eight o'clock in the central, mountain and Pacific time zones also.

By the late '40s, their prospects were complicated by the need to build or buy television stations and to produce TV programs. Fresh infusions of heavy cash were essential. The old management decided to sell and talked to twenty-six potential buyers.

One of them was a recently divorced theater chain, separated by a U.S. government edict from its Hollywood studios. United Paramount Theatres, under the presidency of Leonard H. Goldenson, had perceptively surveyed its theater business in cities served by TV stations. In each television center, movie business had dropped significantly. The message was loud and clear. United Paramount should get into the broadcasting business.

In 1953 Goldenson paid $8 million for the old Blue network, now the American Broadcasting System. It was the biggest deal in broadcasting history.

"What do those movie persons know about broadcasting?" sneered Radio Row.

ABC replied with Walt Disney, a movie person. Helping Disney to finance his blueprinted Disneyland in California, they persuaded him also to produce a unique Disney-flavored TV series that immediately attracted millions of fresh listeners. Two years later, a second show, "The Mickey Mouse Club," made history by attracting so many advertisers that the new network showed its first profit.

ABC turned adroitly to younger adults and teen-agers. By 1958 they were presenting Ozzie and Harriet, Donna Reed, Pat Boone, Dick Clark, as well as a surprise hit, schmaltzy Lawrence Welk, and a novel breed of cowboy drama called "Maverick." Next they cornered the unexploited sports field. For peanuts—compared with today's prices—they signed up big league baseball, NCAA football and basketball, championship golf, bowling and the "Fight of the Week."

Those movie persons were also partly responsible for the nightly movie-of-the-week now available to most viewers. ABC's presentation of "The Bridge on the River Kwai" in 1966 attracted such a huge audience that it started a new gold rush by networks and stations to buy up old Hollywood films.

Good management, good programming and good times seem to have combined to favor the American Broadcasting Company. Serendipity is the natural ability—says the dictionary—to make favorable and profitable discoveries. You have it or you don't. By 1969, ABC's $8 million investment of 1953 had "discovered" annual revenues for that one year of a half billion dollars. ABC, in 1953, owned two radio stations. Today they own five TV stations, seven radio stations and whatever else the law allows.

Their TV affiliates number 168 stations, plus 1,200 radio affiliates. In every American market with three or more TV stations, ABC competes head-to-head with other networks. And its ABC-owned outlets, it is claimed, have become the most popular of all network stations.

The point of relating these details is hopefully to demonstrate again what has been revealed before: that good management can simultaneously show a pretty profit and serve the nation. With time, executives and staffs mature, developing the public-interest statesmanship required by their difficult assignment. This is also true of NBC and CBS. ABC's dramatic "Marcus Welby, M.D." regularly discusses today's burning issues, such as race, rioting and drug addiction. ABC was the first network to announce its response to a White House request that broadcasters help the public understand the cause

TV developed many unlikely stars. Top: Jack Nicklaus became the idol of a host of golf watchers. Below: Bandleader Lawrence Welk became an authentic favorite by delivering harmony, rhythm and schmaltz.

The money game reached a climax with such big giveaway shows as "Twenty-one" and "The $64,000 Question." Elfrida von Nordroff and Charles van Doren were two of the big winners.

and cure of drug addiction by producing a complete daytime serial on the subject.

One of its properties, KABC Los Angeles, is called the world's first Ombudsman station because it helps its listeners to solve their personal problems, even going to bat for them at City Hall whenever they run afoul of bureaucratic bungling or injustice. Other stations concentrate on community talent hunts among ghetto children, and run annual career expositions that help poor youth to settle on professions while steering them into training programs.

These samples are only a few among many and they pile up no profits, but they pay off in a kind of coin that has never seen a mint. As for the monthly bills, they are paid with income from such sponsored programs as "Bewitched," "Johnny Cash," "Movie of the Week," and—potentially—by the Monday night National League Football games scheduled for the 1970–1971 season.

Broadcasters behave like sheep. Let one producer wander into a green pasture and the remainder follow. The result is often a spate of imitative programs running on all three nets. This happened in 1952 when Jack Webb straight-faced his way to stardom on "Dragnet." Next came "I Led Three Lives" and "Naked City," "77 Sunset Strip" and "The Untouchables." Factual reality was the idea. Most factual and most popular of all was "Victory at Sea," supported by the lovingly composed music of Richard Rodgers, which celebrated the exploits of the U.S. Navy during World War II.

An older generation had worried about the preoccupation of its children with such programs as "The Lone Ranger" and "Little Orphan Annie." In the late '50s, people began to worry about themselves. Their worry was multiplied by the pronouncements of sociologists who had ascertained that an average family was watching TV as much as five hours each day. From that moment on, the medium would never lack for critics or be without a struggle between those who wanted merely to relax while watching an entertaining program and those who felt that TV should "do something."

Color TV began catching the public's fancy in the mid-fifties, and really big screens of twenty-one and twenty-three inches (in console sets) brought the peacock into thousands of homes. An incentive to buy was provided by a new kind of NBC program called a "spectacular." This was a one-shot, ninety minutes long, usually a musical with a cast of famous names and an energetic chorus line. By hard plugging, a spectacular could be built up into something greater than "Show Boat" and more exciting than "Ben Hur." That season expectant audiences deserted their regular favorites in droves and watched spectaculars—which was the big idea. NBC was trying desperately to overtake front-running CBS.

Within a few months, CBS was promoting its own spectaculars, spending more than a quarter of a million dollars on each. They were great treats for the viewer—some of them—but NBC failed to catch up in the Nielsen ratings, so presently their war shifted to other endeavors.

The radio show "Stop the Music," with Harry Salter's orchestra and Bert Parks' vocal jitters, spawned TV counterparts: "The $64,000 Question," "The Big Surprise," "Twenty-One" and others. Bert Parks became Hal March. The big difference was that the winners got real money—a fortune, a king's ransom. A host of big winners who were little people—jockeys, shoemakers, schoolteachers, child prodigies, ministers—came and went, each one a folk hero, each one richer by about $100,000, sometimes more, sometimes less. A viewer felt good, seeing them win. It was only justice. All was well with the world.

Each autumn is a time of high hope for broadcasters, critics and audiences. Within one fortnight, a score or so of shiny new programs are displayed on network screens. Each year most of them are shot down by critics or public indifference. In 1956 a stunning thing happened. Not a single new program got into the Top Ten, that royal family of favorites selected by the rating services.

Other signs indicated that something might be amiss. The popularity of the giveaway quiz began to slip. Sylvester Weaver, president of NBC and responsible for the vogue of spectaculars, resigned. In 1957, more signs of unrest appeared. Frank Sinatra, the Renaissance man of Hollywood's Wolf Pack, attempted a thirty-minute song series and flopped. Jackie Gleason retired. Sid Caesar left NBC.

On the up side, the Rose Bowl parade was televised in glowing color, and audiences were delighted with a spate of intellectual Westerns—some called them nervous Westerns—such as "Wells Fargo," "Zorro," and "Have Gun Will Travel." Producers were delighted, too. In "Maverick," they had a hit to copy. By 1959, thirty-two imitation Westerns were on the air during the same season. Then a new hero emerged in the person of $4,000-a-year Assistant Professor Charles Van Doren, of Columbia University, who won $129,000 on the giveaway "Twenty-One," plus a $50,000 full-time job with NBC.

Turning sour in 1957, the economy had sagged into the recession of 1958. A great shake-out began in broadcasting. "The Kraft Theater," after eleven successful years, was canceled. Ed Murrow's biting essays called "See It Now" were terminated and he began a year's leave of absence. Arthur Godfrey's "Talent Scouts" ran into

Top: Howard K. Smith, an American Broadcasting Company anchorman, built an envied reputation for independent judgment. Middle: The "Mod Squad" was one of the pioneers in presenting an interracial cast. Bottom: Dick Cavett and guests Lynn Fontanne and Alfred Lunt in a memorable tribute to Noel Coward.

trouble and Godfrey entered a hospital for a lung cancer operation. The "Bell Telephone Hour," with a distinguished service record of 935 concerts over eighteen years, locked up its music scores and was heard no more. The "Voice of Firestone" celebrated its thirtieth birthday and quietly expired. "Omnibus," a quality product that had surprised everyone by lasting seven years, gave up the ghost.

Surveying the wreckage of its once omniscient Red network, NBC announced that its radio losses over the last few years totaled $9 million. And the Mutual Broadcasting Company, with no TV stations to attract audiences or income, turned up its toes and declared itself bankrupt.

The biggest crusher of all, however, was the quiz show scandal. It began in August 1959 when the Colgate-Palmolive Company suddenly canceled its giveaway program called "Dotto." Their move ignited a bomb. When the smoke cleared, dozens of former contestants admitted that program producers had secretly given them answers to money-winning questions. Newsmen told of rumors of corruption that had floated through New York studios for months. Investigations were scheduled and hundreds of persons were questioned. A few producers confessed. Others were indicted for perjury. Network presidents insisted that they had known nothing about the rigging.

Many contestants said they had won honestly, among them Public Hero No. 1, Charles Van Doren. President Eisenhower asked the U.S. Attorney General to put Department of Justice sleuths on the case. On its own, Congress acted when the House Special Subcommittee on Legislative Oversight called Van Doren, among others, to Washington for a hearing. The public held its breath, refusing to believe that so many nice people would have deceived them. Certainly not young Van Doren, the scholarly son of a proud and distinguished American man of letters, Mark Van Doren.

The bubble burst in a Congressional hearing room with Van Doren on the stand. He confessed that his denials of wrongdoing over the past years were lies. He admitted that he, like so many others, had been given information to enable him to win his quizzes. Within hours, Columbia University "accepted his resignation." His pleasant job with the National Broadcasting Company—and its salary of almost $1,000 a week—was discontinued, and he returned to obscurity.

Van Doren's shocking confession was a body blow to public confidence in broadcasting morality. Hard probing by the New York district attorney had also uncovered a smelly trade custom. It was the tendering of "payola," an under-the-table cash gift to a disc jockey in exchange for his playing certain phonograph records. To be blunt, it was a commercial bribe.

Now broadcasting's top echelon was worried. Faith in the integrity of claims made for advertised products is the foundation of radio and television. "The American people were devastated," wrote Irving Settel and Williams Laas in their book, *A Pictorial History of Television*. "Neither the people nor the medium would ever regain their innocence."

Top executives moved to clean up the mess. Obviously, if contests were rigged, why not products? Each network took a hard look at itself—probably the first in years—and acted according to its lights. Stations all over America inspected the accounts of their disc jockeys and made interesting discoveries. In a half dozen cities, disc jockeys were replaced. Dr. Frank Stanton banned all quiz-type give-aways on CBS, as well as more conventional types of deceit such as the use of taped laughter to warm up a cool comedy. Applause, he decreed, must always be authentic and never supplemented by a sound track. ABC's teen-age idol, Dick Clark, who owned a prospering recording and music publishing business, was told: "Sell out or leave the network." He sold out.

Meanwhile, television was improving its ability to bring slices of life into the home. Smaller cameras, better lenses and more perceptive reporters combined to create an entertainment built on real people and their antics. With such improvements, the world became a stage.

History cooperated extravagantly. Premier Nikita Khrushchev, attending a United Nations session, indignantly beat his desk top with his shoe. Adlai Stevenson, running for the Presidency, bounced ideas off millions of skulls—no matter that they won few votes. Segregationists rioted in Little Rock, Arkansas, and federal troops were required to reestablish law and order. Sputnik I rose into the Russian sky, lighting up the extent of American scientific complacency. Hungarian students revolted and were crushed by a Soviet army. Israeli columns chased Egyptians from the Sinai desert in a devastating "instant war." And Wernher von Braun and his fellow scientists finally got an American rocket off the pad in 1958, initiating the greatest scientific rivalry in mankind's history. Later, newsman Walter Cronkite would dub it "the race to the moon."

When the decade of the '60s dawned, American audiences still had a bad taste in their mouths but they were also hungry for something new. When they got it, they got it in full measure, and it was almost too much to bear. Its chief prophet and protagonist was a young politician named John F. Kennedy.

10
To Serve a Nation

S o what happened in the '60s? The Great Debates between Vice President Nixon and Senator Kennedy ended in an election that put the latter in the White House. His campaign talks had insisted that the American way of life was a disgrace, that our young people were being cheated by a slowing economy, that we disregarded our poor and uneducated, that our streams and air and earth were polluted, and that our national idealism was corrupted by lack of purpose. His inauguration speech challenged every American with: "Ask not what your country can do for you. Ask what you can do for your country."

It was the beginning of a fascinating, frightening era, one in which John Kennedy would use television like a surgeon's scalpel in his effort to excise the nation's malignancies.

West Virginia had taught him the rudiments. Going into that state's primary against Hubert Humphrey, he had been a poor second. By buying large chunks of broadcasting time, he managed to put his face and voice into almost every home in the state. He won, going away.

Once installed in the White House, Kennedy turned the presidential news conference into a tool of leadership. President Eisenhower had permitted the filming (and editing) of his interviews. J.F.K. invited *live* TV coverage, an unprecedented step. And he would hold, a later count revealed, an average of twenty-one conferences a year.

Respecting the power of the media, he knew the danger of a

Opposite: Senator John F. Kennedy campaigning in 1960. His early use of broadcasting was credited with gaining him the Democratic nomination— and his debates with Nixon the Presidential election.

SEPT 21
I'D VOTE FOR
NIXON

wrong answer, so he prepared himself before each conference with an exhaustive breakfast meeting attended by a half-dozen associates who brought with them the knottiest questions any newsman might ask and the answers. When he went before the TV cameras, he was assured, at ease and letter-perfect.

His thin skin did not readily tolerate unfriendly stories however, and he often protested alleged "inaccuracies." Following one unhappy experience, a newsman at a conference asked: "Now that you're in the White House, what do you think of the press?"

Kennedy replied, grimly: "I'm reading it more, and enjoying it less."

Frequently he asked friends in broadcasting how he could improve his use of the medium. The complacency of people distressed him. He was convinced that only a national scandal would arouse their anger to a pitch that would enable them to act. "The nation will listen only if it is a moment of great urgency," he said.

The Kennedy years gave the people their closest view of their President at work and play. And because he knew how to communicate, they began to examine their own style of life—as he examined his—and they learned about many things, among them thalidomide, pesticides, cigarettes and Soviet expansionism.

With the benefit of hindsight, the bullying tactics of the Soviet Union can now be seen to follow a clear and accelerating course. Over the months, news commentators fed its details into the American stream of consciousness: the U-2 incident, the success of Sputnik, the Berlin Wall, the Cuban missile buildup, the Bay of Pigs. The offensive seems to have begun with the shooting down of the U-2 spy plane over Russia during the Eisenhower presidency. It picked up speed with the aborted summit meeting of world leaders when Premier Khrushchev angrily denounced the United States for spying and refused to sit with President Eisenhower. Khrushchev's press conference, heated and rude, showed the world a fierce, contemptuous adversary.

During the first months of his administration, Kennedy met Khrushchev in Vienna, hoping for a détente. Instead, the shaken young leader returned home to describe on television and radio the bold thrust of growing Soviet militancy and to initiate the building of countless bomb shelters.

In TV studios across the country, producers tried with little success to repeat their old program triumphs or to invent new ones, but a new mode of TV fare was grabbing the big audiences. Nobody had a name for it; but people watched—how they watched—as events unfolded around the world. Arthur Godfrey, healed after a harrowing operation, returned and settled down on CBS radio. Ed Murrow came back, rested and eager for confrontation. Suddenly the big story on TV was human conflict and global violence; and the big wheel of broadcasting was the anchor man.

Within months, TV viewers began to see the world as a place altogether different from what it had been. Anarchy and malevolence struck into hearts and minds from millions of screens and loudspeakers. In the Congo, a black leader named Patrice Lumumba was murdered. Overhead, Cosmonaut Yuri Gagarin circled the earth in a Russian spaceship, the first man ever to do so. Months later, a second Russian made seventeen orbits and the Communist press, radio and TV crowed in triumph. Against such feats, the U.S.A. rocketed Astronaut Alan B. Shepard 116.5 miles straight up and back to a splashdown into the Atlantic Ocean. When Gus Grissom did much the same thing in July, his multimillion-dollar capsule sank.

Broadcasting played a significant role in every American space flight. Networks sent their best camera crews and commentators to cover every moment. Commander Shepard's welcome home thrilled millions. TV showed him at the White House, at the Capitol and in an intriguing news conference. Chests swelled in most American homes.

These smiles at Vienna in 1961 changed to scowls when Premier Khrushchev secretly tried to plant his Russian rockets in Cuba.

TV and radio news won huge audiences when Russia's Khrushchev pounded his U.N. desk top with a shoe and when the U.S. spy plane U-2 was downed while flying over the Soviet Union.

If science could send a man into space, surely it could solve other problems. Presently, John H. Glenn, Jr., orbited the earth in Friendship VII and became a national hero. Television cameras covered him, the Cape, his family and his return, for twelve straight hours.

President Kennedy's thoughts about the future were soon revealed to a nationwide audience. "Now is the time to take longer strides," he said. "Space is open to us now. I believe we should go to the moon."

The space race was on.

Scott Carpenter followed John Glenn. Then Walter Schirra, Jr., went into space. In the meantime, the Soviets had lofted a spacecraft carrying three cosmonauts. Similar flights would color broadcasting for the remainder of the decade.

For most of its years, the Federal Communications Commission had discharged its duties along lines originally practiced by Secretary of Commerce Herbert Hoover. Supervision was technical, not ideological. The law has clearly proscribed interference with programming.

In 1961, President Kennedy named Newton Minow—a young Chicago lawyer and a partner in Adlai Stevenson's law firm—to be chairman of the FCC. And the broadcasters, as had been their traditional practice, invited the new chairman to address their annual convention. It was in this speech that Minow described most of television's fare as "a wasteland."

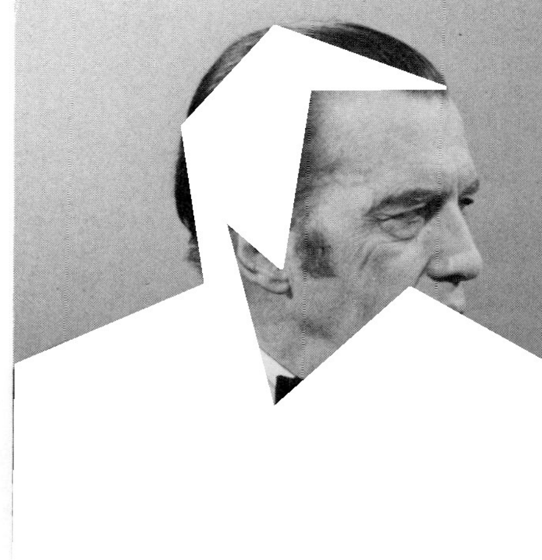

Top: Newsman Ed Sullivan assembled acts from all over the world to become a top CBS programmer for over a decade. Left: Jack Paar and Dody Goodman on an early "Tonight" show.

The "wasteland" phrase was immediately seized upon by television's critics and the FCC's mailroom began to bulge at the seams with thousands of letters from viewers agreeing with Minow's charges. Little was reported of the thousands of letters received by broadcasters across the nation disagreeing with the energetic new chairman or of the warnings by industry officials of the incompatibility of radio and television's program content and politics.

On Capitol Hill, members of another arm of the federal government cocked a jaundiced eye at certain television programs. A senate subcommittee began to inquire into televised violence and its relationship to the unrest that simmered on campuses and in ghettos. Hearings were held. Witnesses presented by both sides canceled each other out, as they have to this day. The experts, it turned out, thought that too much TV violence was bad for children but nobody could prove it.

In New York, Jack Paar enlivened his "Tonight" show by feuding with Ed Sullivan, the long-running anchorage of CBS's Sunday night. Both men depended on visiting celebrities. Sullivan paid up to $7,500. Paar paid the minimum permitted by the actors' union, a princely $265. The difference was made up supposedly by the publicity value of exposure to Paar's midnight fans. Another difference was that guests performed for Sullivan, for Paar they talked. Midnight talk shows ("they watch us through their toes") were becoming a vogue. One day Sullivan let it be known that stars who talked first for Paar would be blackballed by "Talk of the Town," Sullivan's newspaper column. Paar, who was developing a feisty temper, yelled "Un-American!" A personal confrontation was arranged, a show-biz showdown with dirty linen waving. Thirty minutes before air time, it was canceled. Each star accused the other of backing out. The feud died—but there would be others.

At the early end of the NBC day, Dave Garroway, maestro of the "Today" show for ten years, raised his hand in the universal sign of goodwill, uttered a solemn "Peace" and left the air to dedicate himself, he announced, to the world's more pressing needs.

Idealism was rearing its head in many strange places, perhaps inspired by President Kennedy's Peace Corps. Even physical fitness was incorporated into the New Frontier. "The President did his back exercises . . ." Hugh Sidey wrote in *John F. Kennedy, President*. "He frequently challenged his chubby press secretary to do pushups . . . he prodded his own desk-bound military advisers into a fitness course . . . Every activity had to be at full throttle."

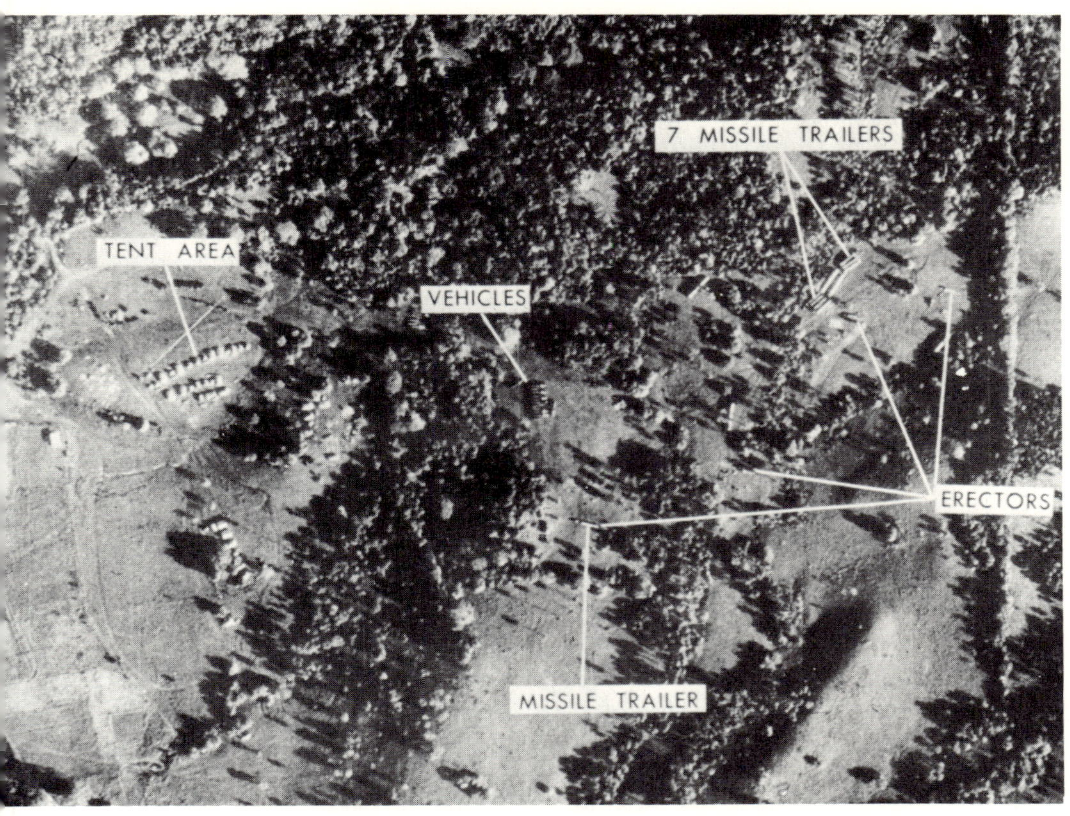

These photographs confirmed the rumors that Russian missiles were being planted on Cuban soil, pointed at the U.S.A. While the world held its breath, round-the-clock communications prevented panic and arranged a settlement.

Top: Night people have never had it so good. Johnny Carson, Croesus of the current crop of "talk show" impresarios. Above: Joey Bishop, who worked a rival West Coast version.

By midsummer the euphoria of Camelot was diluted by rumblings from Cuba. Fidel Castro's Communist regime had caught the fancy of Premier Khrushchev and he was jam-packing the island with technicians, electronic equipment and a dragon's brood of rockets. Friendly Cubans, at the risk of their lives, whispered a warning. At first nobody believed them. The Russian ambassador, called to the White House and backed against a wall, swore that the weapons were small, defensive and of no consequence. General Curtis LeMay, a no-nonsense veteran of innumerable combats on and above the ground, ordered photographic flights by Air Force reconnaissance experts. Their pictures showed clearings in remote forests, concrete pads and silo-size cylinders lying on their sides under camouflage. Other intelligence confirmed the bad news.

The President called up the reserve, canceled all military leaves and poured troops into southern bases. His phone call to the networks asked that the air be cleared for a special announcement. On the evening of October 22, 1962, he told U.S. citizens:

"The government feels obliged to report this new crisis to you in fuller detail." Sitting in his office, his boyish face like iron, he described the discovery of two kinds of missile sites. They were capable of mounting rockets that could strike north all the way to Hudson Bay, south as far as Lima, Peru. "The 1930s taught us a clear lesson," he said. "Aggressive conduct, if allowed to go unchecked and unchallenged, ultimately leads to war." The steps he intended to take rumbled from millions of loudspeakers. First, he would demand that the offensive buildup be halted. Second—and these were his words —"a strict quarantine on all offensive military equipment under shipment to Cuba from whatever nation or port will, if found to contain cargoes of offensive weapons, be turned back."

America shivered. Stopping a Russian vessel, boarding her to examine her cargo and turning her back—this was an act of war. Already, dependents at Guantánamo Naval Base were being evacuated. "This is a difficult and dangerous effort on which we have set out," the President said clearly. "No one can foresee precisely what course it will take or what costs of casualties will be incurred."

The threat of atomic holocaust had never been so close as it was at that moment.

For days a complex of southern broadcasting stations beamed messages directly to the Cuban people. All over America, commentators flashed each new development to a tense nation. Letters were exchanged between Washington and Moscow, calling a bluff but closing no doors to peace. Soviet freighters at sea, laden with missiles, steamed steadily onward. U.S. troops waterproofed their invasion gear. Newsmen displaced entertainment programs for long periods as the crisis deepened. Finally, the Soviet freighters halted, turned about and headed home. The work of dismantling the Cuban missile sites commenced. The iron Irishman in the White House had outfaced the foxy grandpa in the Kremlin.

After the missile crisis, something new had entered the nervous system of broadcasting. Every owner of a radio or TV set sensed, perhaps subconsciously, that the so-called "boob tube" was not so boobish after all. Sitting there in the living room or bedroom, it was different from other appliances that made life easier. In fact, it frequently made life harder, for it reflected the toughness of the world into which America was moving. An essential part of the family, it kept watch on the universe, extending human eyes and ears to take in both convocations and confrontations.

Programming would never be quite the same, for too many events pressed against history's door, enforcing a need for almost instant understanding if democracy was to survive. From now on, broadcasting would follow three broad highways: first, that of the conventional entertainment series; second, the exposition of a concept or idea; third, the close-up coverage of meaningful events all over the world. This last was assured by miniaturized, complicated flying objects whirling endlessly through global orbits and bearing such names as Tiros, Midas, Nimbus and, later, Telstar and Early Bird.

For the remainder of the decade, a common blight seemed to afflict conventional programming. Each new season would see the return of scores of old favorites plus the premieres of two or three dozen new shows, but frequently not one of the latter would attract an audience large enough to reach the Top Ten. Among those that survived a high casualty rate were "The Beverly Hillbillies," "Bewitched," "Hogan's Heroes," "Green Acres," "Laugh-In," "Julia," and "Marcus Welby, M.D."

Every year professional critics used almost identical words: "No standouts, no surprises, mostly based on established patterns of spies, screwballs, families, Westerns." Some of them wondered in print what had happened to creativity, and if broadcasting might need a new infusion of youth and originality.

Probably the best example of network copycatting was demonstrated when all three broadcasting giants ended the decade fighting for public preference with bedtime programs as alike as three peas in a pod—the so-called "desk-and-couch" show, a format consisting of nightly chitchat among a master of ceremonies, his pitch-

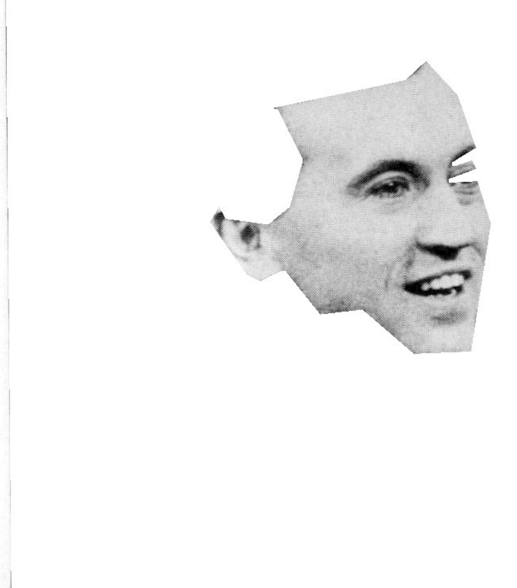

Top: Merv Griffin, who seems like the boy next door, added a fine singing talent to his interviews. Above: The Great Briton, David Frost, dug, not for dirt, but for meaning—and built a smashing audience.

man-announcer and a half-dozen famous or oddball guests, plus an orchestra.

Historically, NBC was the originator. Master of ceremonies Steve Allen was soon succeeded by Jack Paar who was succeeded by Johnny Carson who turned "Tonight" into a bonanza for himself and NBC. Rumor guesses that his salary is at least $25,000 a week, including insurance and deferred compensation, plus thirteen weeks of annual vacation. A one-minute advertisement on "Tonight" costs an advertiser $17,000.

After the success of "Tonight," several different formats were tried by rival networks and abandoned. Old movies held up for a while, but the supply was limited. Already, such stalwarts as "Stage Coach" and "War Correspondent," it was estimated, had been shown on New York stations at least seventy-five times. ABC was the first to fight fire with fire. Joey Bishop became helmsman of "The Joey Bishop Show," which, except for originating in Hollywood, was a facsimile of "Tonight." Meanwhile, the Westinghouse Broadcasting Corporation, an independent syndicate, put young Merv Griffin behind an identical desk, gave him a couch, a side-man, a guest list and an orchestra, and sold the taped result to individual stations across the country. A tremendous audience responded.

Dan Blocker and Lorne Green, of the perennial adult Western, "Bonanza." Below, right: Richard Chamberlain starred in "Dr. Kildare" with Raymond Massey in a long-lived "doctor" show.

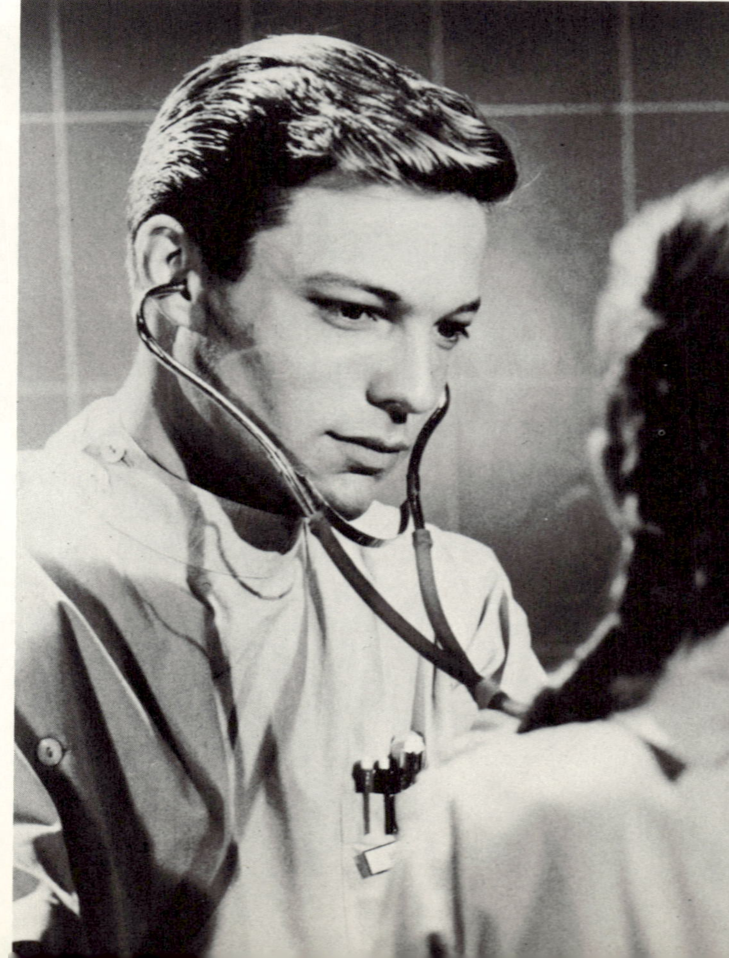

Unable to come up with a better mousetrap, CBS executives decided to buy one. They bought Merv Griffin. So the autumn of 1969 saw Johnny Carson, Joey Bishop and Merv Griffin in a three-horse race.

As the '70s dawned, late-breaking changes slightly altered the lineup. Joey Bishop was replaced by Dick Cavett, a sharp-witted Ivy Leaguer. Westinghouse filled the vacuum left by Griffin's move to CBS by importing an English intellectual named David Frost, whose spirited interviews broke the desk-and-couch format by eschewing vaudeville gags and offering literate talk. Johnny Carson continued to set the pace.

A coincidental development was a daytime, 90-minute session in Cleveland at Station KYW, since moved to Philadelphia. The Westinghouse TV-Radio interests (descendants of the pioneers who had given radio its first big bang at KDKA) hired a young singer named Mike Douglas to create a show for young housewives. It caught on so well that it was first supplied to other Westinghouse stations and then, via syndication, to anyone interested. Scores of stations bought it, and its average list for 1970 was about 125. Mike, a solid performer, shares the top spot with a co-host celebrity, a different one each week. Other guests in-

Raw protest and racial dissent invaded parlors and playrooms with Martin Luther King's marches. This 1963 march in Washington, D.C. was called his greatest contribution to peaceful protest.

clude such prominent people as Dr. Spock and Barry Goldwater and such entertainers as Sammy Davis, Jr. and Joan Baez. Perhaps because it is produced in an ordinary studio in a nonnetwork climate, it also projects a homey, lighthearted image of its star.

The decade of the '60s also saw the emergence of "Bonanza," destined to become America's highest-rated program for many seasons. Then "Doctor Kildare" came along with its contagious idealism and dedication to humanity. Both were much imitated.

Soap operas, which had moved from daytime radio to television, touched only gingerly on forbidden themes for a while, but when *Peyton Place,* the sensational novel, became an ABC soap opera, a new level of sexual candor was reached. *Variety,* the show-biz bible, made this 1968 comment:

"The daytime soaps . . . have already done nymphomania, abortion, homosexuality, frigidity, and miscegenation, and one of them recently has been fooling around with incest . . . 'Peyton Place' which had seemed so over-sexed when it premiered four years ago, looks mild in retrospect."

If the excellence of most entertainment lapsed, however, the so-called "special" began to thrive, embracing every kind of subject from art and architecture to Zen Buddhism. One of the best was a 1962 tour of the White House in which a poised First Lady, Jacqueline Kennedy, explained its treasures and traditions to CBS's Charles Collingwood and 46 million viewers. Another triumphant "tour" was NBC's full-color visit to the Kremlin in Moscow and its treatment of Russia's priceless art treasures.

Not every new idea pleased. A CBS dramatic program discussed the growing problem of abortion. Cautious network executives showed it to their affiliates via closed-circuit TV. Thirty-five station managers turned it down. But times were changing. By the late '60s, several states had passed laws permitting abortion, and the subject could be freely presented by any mass medium.

NBC set a record by devoting three hours to a single treatment of what they called "The American Revolution of '63." ABC offered a five-part series of social analysis. CBS presented a probing documentary called "The Other Face of Dixie." Unanimously, the networks began to look closely at the implications of racial unrest.

As the decade sped on, several other outstanding ideas and programs surfaced, stirring the nation. Concerned about highway deaths, CBS broadcast a national drivers' test taken by millions. Later, they broadcast tests on citizenship, health and environment.

The race to the moon provided many unforgettable broadcasts. Thousands of close-up photos of the lunar surface were televised back by near-human satellites. Both American and Russian spacecraft made soft landings in 1966. The Apollo 9 flight, testing the endurance of astronauts and machine, orbited the earth for ten thrilling days at a cost, someone figured, of $300 million.

But the sight that 125 million viewers will never forget was the blast-off of Apollo 11, which reached a climax when Neil Armstrong and Ed Aldrin piloted their LEM, named the Eagle, to man's first touchdown on the lunar desert in 1969.

The spectacle that followed will never be surpassed. Its immense audience saw history made as Armstrong and Aldrin, in their Buck Rogers space suits, collected samples of moon rock and bounded weightlessly over the lunar terrain like two exuberant kids. Then, to add one miracle to another, they put in a radio call to the White House and talked to President Nixon while the whole earth listened breathlessly.

Earthlings remained transfixed before their sets, a poll discovered, for an average of more than fifteen hours each. It was a show without precedent, with each network trying to sense the mood of its audience. That night Walter Cronkite was on the air for seventeen continuous hours. The public was served—and it cost a bundle. *Broadcasting Magazine* commented: "It took a minimum of $11 million in expenditures and in revenue loss, and an estimated 1,000 personnel for the networks to produce what had to be the biggest show in broadcast history."

Only one other ascent provided such emotional wallop. It was the aborted Apollo 13 mission in April 1970. Its launching began as a twice-told tale. But 205,000 miles out, Captain James Lovell's voice cut through a conversation with Houston Ground Control to say, "I believe we've got a problem here." A fuel cell had exploded, rocking the ship and rendering the command module useless. Their return to earth, if at all, would have to be achieved via the LEM moon lander, using its engines like an outboard on a disabled motor cruiser.

The drama was played out on television screens before a world alerted to tragedy. The yawn turned to the thrill of the decade. Even critics of TV lost their cool. Columnist Max Lerner, of the New York *Post*, wrote: "I watched the idiot box as if, by sheer will, I could mesmerize the TV reporter into telling us that all was well."

Time said: "Any place with a television set became a magnet, even after the safe landing seemed likely. In Atlanta, a drive-in near

Georgia Tech set up five television viewing rooms." In a few minutes, they were jammed.

And now the world prayed. American churchmen said prayers at Sunday services. The Pope in Italy sought God's protection. Orthodox Jews at the Wailing Wall in Jerusalem pleaded for divine intercession.

At the end of several agonizing days, a camera on the pickup ship, the *Iwo Jima*, sighted the capsule swinging gently beneath its great parachutes. The splashdown in the South Pacific was perfect. And the citizens of a concourse of nationalities were united briefly by a surge of thankfulness and fellowship and the realization that all mortals are brothers.

Along with space exploration, watching sports has become an American TV compulsion. *Sports Illustrated* magazine says: "The epoch of Super Spectator is upon us, and it is stupefying to behold."

During the '60s, sports changed from a few ragtag exhibitions between rival clubs to a golden bone to be fought over by the networks. The mind boggles at trying to understand the soaring flight of broadcast rights. It is almost beyond belief that an Orange Bowl Committee in Miami once *paid* a network $500 to originate a broadcast at a New Year's game. In 1969 NBC paid this same committee $500,000 for the privilege. Baseball tycoons once charged Ford and Gillette only $65,000 to broadcast rights of all seven World Series games. Those same rights today are worth millions. To buy merely a one-minute commercial during any World Series broadcast now costs $80,000 or more.

The U.S. Olympic Committee charged CBS $660,000 for rights to broadcast the Rome Olympics. ABC has concluded a deal for the Olympics to be held in Munich, Germany, in 1972. They are paying $13.5 million.

Managers and coaches admit that TV money is what makes the mare go. Calvin Griffith, owner of the Minnesota Twins, says: "TV is a matter of life and death. We couldn't operate without it."

Bear Bryant, famous football coach at the University of Alabama, says: "We think TV exposure is so important in our program, and so important to this university, that we will schedule ourselves to fit the medium. I'll play at midnight if that's what TV wants."

Almost any championship game is likely to carry a million-dollar price tag. To get the broadcasting rights of an early Super Bowl game, NBC paid only $926,000. The 1970 play-off between the Cleveland Browns and the Minnesota Vikings cost CBS $2 million. Gate receipts for the game, by the way, were slightly in excess of one-fourth of that amount. For a new series of National Football League games to be played on Monday nights in the fall of 1970, the American Broadcasting Company is said to be paying $8 million.

The availability of so much TV money has multiplied the value of every team's franchise. In the good old days, a football team was a millionaire's plaything. Today, it is Big Business. For example, the Los Angeles Rams, which one of the current owners bought years ago for $100,000, is now appraised at a rousing $20 million.

Who watches these expensive spectacles? *Sports Illustrated* calls a member of the audience Super Spectator: "He is a conglomerate being conceived in the bloodless circuits of MassCom [mass communications], an offspring of the passionless miracles of engineers, a product of the frigid market research and performance requirements of advertising men. But sport as we know it today can no longer do without Super Spectator."

The networks carry more than 700 hours of sports events each year—and pay about $150 million for them. Because of the huge audience, advertisers are willing to pay around $300 million for commercial announcements on sports shows. Everyone profits—sports promoters, networks, athletes.

"Super Spectator" demands his rights. In 1968, the Oakland Raiders and the New York Jets game was in its closing moments, the Jets ahead. NBC switched from the game to a commercial, then to the movie, "Heidi," scheduled for that time slot. Meanwhile the Raiders scored two last-minute touchdowns and won the game—and not one TV fan saw it! Angry telephone calls came in by the thousands. "The Heidi Affair," as the mixup came to be known, is remembered in broadcasting circles as a way not to win viewers and influence sponsors.

In the decade of the '60s, more than half of all network programming came to consist of sports and news. The change evolved with passing events. Big stories broke again and again under the noses of network newsmen, pushing regular programs off the air.

There were the assassinations of President Kennedy, of Martin Luther King, of Robert F. Kennedy. There was the racial violence in Selma, Watts, Detroit, Newark, Washington, D.C., and a hundred other cities, and the anti-war, anti-Establishment violence at Berkeley and Harvard and Kent State and other campuses too numerous to count. There were the peace marches and the Moratorium, the political conventions, the Black Panther trials. There was the Pope's visit and the tragedy of Mary Jo Kopechne. There was the political end of L.B.J. and Charles de Gaulle, and the funeral of General Eisenhower. There was a Presidential election narrowly won by Richard Nixon. Finally, there were the wars: the Israeli-Arab struggle with atomic escalation implicit in every air raid and guerrilla strike; the war in Vietnam, endless and winless, from which news of U.S. casualties trickled in, in a steady, tragic stream.

The most relevant aspect of modern broadcasting is its thorough reporting of global news. This is something fairly new, and will be discussed elsewhere. However, in concluding this historical review of broadcasting, it is pertinent to note that its content was being challenged as the decade ended. The challenge came from Vice President Spiro Agnew.

For better or worse, all barometers continue to indicate a growing public satisfaction with the service it receives. People do not buy radio or TV sets to listen to that which irritates or demoralizes. Seeking satisfactions that are hard to come by in the world of today, they spend their money judiciously.

In the '60s, one can find no better index of the importance of broadcasting to Americans than the record of purchases.

TV Sets Bought in the United States

1960	5,829,000
1961	6,315,000
1962	7,134,000
1963	7,983,000
1964	9,762,000
1965	11,447,000
1966	12,714,000
1967	11,564,000
1968	13,211,000
1969	13,308,000

Radio Sets Bought in the United States

1960	24,463,000
1961	29,222,000
1962	32,030,000
1963	31,548,000
1964	31,871,000
1965	41,726,000
1966	44,173,000
1967	41,211,000
1968	46,833,000
1969	51,353,000

The little black box that Guglielmo Marconi took to England so many years ago has multiplied itself by the billions. Men have adapted nature's laws to such a multitude of services that no part of the earth is without its electronic eyes and ears.

Some critics assert that our technology has assisted violence more than peace, factionalism more than unity and selfishness more than selflessness. To an extent, they may be right.

But in the long view, it must be otherwise. Given today's instruments, modern leaders have the means of pacifying man's fevers, of healing his sick spirit and of achieving the impossible dream of lasting freedom and peace.

Today, a new generation of young people are moving into positions of power. The old order has handed them a uniquely omniscient and omnipotent instrument.

11

The First Golden Age of Newscasting

The scene was Washington, D.C. The government official was very angry. He said, "Your commentator is unfriendly to this administration. He is biased and unfair and his broadcast last night proves it. I want to know what you are going to do about it." The radio station manager uttered soothing words—and privately tore his hair in frustration.

Again, the scene was Washington. The government official was both angry and grim, and he spoke into a microphone and looked into a camera that connected him with millions of Americans. His address attacked newscasters as "a tiny and closed fraternity of privileged men." He criticized their "instant analysis and querulous criticism," charging that their minds were made up in advance. He even suggested that the right of free speech guaranteed by the First Amendment might not apply to the broadcast medium.

The first instance took place in 1924. The official was Secretary of State Charles Evans Hughes, and the broadcaster was a Brooklyn newspaperman, H. V. Kaltenborn, speaking over WEAF New York. In short order, Kaltenborn was fired.

The second incident happened forty-six years later and the official was Vice President Spiro Agnew. No heads rolled at the networks, but the consequences may ultimately be much more serious.

ABC's Edward P. Morgan, winner of a half-dozen awards for newscasting excellence, said: "That was one of the most significant and one of the most sinister speeches I have ever heard."

G.L.
Pilot
KDKA

Giants of the anything-goes era. Top: Gabriel Heatter helped turn the Lindbergh kidnapping trial into a circus. Norman Brokenshire (center) described Democratic Convention fistfights. Walter Winchell (bottom) turned his machine-gun delivery on stockmarket booms and busts.

Chet Huntley, of NBC, said: "This is a concerted drive on the part of the administration. It could get very vicious and very bloody."

The point to be made is that nothing much has changed so far as official pressure on the free flow of news and opinion is concerned. What is changed is the role that newscasting plays in American life.

Broadcast news has become a daily necessity to millions of listeners. A study by the A. C. Nielsen Company has found that 75 million people watch the various television dinner-time newscasts each week.

Such dependence imposes a twofold responsibility on networks, stations and newscasters. The first involves the manifold problems of choosing, processing and presenting a balanced reflection of the truth. The second is the moral imperative underlying the performance of any man of consequence. William Paley, chairman of the board of CBS, once told Fred W. Friendly, then the CBS news chief, "You have in your hands the most sacred trust that CBS has. Your job is to keep CBS news holy—and I expect you to do it."

When Robert Kintner, an ex-newsman himself, was president of the National Broadcasting Company, he spelled out precautions taken by his company. "All these programs must be ours from top to bottom. . . . We must have someone to hold accountable for every piece of work that goes into the show. . . . We cannot know enough about where the information came from."

Newscasters themselves, both national and local, have evolved a creed to which hundreds of professionals subscribe. It reads:

"My job is news, reporting it and interpreting it.

"To this assignment today, I pray that I may bring honesty, integrity, and a respect for the public that I serve.

"The truth to me shall be precious, and thus treated; and because it is precious, I will share it with others, for truth is the health of freedom.

"I will strive to set aside prejudice during the hours that I give to this hopeful task, for prejudice is a whip that scars the mind.

"My loyalty shall be to the fact, and my purpose to make it known. But to that rigid loyalty, I pray that I may bring a compassionate understanding of the importance of the fact to the peaceful and faithful pursuits of the people who dwell in this place.

"Whatever talent I have, I will give to relating faithfully this day's events.

"And this evening, when it is done, I will seek tomorrow and hope to find in it the reward of yesterday."

Are newscasters really that idealistic? Author John Swallow, after much investigation, wrote a book called *Factual Television*. He stated: "In what is known mysteriously as the free world, news next to education, is the most honorable and least corrupt form of television, apparently uninfluenced by the pressures of the advertisers and the glances of the government."

Clearly, newscasting has demonstrated an ability to communicate with people. Moreover, it has given millions their brightest memories. Few who followed Astronauts Neil Armstrong and Buzz Aldrin to that awesome touchdown on the moon will ever forget it, or the fact that they were a part of the largest single audience in history.

Nobody who saw it will ever forget the immense nighttime façade of the Castel Gandolfo, and its single lighted window where beloved Pope John lay dying.

Or the funeral of President Kennedy, or the assassination of Bobby Kennedy, or Martin Luther King standing before that peaceful crowd in Washington, D.C., declaiming, "I have a dream . . ."

Or the sound of radio in pre-TV days when New York gave Charles Lindbergh a hero's welcome on his return from his flight across the Atlantic to Paris.

Or the melancholy sentiments of King Edward VIII as he stepped down from his throne: "At long last I am able to say a few words of my own. You all know the reasons that have impelled me to renounce the Throne, but I want you to know that in making up my mind, I did not forget the Country, or the Empire, which as Prince of Wales and lately as King, I have for twenty-five years tried to serve.

"But you must believe me when I tell you that I have found it impossible to carry the heavy burden of responsibility and to discharge my duties as King, as I wish to do, without the help and support of the woman I love.

"And now we have a new King.

"God bless you all.

"God save the King!"

Broadcasting also leads and comforts. After viewing television coverage following the murder of Martin Luther King, Michael J. Arlen wrote in *The New Yorker:* "All over the country now the members of the global village sit before their sets, and the voices and the faces out of the sets speak softly, earnestly, reasonably, sincerely to us, in order once again (have four and a half years really gone by since Dallas) to bind us together, to heal, to mend, to take us forward."

Another occasion comes to mind: the 1962 showdown in which the American eagle and the Russian bear confronted each other over those Soviet rocket installations in Cuba. Hardly any of us took a deep breath until the crisis ended. And who was the hero? The Manchester *Guardian* of Great Britain said it was the transistor radio. "As America waited for the Soviet reaction, as the Soviet ships crept up to the American sentries, as the drama switched to the U.N., the American Everyman was able to keep constantly in touch as he went about his business."

Electronic journalism has made a proud record; its position should be secure. Such is not the case.

Wally Simpson of Baltimore and King Edward VIII, who made back-fence gossip in Great Britain. Then, when the king doffed his royal crown, the broadcast made one of the most poignant of all programs.

Newscasting has many natural enemies. The foremost is the American press, newsmagazines included. This enmity is rooted in the battle for the advertisers' dollars.

In the '30s, newspaper publishers saw large sums of ad money flowing to radio stations. Hundreds of them promptly stopped publishing program logs. Their next thrust was an effort to deprive radio of the raw news needed for its newscasts. Newspaper influence persuaded both the Associated Press and the United Press to deny its dispatches to radio stations. For a time the embargo was total, so the networks established their own news-gathering facilities. In the end, the press blockade was broken and the effort defeated. Today, all press services are available—for a pretty penny—to radio and TV.

Again, when radio reporters sought a seat in the press galleries of the American Congress, they were rebuffed. Time and honest reportage opened some minds and a few doors in 1939, and today five hundred radio and TV journalists are using those press galleries. But the fight is not finished. Television cameramen are still denied access to the U.S. Senate and the House of Representatives.

Federal courts and most state courts also prohibit the presence of cameras. The theory is that a newsman with a notebook bothers no one, whereas a lightweight camera could prove upsetting to politicians or provide a stimulus to showboating attorneys. Experience in three enlightened states, Colorado, Oklahoma and Texas, negates that argument. They allow trial scenes to be photographed.

At the fifteen-week trial of Sirhan Sirhan in Los Angeles, the trial judge allowed a TV camera to run continuously through every minute the court was in session. The closed-circuit picture was transmitted to a supplementary chamber for newsmen. The California Freedom of Information Committee asserts that the test established five facts:

1. An inconspicuous camera will be ignored as much as any other article or piece of furniture.

2. Lawyers and witnesses will pay no attention to it.

3. Reporters will virtually ignore it.

4. Through TV, a courtroom can be enlarged to almost any size and the judge can maintain full control.

5. The camera, running along by itself, requires almost no supervision.

An odd contradiction to the rivalry of broadcasting and the press appears in the fact that scores of newspapers have either built or bought their own radio and TV stations. Perhaps the principle "if you can't lick 'em, join 'em" applies. As of 1967, newspaper publishers were said to have interests in about one third of all commercial TV stations, plus approximately half of the AM and FM stations. Even this alliance was to run into trouble. As detailed elsewhere, the FCC and the Department of Justice—in the late '60s—began looking askance at any company that owned more than one information outlet and were considering the practicability of dissolution. The threat that newspaper owners would have to divest themselves of their control of electronic media was no longer beyond the horizon.

Another antagonist is the well-meaning critic who represents some special interest or point of view. Many are intellectuals, sincerely concerned about what is happening to society, who make broadcasting their whipping boy. Errors abound in every learning situation and, as this volume insists, broadcasting has been the biggest, most persistent and most puzzling learning situation on which the free enterprise system has ever embarked. Targets are easy to find.

Typical is a small volume called *Survey of Broadcasting Journalism, 1968–1969* and copyrighted by the Trustees of Columbia University. It contains these words:

"Thanks to the new leisure . . . the broadcasters' portion of

the country's waking hours is indeed staggering. The television set is on in the average American home for over six hours every day. The radio accounts for another two to five hours. . . . Into this vacuum broadcasters . . . pour a torrent of situation comedies, adventure-detective-westerns, soap operas, ball games, variety, audience participation and talk-talk-talk shows. . . ."

Few will quarrel with such generalities. But the criticism overlooks totally broadcasting's good side—its good music and documentaries and its coverage of historic events. Surely the listening and viewing experiences of so many millions over so many hours is not all a "hideous waste." Sensible people do not turn from newspapers to the broadcast media if its programs are either hideous or wasteful of their lives.

Then there is the bureaucrat. This adversary of broadcasting may be a member of Congress or a member of a regulatory commission. The body that regulates broadcasting, the Federal Communications Commission, has seven members, three from one major party, four from the other. Since it was created by Congress, some congressmen get in the habit of thinking of it as their own creature. If a con-

Senator Joseph McCarthy used broadcasting to build up his image as a "Communist hunter" determined to clean out the bureaus of government—and then was revealed in his true light by Ed Murrow's crusading revelations.

stituent complains, they are quick to apply pressure. This leads to unpleasantness.

Overworked FCC commissioners have struggled with might and main to chaperone broadcasters since the radio act of 1927. Their mandate, however, is foggy and their decisions often are forced as much by the accumulation of real or fancied inequities as by the law. This lack of a firm base still threatens the well-being of newscasting.

The Radio Law of 1927 barred the commission from tampering with program content. But in practice, their findings inevitably affect programming policy. In the early '40s, the Mayflower Broadcasting Company of Boston gave its wholehearted support to a political party and its candidates. Opponents objected that they had no mouthpiece through which to tell their story. The FCC decided that such editorializing in behalf of one political party was against the intent of the law. So they banned advocacy. Henceforth, no station could have an opinion. That was Act I in the famous Mayflower case.

Act II came when the commission reversed its earlier decision and decided that a station owner had the same right to free expression as any other American. In fact, they said that owning a station gave him an *obligation* to express his opinions. During the Kennedy administration, FCC Chairman Newton Minow campaigned so ably for this policy that hundreds of stations began to broadcast opinions almost daily. But there was a catch. The FCC demanded fair play. If any station presented one side of a controversial issue, it was obligated to offer air time to a spokesman for the other side.

About one-third of all TV and radio stations are said to be broadcasting editorials, some with salutory results. Ex-Commissioner Minow, in his book *Equal Time,* wrote that WTVJ Miami was probably the first TV station to editorialize regularly. It happened when three of the five city commissioners voted to fire their city manager.

Melvin Reese, the station's news executive, went on the air immediately to challenge the action. His treatment was fair but hardnosed. Perhaps, he suggested, the city manager was too honest for his own good. Anyhow, the city needed him. For some reason, a second vote was ordered to complete the firing on the following Tuesday. Each intervening day, over the airwaves, Reese hammered out editorials supporting the city manager. The public began to respond. When the commission gathered on Tuesday, TV cameras were in the chambers. With every move visible on television, the commissioners reversed their dismissal.

"You *can* fight city hall and most effectively, too, with TV cameras," Minow concluded.

Today many broadcasts end with a statement similar to Pittsburgh's KDKA's sign-off: "This station recognizes its obligation to present over these facilities the opposing views of responsible spokesmen in order to achieve a balanced presentation of the issue."

Another regulation applies to newscasting. It is the "equal time" requirement, and it is written into the Radio Act. Section 315 says: "If any licensee shall permit any person who is a legally qualified candidate for any public office to use a broadcasting station, he shall afford equal opportunities to all other such candidates for that office in the use of such broadcasting station. . . ." In 1959 Congress exempted news broadcasts from the "equal time" requirement. In 1960 Congress temporarily suspended the same law for nominees for the office of President and Vice President, which made possible the famous Kennedy-Nixon confrontations. The industry would like to have the suspension made permanent—and so would listeners.

Equal time and fairness, at best, have not increased the possibility of good programming. Because of them, subjects have been bypassed and interesting personalities kept off the air. But TV and radio news continues to grow in popularity.

The process has been one of learning. Stage one was the simple act of an experimenter reading a newspaper on the air, hoping that some listener would send a postcard as evidence of how far his "spark" could travel. Others did the same. An old WOR program log still extant carries the line: " 'Newark Sunday Call' read by Thomas Cowan."

As radio matured and news proved popular, broadcasters either read bulletins contributed by cooperative newspapers or brazenly pirated their stories. Few stations employed their own reporters.

News programs presently discovered an added box-office value in going outside the studio. Some announcers who did this, and survived the ordeal, became famous. Today's television public finds it difficult to name even two or three announcers. A radio listener of the '30s could rattle off a dozen favorites: H.V. Kaltenborn, Ted Husing, Graham McNamee, Milton Cross, and later, in a mounting crescendo of popularity, Gabriel Heatter, Boake Carter, Edwin C. Hill, Floyd Gibbons, Lowell Thomas, David Ross, Ford Bond, Ben Grauer, Alois Havrilla, Walter Winchell. Then came World War II and listeners heard Ed Murrow, Elmer Davis, Raymond Gram Swing, Quincy Howe, Howard K. Smith, William Shirer, Max Jordan, John Daly, Eric Severeid, Robert Trout. Any listing must be incomplete for they were a wide-ranging and beloved tribe.

Women reporters serving daytime audiences created their own kind of news. Usually they probed for human interest, for the whys and hows of life. Queen of them all was Mary Margaret McBride, who brought newsmakers to her studio and gently picked their brains. Named one of America's "ten most successful salesmen," she was paid the highest salary ever granted a woman anywhere. When NBC decided to honor her with a birthday party, they rented New York's Yankee Stadium and filled it to the brim with 50,000 delighted guests.

And there was Murrow, the cigarette-smoking news giant who took listeners with him through World War II, from the fire-bombing of London to the war's final weeks and his visit at the concentration camp called Buchenwald. His comments from the horror camp were not really unexpected, yet the raw facts of man's inhuman-

Huntley and Brinkley teamed up at a political convention and went on to cover the universe. Chet Huntley retired late in 1970.

Fred Friendy (left) and Ed
Murrow (center) began a
partnership in 1946 with
"Hear It Now" and spent
subsequent years tackling
international issues.

ity are always a shock. He said: "Permit me to tell you of Buchenwald . . . let me tell you this in the first person. . . . There surged around me an evil-smelling horde. Men and boys reached out to touch me; they were in rags and the remnants of uniform. Death had already marked many of them, but they were smiling with their eyes. . . . As we walked out into the courtyard, a man fell dead. . . . There were two rows of bodies stacked up like cordwood. They were thin and very white. Some of the bodies were terribly bruised, though there seemed to be little flesh to bruise. . . . I tried to count them as best I could and arrived at the conclusion that all that was mortal of more than five hundred men and boys lay there in two neat piles . . ."

Yesterday, such an eyewitness report was an extraordinary feat. Today, we expect it.

After the war, Murrow became a CBS vice president in charge of news. No network team has ever equaled the staff he assembled. Very early, he sensed that headline news alone could not fill the needs of an informed public, so he invented his own form, a series called "See It Now!" It was part reporting, part documentary film-making, part feature-magazine photography, and all of it was illuminated by his love of justice, freedom and country.

No subject was taboo. The first "See It Now!" broadcast to strike fire was a CBS presentation (with Murrow's partner, Fred Friendly) of the case of Lieutenant Milo Radilovich. Because the young officer chanced to have a sister and a father who were alleged by anonymous accusers to be Communists, the Air Force was about to fire him. The decision had been made arbitrarily after a trial at which no witnesses appeared. When Murrow heard that the youth was being railroaded he set his staff to work.

Jack Gould of *The New York Times* wrote of the production: "The program marked perhaps the first time that a major network, the Columbia Broadcasting System, and one of the country's most important industrial sponsors, the Aluminum Company of America, consented to a program taking a vigorous editorial stand in a matter of national importance and controversy."

The resulting furor gave rise to a pertinent question: Who was responsible for the show's editorial opinion—was it the news team (Murrow, et al) or the network that hired them? This fuzziness persists to this day. When the lieutenant was exonerated and restored to duty, the honors heaped on Ed Murrow's head made the issue seem relatively unimportant—but it would explode thunderously within a decade.

One fact stood out. By taking a forthright editorial stand, by illustrating and documenting his theme with imaginative photography, Murrow had established a precedent for the finest use of the power and persuasion of the medium. While other producers were using what they called "careful courage," he became an exponent of "advocacy by reporting."

Nor did he pull his punches in 1954 when he addressed himself to the menace of Senator Joseph McCarthy's inquisitorial bullying. With wild claims of Communist infiltration in our government and wilder denunciations of scores of little people (who could not fight back), the Senator seemed untouchable. Ed Murrow's telecast coolly dissected fact from fiction, leaving nothing but the naked web of the man's vanity. That program, many say, initiated the McCarthy decline. Certainly it sparked other memorable newscasts, the Army-McCarthy hearings. What rival politicians had feared to do, what the Eisenhower administration had failed to do, Ed Murrow and television did.

Week after week, Murrow's scrutiny of what was right and

what was wrong in America blazed on the home screen. His "Harvest of Shame" program was the first barefisted mass media attack on the horrible plight of migrant labor. Soon NBC and ABC gave their own talented young men orders to recoup their lost prestige by creating their own exposés.

What finally happened to Ed Murrow at CBS is the subject of a book by Murrow's partner and successor as head of CBS News, Fred W. Friendly. In *Due to Circumstances Beyond Our Control,* Friendly describes the high cost of investigative reporting, the growing timidity of sponsors under pressure from their dealers, and ultimately of the corporate decision by CBS that Friendly interpreted as a move away from subjects that caused trouble. He was no more than partly right, for subsequent CBS programs over the years have torn into many touchy subjects for which the network has had to stand up against both public and governmental critics.

At any rate Ed Murrow decided to take a long vacation. When he came back John Kennedy was campaigning for the presidency. Following his victory, Chester Bowles, former ambassador to India and a Kennedy backer, called Ed. "We need you to run the U.S. Information Agency," he said. "How soon can you come to Washington?"

"Anytime you say," Ed replied.

He knew what was happening to the medium and he agonized over it. Speaking to the Radio-Television News Directors Association in 1958, soon after the demise of "See It Now!" he said, "If a hundred years from now . . . there should be preserved the Kinescopes for one week of all three networks, they will find recorded, in black and white or color, evidence of decadence, escapism, and insulation from the realities of the world in which we live . . . If we go on as we are, then history will take its revenge and retribution will catch up with us."

As a government official appointed by President Kennedy, Murrow stirred up his agency, sharpening its focus on dozens of national goals, but his real talent found no market.

Presently he fell ill of lung cancer. Of his death, Friendly wrote: "Ed Murrow, who slept too little and worked and smoked too much, had always said that he wanted to 'wear out, not rust out.' He did! He went to his grave with nothing . . . but for a man with no pockets in life, he died the richest man I've ever known."

William Paley, Murrow's old friend and chairman of the board of CBS, said: "His death ends the first golden age of broadcast journalism."

12

The Evolution in Newscasting

The modern age of electronic reporting was spawned by our national political conventions. Their dates were preset, their import concerned every citizen and their dramatics were frequent. Behind their façade, network rivalry rose to a climax.

In 1952 American business was first persuaded to sponsor these extravaganzas. Reports say that Admiral Television paid $2 million to the American Broadcasting Company, Philco paid $2.5 million to NBC and Westinghouse paid $3 million to CBS—and the nets still lost money.

Convention coverage also produced the concept of the anchor man, a central reporter who sat Jove-like on his throne punditing or prattling, while his outriders patrolled the aisles.

In 1956 NBC decided on twin Joves and named David Brinkley and Chet Huntley to the central post, where their performances evoked wide support among listeners estimated at 33 million. Quick to smell a trend, NBC promptly paired them on a regular newscast and their fortunes were made. CBS continued to rely on the reassuring resonance of their prime-time reporter, Walter Cronkite. ABC countered with Howard K. Smith, followed by various formats and personalities.

Over the years, NBC and CBS newscasts have run neck and neck, one leading for a while and then the other in the ratings race. Just as consistently, ABC has provided some of the best and brightest

206

Opposite: This is the moment that astounded the world. As millions watched, Jack Ruby pumped a bullet into the stomach of Lee Harvey Oswald, accused assassin of President Kennedy.

coverage, but its evening audience still remains somewhat smaller.

Is the news they put on network newscasts relevant to today's needs? In choice of subject, yes. In depth, perhaps. Robert Macneil, formerly an NBC newsman and later with the British Broadcasting Corporation, in his critical book about newscasting, *The People Machine,* wrote: "What a television viewer is getting essentially is headline service."

On the other hand, millions of listeners have been stimulated to undertake additional studies and to join discussion groups. No polls are available to solve the dilemma of depth versus quantity, but adult

education courses are more crowded than ever with students demanding an unusual breadth of subject matter. A news item in *Broadcasting* reports that stations across the nation have doubled, on the average, their financial budgets for news in the year 1969.

While big-time newscasting goes its way, a revolution has spread from coast to coast to make almost irrelevant much of what networks present. The evidence was first summarized in 1968 in "The Land Report," a study prepared for the President's Task Force on Communications Policy and commissioned by the National Association of Broadcasters.

Herman M. Land Associates, an independent research firm, was asked to explore the programming implications of a change in the mode of transmitting radiomagnetic signals. To gauge what might happen, they first had to find out what actually was taking place. When they looked into the area of local newscasting, they made an important discovery.

"In a comparatively short time," they reported, "television news had experienced a dramatic change. . . . Today, news is *the* major element in local programming, and the local television station has become the chief source of information for the country."

A few years ago, the average local newscast was fifteen minutes long and was tucked into some inconspicuous part of the schedule. Today it is often forty-five or sixty minutes long and is the station's bid for prestige and audience. Instead of from a half-dozen newscasts per week, the average one-station community, by 1968, could choose from among 13 to 32 half-hours. In cities with six channels, the audience could watch from 89 to 169 half-hours. In news-happy Los Angeles, stations were pumping out a total of 264 half-hours.

What brought about this change? Listener demand seems to be the answer. When WBZ Boston surveyed their audience, they felt impelled to make a drastic change. "It was decided to expand from 30 minutes [of local news] to an hour, and to package this in two 30 minute segments on either side of the 'Huntley-Brinkley Report.' The additional 30 minutes of local news began during October of 1967."

Staffs have expanded, too. WFIL Philadelphia has a typical modern staff for a medium-size station. They employ forty-five professional newsmen, from writers to sound engineers. Their camera crews roam through four states, assisted by eight stringers, and are directed by two-way radio. Their newscasters are the same reporters who cover a story, telling what they have seen.

Walter Cronkite, CBS anchor man, is at home reporting the news from a tumultuous political convention or a war-shattered village.

A memorable news scoop
was the NBC Tunnel
broadcast, filmed during the
digging of a secret passage
beneath the Berlin Wall.
News Correspondent
Piers Anderton (right)
was narrator of one of
broadcasting's most
dramatic moments.

KDKA Pittsburgh says: "We use the beat system, assigning one man full time to coverage of the city-county government. We also hired a full-time investigative reporter who would not be hindered by daily deadlines. One of our reporters began to specialize in an ombudsman role, doing daily features on the little guy versus the establishment. One became a daily reporter of business and politics. Still another emphasizes reporting the problems and achievements of youth."

A few staff jobs are unique. WSB Atlanta has an editorial cartoonist. WSJS Winston-Salem has a daily news program for the deaf. As the newscaster speaks the lines, the interpreter uses sign language. The audience is small but very grateful.

Even coverage is different today. WALA Mobile reports: "Channel 11 deliberately challenged itself to a specific task." It doubled its staff, equipment, budget and air time, and then set out "to arouse the citizens of our viewing area to an awareness and concern as to what is going on in the community. We decided we would cover every important meeting of a public body with our own staffers. What's more, we made the decision to give our reporters a certain editorial freedom to comment on the real meaning of what's happening."

Bright, fresh minds in many stations are devising new ways to interest the public in important issues. One device is the mini-documentary, or "five-minute feature," that runs as a part of the regular newscast.

"By breaking a long report into short takes," one news director asserts, "we know we are getting many more viewers than would look at a full-hour special."

WCKT Miami Beach has used this technique in an eight-part "mini" on local education, a seven-part "mini" on local extremists and a five-part "mini" on University of Miami campus demonstrations.

WSB Atlanta talks about race relations in frequent "minis." "It's the best way we know of getting through to segregationists."

Vigorous hometown newscasting—which developed in the '60s—is apparently here to stay. The movement is spreading and the audiences are growing.

WLOX Biloxi used public opinion polls to discover its hometown preferences, added news as a result and saw their ratings grow to "nearly triple those of last year."

WLDS Asheville says: "We feel very deeply our responsibility to present accurate, unbiased, comprehensive and thorough reporting of the events which reflect our community. The citizen's

Top: Robert Sarnoff, son of the famous David Sarnoff, worked his way up to the presidency of NBC, then became head of the Radio Corporation of America. Above: Dr. Frank Stanton succeeded William Paley as chief executive of CBS.

right is to know what is going on. It is our privilege to help him exercise that right."

NBC established a morning news beachhead during the early sixties with its program called "Today." Broadcast from a goldfish bowl, it featured, among other things, a sight of tourists pressing their noses against the studio's plate-glass windows. Dave Garroway, trained in the free-and-breezy style of Chicago, came to Manhattan as master of ceremonies and soon became a national institution. His assistants were a news reporter, sports reporter, women's interest reporter and J. Fred Muggs, a baby chimpanzee.

From the beginning, "Today" was meant to be more than a headline report. It tried to cover the contemporary scene, using celebrity interviews-in-depth, book reviews, pop science and pop art. It was masterminded by a professional newsman named Abe Schecter and its audience soon included professors, tycoons, most of the members of the U.S. Congress and the President himself.

When Garroway resigned, he was replaced by literate, low-key Hugh Downs who, while acting as announcer for Jack Paar on the "Tonight" show, had won a reputation as the unflappable man. Through the years, he maintained that image and helped build the show's perennial popularity.

Dr. Frank Stanton, president of CBS, once discussed the woes that can result from earnest journalistic effort. Speaking to Sigma Delta Chi, the nation's largest journalistic fraternity, in 1968, he said: "Last May, CBS News produced a hard-hitting, one-hour broadcast, 'Hunger in America.' The main point of this broadcast was that of 30 million impoverished Americans who earn less than $3,000 a year, 10 million—or five percent of our total population—are hungry.

"The official reaction was immediate and vehement. Secretary of Agriculture Orville Freeman accused CBS News of 'shoddy journalism' and of blackening the good name of his department; from there he went on to demand equal time to defend his food program. Because we had dealt fairly with the issues, we refused the request.

"So Secretary Freeman wrote us again; this time, he threatened the imposition of what he called 'even more stringent statutory requirements' against our medium. While he was thus attacking the broadcast, however, Secretary Freeman was officially conceding its main point—that Federal programs were inadequate to the needs of America's hungry. I have no doubt that Secretary Freeman and many of his top aides—insulated as they are from many of the unpleasant realities that our broadcast depicted—had no idea how serious the problem of American hunger really is."

And he added, "Thus, the value of such hard-hitting reporting is not only that it keeps the public informed—but it keeps the government informed, as well."

CBS's other tribulations for that season included the FCC's demand for an answer "within 20 days" as to why the network had made the news judgments it did during the 1968 Democratic convention, with special reference to the Chicago street demonstrations. A federal grand jury decided to investigate the same matter, as did subcommittees of the U.S. Senate and the House of Representatives.

Finally, there was the "Pot Party at a University" broadcast. A CBS reporter had been invited to attend—with camera—a party where marijuana actually was being smoked. The bid was accepted and the story was broadcast. Dr. Stanton says, "Both the FCC and the House Special Subcommittee on Investigations charged WBBM-TV with 'staging' the party."

After days of investigation in Washington and Chicago, nothing was turned up that indicated that the CBS operatives had deviated in any way from proper journalistic standards. Eventually, the charges were dismissed, but the effects linger on. The accusation must have reduced public confidence in the medium to some extent. And the harassment by government agents undoubtedly affects producers and others involved in "depth reporting." Next time around, they may be tempted to pick a less controversial—and perhaps less meaningful—topic.

Official interference by another government department almost caused NBC to lose one of its most dramatic news programs. The story began in West Berlin when students approached both CBS and NBC and offered to sell each of them the right to film separate tunnels that were being dug under the Berlin Wall. Both companies accepted and cameramen were assigned to the crews that were doing the digging. Within a short time, West Berlin police discovered the tunnel CBS was covering and closed it. The NBC tunnel remained undetected.

The tunnel being filmed was finished and was the escape route for the largest single group of refugees since the Wall was built. But when NBC announced it would show the film on television, great excitement arose. The State Department said it disapproved of NBC's action. Pressure mounted continuously for a month. After viewing the edited film NBC executives were certain that showing the film would not endanger those who had built the tunnel, those who escaped by means of it, nor those left behind in East Berlin.

But the State Department continued to object, calling the

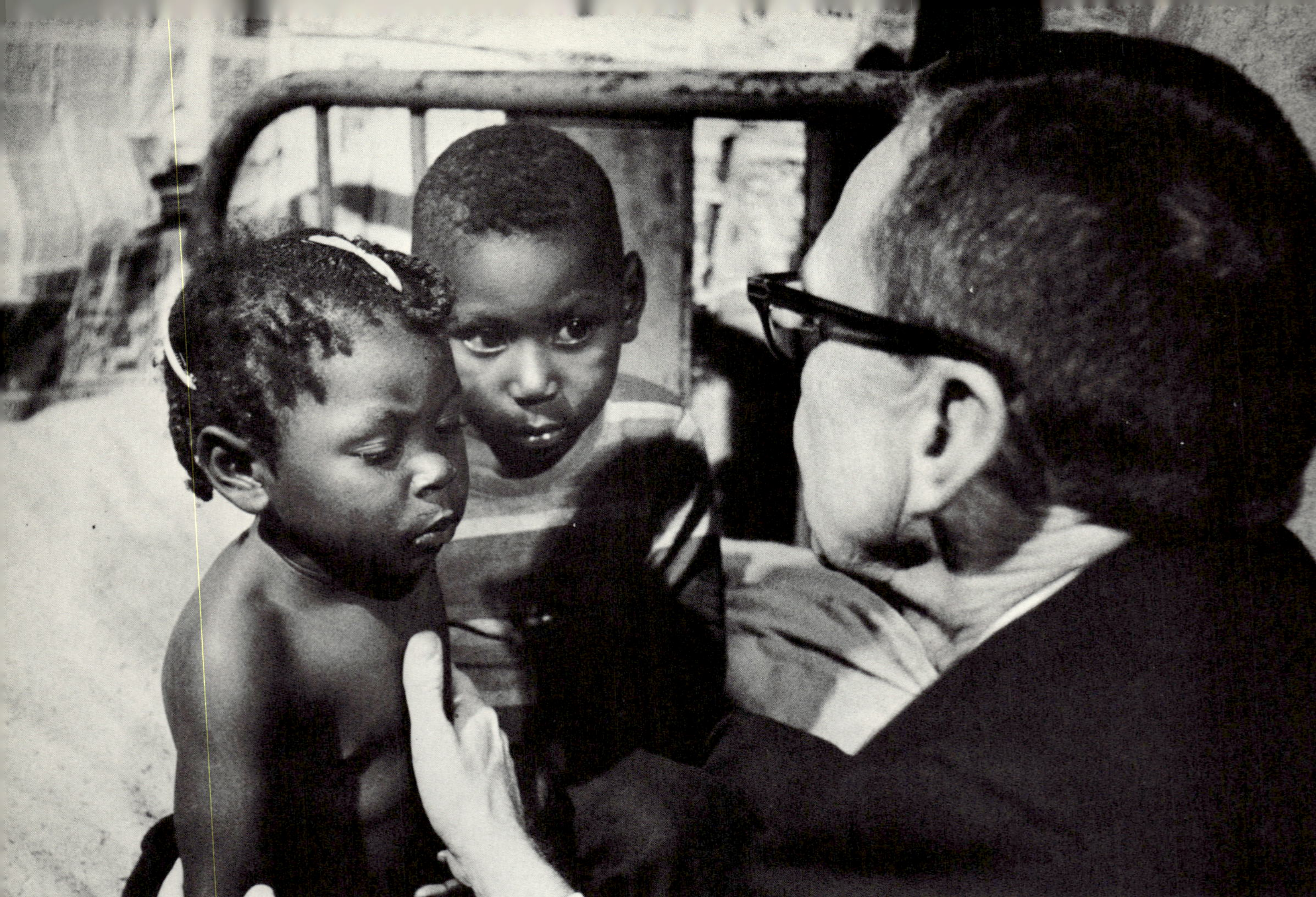

project risky, irresponsible, undesirable and not in the best interests of the U.S.A. In Germany, the Berlin Senate got a firsthand look at the film. And they asked that it be broadcast "in the interest of Berlin." So the program went on the air. Kintner says, "I consider 'The Tunnel' to be one of the greatest achievements of broadcast journalism, and it had one of the highest ratings ever recorded by a public affairs program."

Ironically, another branch of government, the U.S. Information Agency, promptly borrowed NBC's negative, edited it down to a thirty-minute program, and sent prints all over the world.

A half century of newscasting has seen four major periods: that of the bulletin reader (and a few of the "rip-and-read" school are still with us), of the analyst who interprets, of the crusading documentary producer and of today's giants who in person or by proxy range the world to skim headlines off its troubled face. Their technical performance is superb, but many observers wish they would pay more attention to gut issues.

On the other hand, one gut issue of growing importance to the broadcasting industry is the Nixon Administration's harnessing of the medium for its special purposes. Allegedly, this harnessing began during Nixon's candidacy, and a book called *The Selling of the Presidency* has described the process by which skilled TV technicians changed the candidate's image from that of a loser to a winner. Following the 1968 election, three events bore witness to the expertise of the new team in the White House.

The first was the swearing in of the Nixon Cabinet and Nixon's introduction of its members to the nation. This was seen by one of the year's largest audiences. The second event was the President's first stand-up press conference, without notes and without a lectern, wherein he gave plausible answers to questioning newsmen. (But which followed the Presidential prerogative of barring "follow-up" questions which might have probed for nitty-gritty news.) The third was his commandeering of TV on the evening of January 26, 1970, in order to explain his opposition to the multibillion-dollar Health and Education Department appropriation bill, and his veto of the bill "on camera."

Significantly, the Nixon Administration also moved strongly

into the regulation area when it established its own in-house crew of experts under the name of the White House Office of Tele-communications Policy. As explained to Congress, its function is to provide guidance to the President on the complex problems before the Federal Communications Commission—matters such as the federal policy on international satellites, the spectrum shortage and the reorganizing of those mixed-up kilocycles assigned to cars, boats, trucks, motorcycles and "citizen band" users.

Some objections were raised, based on the fear that this was a power play intended to reduce the importance of the Federal Communications Commission. Reassurances came quickly from White House spokesmen and the FCC chairman, Dean Burch, a recent Nixon appointee.

Finally, any account of the Administration's use of broadcasting must include the bareknuckle attack of Vice President Agnew, mentioned earlier. His charge of tacit conspiracy made international headlines. That he was playing for keeps became apparent a few days later when he repeated his original charges and added two of the nation's leading newspapers to his blacklist.

So history repeats itself. The tug-of-war resumes when officials attack and broadcasters defend. In this instance, however, an interesting split appeared among spokesmen for broadcasting. Many—some believe a majority—agreed with Mr. Agnew's assertions, though most felt that he was probably the wrong man to present such material. For a White House official to do so suggested an Administration intent to intimidate, whether or not the Vice President was expressing only his own opinions.

Top network anchor men split among themselves. Eric Severeid and most of his colleagues pleaded not guilty. Every network denied the charge, but ABC's Howard K. Smith told *TV Guide:* "I agree with what Mr. Agnew said. In fact, I said some of it before he did." He pointed out that most reporters are liberal and given to reporting things in a liberal light. He pinpointed another shortcoming: "As reporters, we have always been falsifying issues by reporting on what goes wrong in a nation where, historically, most has gone right. That is how you . . . win a Pulitzer prize."

At the 1970 NAB convention, NAB President Vincent J. Wasilewski described the real issue by asking: "Did the Vice President's words constitute the beginning of a campaign of intimidation, a do-it-my-way-or-else approach to broadcasting?" Answering his question for the assembled broadcasters, he added: "I am happy to say that the answers . . . appear to be no."

Beneath the talk is a vital issue, that of the freedom of speech guaranteed by the First Amendment. But does it apply to a medium like broadcasting, which affects the public interest, convenience and necessity? Most journalists feel that it does, and that the widest possible diversity of voices is essential to successful democracy.

Dr. Frank Stanton has said: "Judge Learned Hand saw this clearly when he said that the First Amendment 'presupposes that right conclusions are more likely to be gathered out of a multitude of tongues, than through any kind of authoritative selection.'" Stanton quoted Walter Lippmann as saying, "'This theory of a free press is that the truth will emerge from free reporting and free discussion, not that it will be presented perfectly and instantly in any one account.'"

Viewers-with-alarm exist in every profession, and broadcasting has its share. After a series of blows from critics, official and otherwise, in 1969, *Broadcasting* magazine, the industry's bible, published an editorial with a pertinent message:

"Broadcasting in the United States stands in grave jeopardy. Politically powerful and efficiently organized groups, actuated by selfishness and with a mania for power, are now busily at work plotting the complete destruction of the industry we have pioneered and developed. These groups give no thought to the effort and the money we have expended nor the services we have rendered the American public in the development of the greatest broadcasting system in the world. They speak of our business as if it could be cut down by the mere wave of a legislative fiat. To protect the present system of broadcasting is a definite obligation which we as broadcasters owe to ourselves and to the millions of the public whom we serve. And adequate protection can only be achieved through efficient organization. In other words, American broadcasting today is given its choice between organization and destruction.

"The paragraph you have just read (if you managed to get this far) is a classic, in a way. What reads like a cliché-ridden overview of conditions in broadcasting today was printed 38 years ago in Volume I, Number 1, of 'Broadcasting.'

"It was a blurb accompanying an article about reorganization of the National Association of Broadcasters. The quotation was from the late Walter J. Damm, general manager of WTMJ, Milwaukee, the outgoing elected president of the then NAB.

"The NAB emerged from its reorganization crisis and held reasonably firm for seven years before the next one arose. The script was the same.

"So what else is new?"

13
The Future

When does the future begin? For TV viewers, it began when European scientists decided to find a new way of creating a likeness. Like the invention of radio, it was a step-by-step process that began with light-sensitive materials, concave and convex lenses and finally a box uniting all the elements into a camera. William Henry Fox Talbot, the British father of photography, is usually named as the source of electronic picture-taking, for his work inspired the effort which eventually discovered the photon and the amazing ballet of light waves and sound waves that, when harnessed, became the Hollywood movie, the TV show, the laser beam and all their marvelous progeny.

Where does the future lead?

A perceptive writer in an issue of the *Kaiser Aluminum News* wrote of what he calls "telemobility." He asks us to imagine a time circa 1986. "A home is in the suburbs of Phoenix. A man is sitting in the middle of a circular room and on the curved walls around him he can see the ocean—surf breaking over the rocks. . . . Across from him sits another man. . . ."

The writer asks us to imagine that the room is underground, and that it has no view at all. What is on the curved wall is an image on a television screen, taped in Hawaii and now being shown electronically. More, he proposes that the first man is real—but the second man is being broadcast by laser beam from a satellite and re-created in color by holography. He seems to be there in Phoenix, but in reality

Opposite: The moon-walk telecast gathered one of the largest audiences in history. The picture was taken with a special lunar surface camera.

he is sitting comfortably in his study at the University of Edinburgh.

Where, in such a situation, does reality begin—and end?

The next question is: Do we want this unreal "reality" to happen? And the answer is: Perhaps it *must* happen, otherwise we all shall perish.

The enormity of the world's population explosion and mankind's pollution of the environment are familiar stories. Less known are animal experiments that demonstrate our danger. A scientific investigation of rat behavior is typical of many similar projects. Three rats were placed in a cage with adequate food and water. They lived harmoniously. Three more rats were placed in the same cage with the first trio, with extra food and water. The six lived harmoniously. Next, the number of rats was raised to twelve. They were given extra nourishment, but still confined to the original space. Now conflicts began, cliques formed, tempers erupted. Finally, the rat population was doubled again. The twenty-four could eat their fill at any time but their living space was only what had originally accommodated three. The result was catastrophic. Some rats began homosexual practices. Some apparently went insane. Some began killing other rats. Why? Scientists say it was lack of sufficient living room.

Cynics have described modern industrial life as a "rat race, a race that is always won by a rat." Certainly our world has experienced a population boom. The rate of increase has doubled in this central third of the twentieth century. Today, about 25 percent of all human beings who ever lived are alive. Of scientists, about 90 percent of history's total are alive.

This massive and changing society must be supported, which imposes a colossal burden on our economic system. To survive, we manufacture things and sell them, turning enough profit to purchase a few of the finer things of life. Apparently we cannot change this system, even though many people have lately proclaimed that we must. So if we cannot change it, can we save ourselves?

Perhaps the technology that has brought us to the verge of disaster can become our savior. An examination of our history points to a blueprint. Once a city was limited in size because it took one thousand farmers to grow enough extra food to support one hundred citizens. After much study, a Greek philosopher once concluded that no city should hold more than 300,000 persons. Ours hold many millions, and the cancers are showing. Once upon a time, life in a city was a pleasant affair, allowing its upper, middle, and lower income groups to live side by side, with the latter, in a democracy, nourished by the trade of the industrial revolution and the possibility of scrambling from the ruck of poverty to a more comfortable status. Then came the automobile.

One observer has noted that man's self-fragmentation and alienation began with travel. Whether he moved by dugout or horseback, "He began a process of separation which, amplified over the centuries by advances in vehicular technology, broke society into little pieces, and made strangers of us all."

With the advent of the auto, society began to disintegrate. Given mobility, the upper income groups moved their homes to the hills and fields. Gradually, those of more modest station followed in search of better air and schools. Into the resulting vacuum, social and industrial pressures sucked a horde of migrants who turned those abandoned city neighborhoods into warrens of violence and misery.

Yet the business world needed many cities. They were necessary centers of communications, transportation and industry. So skyscrapers grew loftier in order to house enlarged headquarters staffs, and factories spread their roofs where raw labor was at hand. We have called it progress.

Industrial technology and applied science have combined to create astonishing products. Advertising and merchandising have created markets all over the world. Communications have tied the empire of commerce together, progressing from the quill pen to the typewriter, from the cable to the microwave and from the calculator to the computer.

For generation after generation, all was well—or so it seemed. However, in the '60s, a sickness broke out for which we were unprepared. Hippies and yippies, the generation gap, the new morality, black power, Watts, bombings—these were symptoms of a profound malaise.

Authorities are saying that the unrest on campuses is less the result of Vietnam than of the frustration of being plunged into an unattractive, institutionalized world without hope of changing it. Hungry children in the South and rotting tenements in the North are no part of the American dream. What appears to be mindless violence may really be a striking out by shackled egos against the fetters of a structured society that pours both men and women into what has become for many a joyless mold.

Few persons living today can remember those early automobile advertisements that equated the motorcar with freedom, the open road and the liberated spirit. Today society has so turned in on itself that owning a car is usually advertised as an avenue to easy sex. For a long time now, perceptive sociologists have condemned the

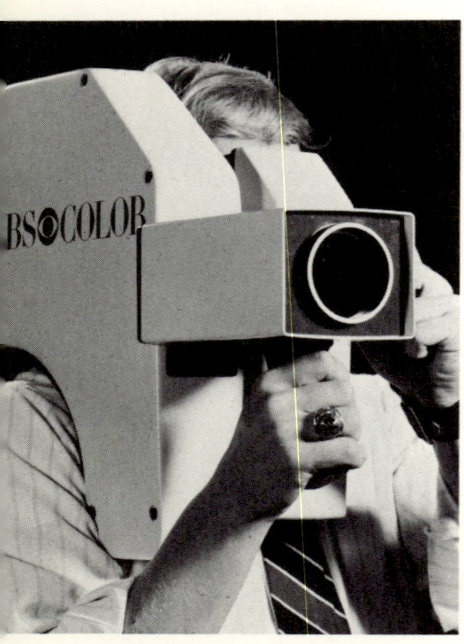

automobile as a fragmentation bomb, uprooting families and disrupting communities. If the going is rough, run away from it. The auto has become a cop-out. So many people are running away today that even our roads have become as dangerously overcrowded as that experimental cage full of rats.

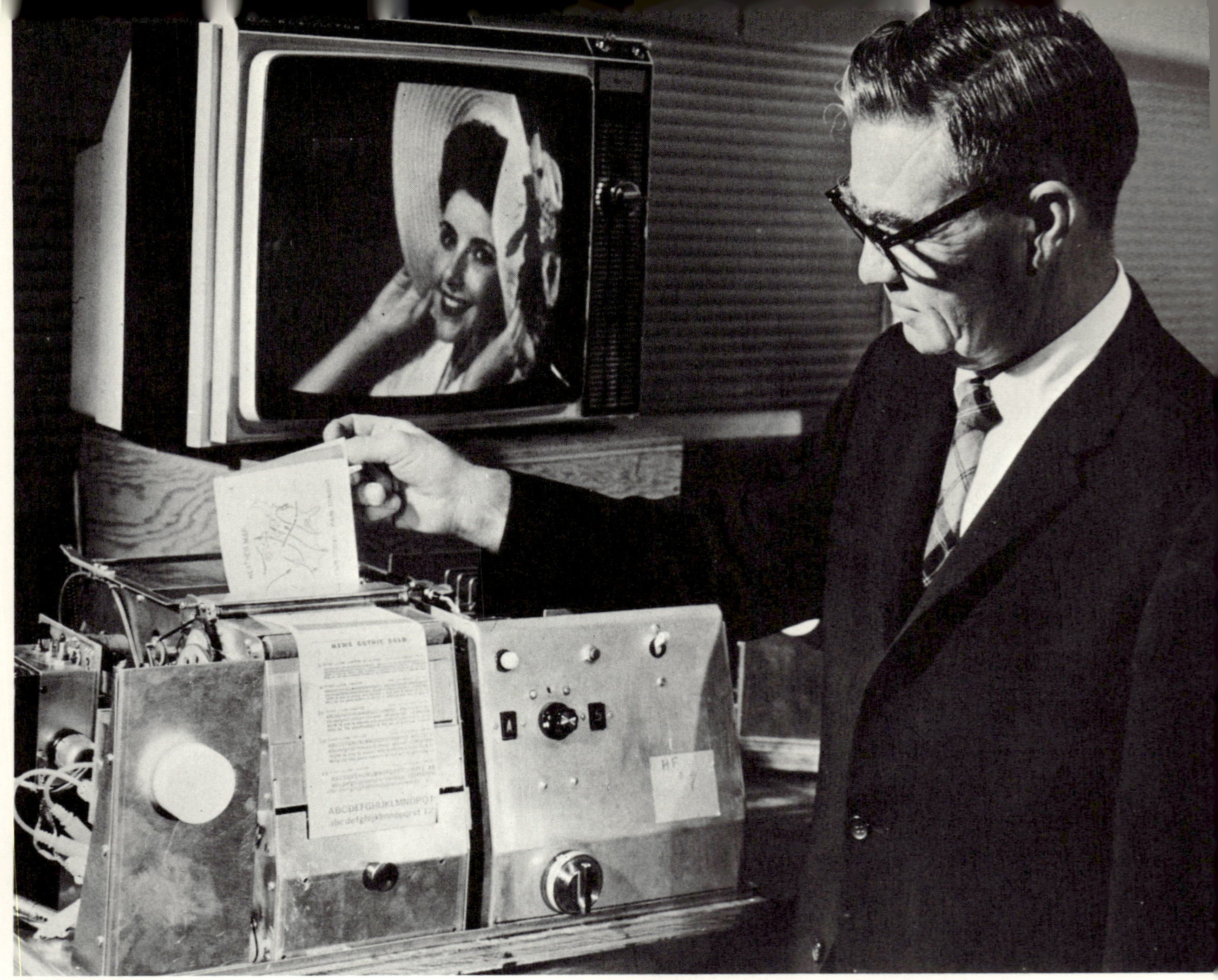

There is a permissible relationship between people and their throughways, if sanity is to survive. Exceed it and the cost is tragic. In the U.S. people are being born three times faster than new miles of roads are being built. At the same time, the cost of a mile of highway has gone up twelve times faster than the amount of mileage.

Every year existing routes must accommodate more cars. In 1950 an average mile of highway was used by 14.8 automobiles. By 1961 the number was 22.2. Estimates for 1970 put 35 cars on each mile. In the horse and buggy days of 1910 a horse-drawn dray averaged 11 miles per hour through city streets. Today motorized trucks average only 6 miles an hour. It is a losing battle.

Aviation planners are already talking about tomorrow's forty-five minute world, meaning that an individual may be transported, by future rocket systems, to any spot on our planet in forty-five minutes.

His speed through the air will be just under 17,000 miles per hour.

The romance between man and the vehicle is ended, strangled by his urge to travel and his commercial need to see for himself. Business has created a treadmill world that nobody really wants, a world with no exits—or so it seemed until recently.

But there may be an escape. It lies with the electron. "By 1975, TV will be an integral part of a vast international communications network built around computers and space satellites," says Wilson P. Dizard, a research fellow at MIT. "These machines will provide any kind of data instantaneously in all parts of the world to meet the need of the new information explosion."

The '70s is the decade in which Uncle Sam will receive a new nervous system. Already his neurons have been shaped by radio and television stations. Presently, his ganglia of long lines will be augmented by wires and satellites capable of reflecting all kinds of electronic information into every TV set in the world.

All of this, planners say, may provide a counterpoise to the fragmenting automobile. Instead of a man rushing off to the scene of his work or pleasure, electronics will bring his work or pleasure to him. The first paragraphs of this chapter examined briefly one form of this phenomenon. Inevitably, every home and office will have its communications console. A small corner will hold solid-state circuitry, a typewriter keyboard and a facsimile printer. In the TV room a flat or curved wall will reflect a picture from floor to ceiling. Or if space is precious, a four by three picture frame will enclose the phospor screen. And the housewife, busy in the kitchen, can glance at the dime-size screen of her wristwatch TV set to note the program to which her small fry are tuned.

"The day may come," David Sarnoff said long ago, "when every person will have his own little radio station in his pocket to communicate with his friends or his office as he walks or rides along the street."

Television, too! Dr. Vladimir Zworykin, father of modern TV, says he conceived his inventions to "visualize an extension of human sight, to let us see what we couldn't see with our own eyes—whatever was too small, too big, too dangerous, or too far."

Can electronics really unclog our highways, restore our peace of mind and defy the treadmill? Look at the record as outlined by E. J. Wattenberg in his study of the 1960 census:

"In 1940, the . . . television sets in American homes could . . . be counted on the fingers of one hand. In 1948, fewer than one household in each two thousand had a set; in 1960, nine out of ten families

223

owned a set. By 1964, fully 93 percent of American households had television."

What happened? *Electronic Age* magazine says that the American people made a commitment in the '50s, creating a tidal wave of approval. "No other single phenomenon in American life has ever met with such acclaim," says Desmond Smith. "It took 80 years for the telephone to be installed in 34 million homes. It took 62 years for electric wiring, 49 years for the automobile, and 27 years for the TV set."

What is the hardware of our electronic future? A look at the TV screen of tomorrow sets the tone. No tube will form its picture. Instead, it will consist of thousands of separate light elements. For a screen the size of a large bridge table, 700,000 individual elements will be needed for a black-and-white picture, almost 3 million for color. Each element will be separately controlled, which is a major problem. "But it won't be too long, things continuing as they are," says engineer Frank Leary, in *The Exchange*, "before the electronics industry will be able to fit this tremendous complex of control circuitry into a package no bigger than today's portable television screen."

And now television must bring—and is ready to bring—the event, local or global, to the individual. To be sure, human complacency still blocks many changes. The old order, anchored in tired minds, rebuffs the innovating newcomer with: "We've already tried it. It won't work!" Philosopher W. H. Ferry says in *MassCom as Educator*, "The most notable aspect of our world of novelty and rapid change is the unwillingness of economists and political scientists to perceive it, and their hostility toward those who do." In time, objectors and objections usually disappear.

If electronics can bring the event to the person, think of the savings in travel, in car mileage, in gasoline for autos and planes. Think of the gain in free time to be used for culture and leisure. Think of the tides of humanity that flow in and out of our cities, a slave-army harnessed to wheels as tightly as captives were once locked to oars in Mediterranean galleys. Their liberation is the promise of the electron.

As we explore these possibilities, keep in mind that the master task of communications has always been to get a message from here to there. Tomorrow the reverse will prevail; the message will move from there to here. What instruments will perform the promised miracles? What appliances must we buy?

First, consider the home.

The cordless telephone. You will carry it in your car, golf bag, fishing creel, briefcase. It will be self-powered. You will not have to push a button to listen, as is now the case with car phones, or say "over" when you have finished speaking.

The forwarding-button phone. You are going out for the evening and want incoming calls forwarded. Just press a button and dial the number of the telephone at the new location. All calls will be forwarded.

The instant-dial phone. If you call numbers with great frequency (hairdresser, daughter, home, office), ask the phone company for a two-tone adjustment. By dialing only two numbers instead of the customary seven you will get through.

The three-party call. Today an operator must arrange each conference call. Tomorrow's phone will call two other persons simultaneously.

The picture-phone. AT&T first developed a picture-tube attachment for its hand phone ten years ago, and set it aside until the time was right. It will become available to most cities during the '70s. Both parties will see each other in full color, with such accuracy of detail that person-to-person confrontations between salesmen and customers may become obsolete. As in real life, a lifted eyebrow, a quizzical glance or a jutted jaw will become clues to conversation, providing better understanding. Eventually, all such phones will have high-fidelity sound, as recognizable (and as informative) as if both parties were in the same room.

Housewives will use the picture phone for shopping. "How are the strawberries?" A clerk in a supermarket will hold up a box, displaying their color and size. "What's the shape of that birdhouse you are advertising?" A pet shop proprietor will demonstrate. "Can you match this color paint for my bathroom walls?" A paintmart clerk will observe the sample displayed by the homemaker, select or mix a matching sample and complete the transaction.

A push-button meter reader. In his office at the electric company or waterworks, a clerk will sit before a console that is connected to the telephone of every subscriber. By dialing a special number, a command is carried by the phone line to a reading device attached to each meter. The call goes through even when the phone is busy. Information is returned at lightning speed to the headquarters computer which calculates the amount due, prints a bill and drops it in a mailbag.

The buttinsky phone. Gabbiness is a national failing, and many a call is missed because the callee is gaily chatting away. This

new phone service will "butt in" with a beeper that sounds the news of an incoming signal.

Quadruple sound. Stereophonic music is now standard in most American homes. It is good enough, but quadruple sound is better. Perfect reproduction requires the addition of those vibrations which bounce off the back wall of a concert hall. Call it the "wrap-around effect." It will be available soon through extra rear speakers and multiplex broadcasting and on records.

The talking bullhorn. This device is equipped with an electronic sensor and a recorded tape that delivers a warning in a voice that can carry for blocks. A community can install it at the curb of a block where children play, with its electron rays aimed to catch the movement of anyone into the street. If the ray is broken, the horn will tell motorists, "Drive with care! We love our children." Security officers can use it so that it automatically shouts: "Take cover. This bank is being robbed." With a heat sensor, the bullhorn can call out, "Fire in the shipping room. Close all doors and windows." At railway crossings, a bullhorn can warn: "Clear the crossing. Fast train approaching."

The sound synthesizer. This black box contains a reading machine much more sophisticated than the check readers now used by banks. After turning printed words into electromagnetic waves, it converts them into sounds that are fed into a loudspeaker. If Grandma's sight is bad but she enjoys novels, history or the Bible, the book of her choice can be placed under the synthesizer's eye, which will convert the page into sound, reading to her just like any human companion. Her only responsibility will be to turn the page.

The MassCom home center. Grant an electronic engineer the right to dream and his vision of the future is bound to include a supply of rainbows. The MassCom (for mass communications) center embraces much more than today's twenty-one-inch screen. Think of it not as gadgetry but as a bottomless source of information, like an all-knowing Sphinx that has learned to talk. Its hardware will include a keyboard for passing queries to a distant computer, a readout screen, a printer for reproducing each transaction so a copy can be filed and assorted buttons.

For the housewife, its timesaving, mind-sparing services are spectacular. Imagine that the family is awake and preparing for the new day. The printer has already delivered a facsimile newspaper,

227

Telstar flies over the Atlantic and transmits pictures from America to Europe. This TV image of Mount Rushmore pioneered the Bell System's service to the Continent in 1962.

Want to jive to your own stereo concert? This headpiece saves everybody's ears yet delivers the big beat that teen-agers love. Above, right: Tomorrow's wires will be tubes or pipes, slightly bigger than an eye, and they will carry high-frequency waves for voice, data, TV and Bell's upcoming Picturephone.

which is placed beside the master's eggcup. While Mother prepares breakfast, a fresh sheet unfolds from the console displaying pictures, prices and descriptions—the day's bargains are coming in from all the supermarkets.

Dad is late so he picks up a pepper shaker (it's really a cordless telephone), touches two buttons and reaches his car-pool partner in order to explain the delay. After he departs, Mother gives the children their school books and bundles them off, making certain that each is tagged with a tiny electronic Locator.

It is time to do the day's shopping. Sitting at the console, she prepares her list, adds bargains selected from the telefaxed ads and contacts her favorite supermarket. A computer lists her requirements, passes the order to a service center where it is filled and put on a truck for delivery. Simultaneously, the computer totes up the cost and sends it to her bank where the amount is charged against her account and credited to the supermarket.

Perhaps she wonders if her bank balance is large enough to cover the order. To make certain, she dials the bank computer. Its metallic voice answers and she gives her name, address and account number. After a second, her name, address and account number glow in small letters on the readout screen. Other words appear, reading, "If this is correct, please proceed."

"What is my balance?" she asks.

The screen fades and a question appears: "You said, what is my balance?"

"Yes," she says clearly.

The screen fades and lights again, showing the amount of her balance.

It is time now to stir up a dessert for the bridge club meeting—something different, something new. She turns again to the Mass-Com center. Through it, she has access to every cookbook ever printed.

In succession, she calls for unusual recipes, reading them on the phosphor screen, and makes her selection. Finally, she presses a button marked "Print-out." The recipe on the screen is transferred swiftly to a sheet of paper.

At midmorning, a bell in the console rings softly. The print-out says, "This is a poll. Please answer yes, no or undecided. Do you favor rezoning the 20 acres in Westport now known as Nyala Farm to accept light industry or research buildings?" She presses a button marked "affirmative," along with thousands of other housewives. A city hall computer counts the responses and delivers the result to the mayor. Later, she will use this button to vote for candidates for political office.

Her dessert is in the oven, the groceries are ordered, but what of the kids? She steps to the console and turns a knob. Small blips appear on the screen, a cluster of them, one for each child. They are all in school. Now the remainder of the day is hers.

Meanwhile, Dad has reached his office 2 or 3 miles down the road, a two-story building set in a park shaded by oaks and pines. He and the presidents of three other corporations have joined forces to create an electronic executive center. His vice presidents and chief aides are scattered around the country in similar buildings, linked by electromagnetic waves. Their office furniture includes facsimile units, picture-phones, TV monitors, graphic consoles, automatic calculators, computers and quiet, high-speed teletypewriters. All the facilities of the MassCom home console are available here, plus extras. One extra is a row of two-foot TV screens mounted along an alcove wall. This is the electronic "conference room."

At an appointed time, these screens brighten, each one showing the head and shoulders of an executive. Their faces are tanned and relaxed. Dad takes his seat before them. "Jim, how are things in Tokyo?" Jim replies and every syllable is as distinct and every wrinkle in his skin as visible as if he were sitting across a conference table. Other men report from Bonn and London and San Francisco. The daily conference is under way.

At its conclusion, Dad's secretary reports that a lawyer in Washington wants to talk. A picture-phone screen shows him at his desk. "I'm worried about that tax case," he says. "I know the Department is wrong but they won't listen. We may have to take it to court."

"Better check the computer for precedents first," Dad says. Every tax law of the United States government—indeed, every law of any kind—has already been recorded on a set of computer discs. An eyesight search would take months or years. A computer can read

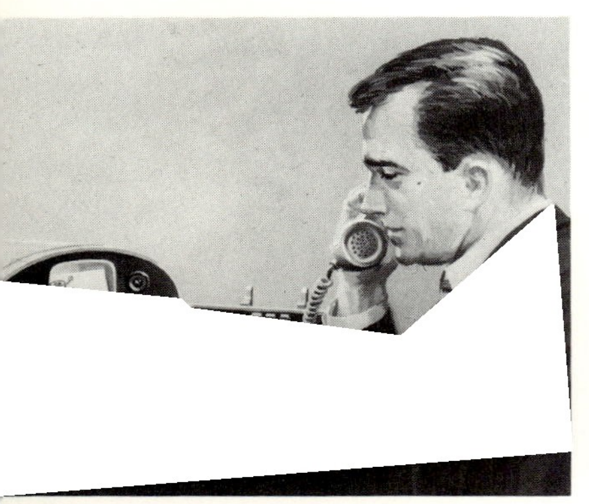

every law on the books and print out precedents in about eight hours. The cost is considerable, but worthwhile when the stakes are large.

The Washington lawyer shuffles his papers. "The Air Force is ready to sign their contract," he says. "How about it?"

Dad asks, "Did they buy those changes in paragraph 10?"

"Here's the way it came out." A screen lights up showing lines of type. Paragraph 10.

Dad reads it and says: "We'd better sign before they change their mind." The type blurs and settles again, showing a place for signatures. He activates an electronic pen and traces his name on a glass plate. In Washington, a facsimile of his signature is electronically recorded on the contract.

"Send a copy to all offices," he directs. In the corner, the facsimile machine begins to whir.

Whereas person-to-person meetings will be less necessary tomorrow, a need for transmitting documents will increase. Many devices are in the works. One researcher has found a way of utilizing a tiny unused portion of the TV spectrum. Viewers are familiar with the phenomenon of a picture that rolls and of the black bar that slides down the screen like a window sash. That blackness represents an electronic waste. Tomorrow it will carry a signal bearing data that black boxes will turn into drawings, layouts, printed specifications and verbatim memos of spoken messages.

Another device: Essentially, it is a picture-phone plus a TV typewriter, an electronic pencil, a box of buttons and a potato-shaped hunk of plastic called a "mouse." Two men with such machines, though on opposite sides of the world, can collaborate in writing a play, working out a new chemical formula or designing a cathedral.

Imagine some simple task, such as a company president and his public relations man, each in a separate city, preparing a statement for the press. As the PR man taps out the story on his TV typewriter, the words appear on screens in his and the president's offices. If they were together the boss would make corrections in pencil. In the offices of tomorrow both pencil and paper are superfluous. Instead, he folds his right hand around the "mouse" and rolls it across a plate on his desk top. A bright dot—a kind of pointer—travels across the screen in accordance with the mouse's movements. He centers it over a word that bothers him. "I'd like something tougher there," he says. "Wait! I've got it." He presses a button and the word vanishes. He touches his keyboard and spells out a new word that jumps into the empty place. He can also do that with phrases and sentences. Looking at each other with electronic eyes, two businessmen or two scientists can argue and debate, amend and delete, until they reach agreement. Then, with the push of a final button, they can turn the finished work into microfilm, tape or just plain paper, and consign it to a resting place in the company computer.

With such gadgetry as this, most executive commuting will become a waste of time. Headquarters buildings in cities will become superfluous. Files will be stored in central computers with coded buttons assuring their instant retrieval. In the office of tomorrow, about the only item left untouched by "progress" will be the coffee break.

At the day's end, Dad goes home. No commuting, no stalled trains, no late dinners. Two TV aerials are mounted on his roof. One is the standard type. The other is an unobtrusive saucer, like one of those aluminum scooters children sit in to slide down icy hills. Both are geared so they can be "aimed" at a wave source. They take him effortlessly to his destination.

After dinner, he and his wife tackle the problem of where to go for their vacation. "Let's look at some places. How about Marrakech?" she suggests. They consult a travel folder that gives code numbers for a score of resorts. Their travel agent's computer never sleeps. Punching a number on their MassCom panel, they watch the TV screen light up, adjust itself until the color is perfect, and then reveal the greens and gold of the fabled desert resort. Camels, the Casbah and Arabian storytellers pass in review. They ask next for Corfu in the Mediterranean and examine its hotels, bars and bedrooms. They visit shops and beaches and golf courses in Bermuda and Hawaii. Six movies later, they have decided to go to Spain.

"We'd better brush up on our Spanish," Mom says. "In the morning, I'll ask the library for a refresher course." Tomorrow the computerized language section of the state library will project a high fidelity sight-and-sound Spanish lesson into her living room at whatever hour she selects. Her teacher will be a famous professor who has taped his instructions and stored them in the computer for future calls.

With two hours to kill before bedtime, they turn on the all-network console. Touching a button brings in all three nets plus an independent station. Games, talk, news, nothing exciting. "How about a play?" he asks.

"I'd like that."

A wall compartment holds a supply of tape casettes, grouped by plays, musicals, variety, sports and so forth. He runs a finger down the titles. "Do you remember 'Death of a Salesman'? It was wonderful."

He slips the casette into a slotted box labeled EVR, for Electronic Video Recording. As the big screen lights up, bringing the wall to life, they relax in deep chairs. Hi-fi sound and ultra-clear images begin to re-create the famous Arthur Miller play. Their seats are front row center. Quickly, they are immersed in the tangled lives of Willy Loman and his wife, which are the lives of all humans.

EVR was demonstrated by the Columbia Broadcasting System in 1970. The Radio Corporation of America will offer a similar device called Selectavision. Both will play cartridge tapes through a regular TV receiver, black and white or color, without the hazard of static or ghosts or snow. Both devices will reach the market early in the '70s with a supply of taped shows—everything from grand opera to the Beatles, current events, travelogues. Many educational subjects are planned. Eventually, EVR will be able to take a live program off the air and transfer it to a casette. With a timer, a person could leave home for an evening out and then return to find his favorite program recorded and waiting to be played.

Speaking of EVR, *New York Times* columnist Jack Gould says: "After tinkering around with an EVR unit at home, the writer concluded that its implications and possible applications border on the staggering." He adds that the tape can be stopped or "frozen" for study of a single frame—for example, surgeons could use it to study a brain operation. Entire movies may be transferred to casettes and rented over and over for home or library use at a cost less than half that of a local matinee. In fact, one movie tape was run experimentally more than a thousand times with no deterioration.

Following a demonstration in London, the *Times* said: "The future was brought in today. Some experts say that EVR means to broadcasting something like what the motorcar has meant to transport. This is a viewer's dream."

A viewer's dream it is. As yet, the TV networks are not afraid of its competition. But if viewers fall away, preferring their own selection of taped programs to those offered by network program managers, they may take notice. Indeed, many critics believe that EVR may provide the incentive for improvement that will stimulate better programming by both networks and stations.

Considering that phone lines are already jammed up in most cities, how can this new circuitry be accommodated? The answer is that advancing technology has the matter well in hand. Mother Bell is already experimenting with "millimeter wave guides," which are two-inch copper-lined-with-steel pipes capable of carrying 250,000 simultaneous telephone conversations. These millimeter waves will not flow around corners, so the pipes must be laid in great arcs that, it is believed, will presently curve their way from city to city and coast to coast. Incidentally, the cost of a long distance phone call will be about half of current rates.

If ever these guides become too crowded, technology will be ready with the laser beam. The astonishing laser is not yet free of electronic bugs, but scientists predict that it will be domesticated sometime in the 1980s. When that happens, one single beam, believe it or not, will be able to transmit 2.5 million simultaneous telephone calls.

Any consideration of tomorrow's broadcasting must include satellites. An offshoot of NASA's space program that put Americans on the moon, they have already started a revolution.

One summer night in 1962, when millions of Americans were watching a CBS TV program about Scotland Yard, an announcer broke in. "We interrupt this program," he said. "The British are ready to bounce a program off Telstar."

Telstar was our prize satellite, a random-orbit bird equipped to relay telephone and television signals. Wilson Dizard described it: "On their screens, viewers suddenly saw an unpretentious control room with three men seated at a table. They made various dull remarks, concluding with, 'It is now half-past three in the morning. Good luck.' And the broadcast ended."

This engineers' experiment originated in a station in the south of England, was bounced off the U.S.-made satellite to a ground station in Maine and relayed from there to American networks.

Presently, there were other birds orbiting the earth, including one called Early. Tomorrow there will be more, all keeping stations in space wherever they can serve best. Three of them are now centered above the Atlantic and Pacific oceans, and all are in regular use. Viewers who saw those incredibly alive color pictures of the Tokyo Olympics in 1964 know what a satellite can do.

Even greater miracles are possible. Given the right satellite flying over Missouri or Illinois, orbiting in step with this whirling world, it is technically possible for a network to bounce a "Bob Hope Special" or a "Bonanza" Western from its transmitter *directly* into every home in the land. Then those endless miles of long lines for which the nets now pay AT&T a reported $100 million per year— with higher rates impending—would become obsolete, or available for land traffic. More important, many areas now beyond TV range would be served—the trapper in the Klondike, the prospector in the mountains, the hermit in Death Valley. Neither tall buildings nor taller mountains would obstruct a signal coming from overhead.

Inevitably, competing interests will object to this change. Perhaps AT&T will fight against its loss of revenue. Perhaps the cable antenna systems now serving landlocked communities will fight to maintain their right to charge subscribers for bringing clear signals over mountain ranges. Time—and political expediency—will tell.

Already, this kind of satellite-to-set broadcasting is planned for India. In that land, where ignorance keeps most of its 530 million inhabitants in poverty, a heroic experiment will be undertaken jointly by the U.S. and Indian governments. Our own NASA will send up a TV broadcasting satellite and position it over the Indian Ocean. The government of India will build a powerful transmitter at Ahmadabad. In five thousand villages, TV sets will be installed in central locations, such as schools or village halls. When the project gets under way, special programs on farming, family planning and nutrition, among others, will be transmitted from Ahmadabad to the satellite, then *directly* to the sets in the villages. Using a searchlight-type electromagnetic beam that will blanket the subcontinent, only one transmitter will be necessary to reach the entire nation without the prohibitive cost of land lines. If the experiment is a success, hundreds of thousands of additional villages will be similarly equipped, so that education may truly be universal. If it works, man will have a formula at last for the elimination of ignorance and poverty.

It is possible, says Dr. Wernher von Braun in *Popular Science*, that "better communications via satellite could even stem or reverse America's trend toward the big city—and alleviate problems like urban decay, smog, polluted rivers, clogged traffic, and crowded airports. . . . the communications satellite may yet turn out to be the greatest thing the space program ever contributed to this country."

Two questions remain:

With our miraculous hardware, what are we going to communicate? *What shall we say?*

And what manner of men are going to do the communicating?

Peter J. Drucker, consultant to blue-chip corporations, says: "Any business that wants to stay ahead will have to put very young people into very big jobs—and fast. Older men cannot do these jobs—not because they lack the necessary intelligence but because they have the wrong conditioned reflexes."

Business Week magazine says: "The future manager will have been tested, analyzed, and selected by electronic means. A new breed will call the shots."

To this new breed, we shall devote our final chapter.

14
Tomorrow: The Electron and You

wo events in life are crucial: choosing a mate and choosing a career.

This chapter is concerned with the latter. The broadcasting industry needs people. Scientists have given mankind unprecedented power to communicate with each other. What man does with that power will decide the fate of the human race.

The broadcasting industry of tomorrow will present even more opportunities for enriching life than it does today and nobody knows what shape it will take. Many political, financial and emotional decisions must be reached before its ultimate direction becomes apparent. In the meantime, a newcomer can familiarize himself with what presently exists.

Today's structure has evolved largely to meet the needs of the man who pays the bill, the advertiser. Here are its broad outlines.

The advertiser

Network programs are usually sponsored by corporations. On local stations, the sponsor may be an individual who has built up a business in automobiles, lumber, real estate and so forth. In either case, this corporation or person usually has within his own organization an advertising department. It may be part of the sales department, though sometimes it is separate. Its function is to create and disseminate advertisements which enhance the sales of the corporation's products. Very large corporations, which sell several products, may

Opposite: This early model of an electronic blackboard will do away with the chalk and eraser of the little red schoolhouse, and enable "conferences" to be held though the principals sit in offices separated by oceans.

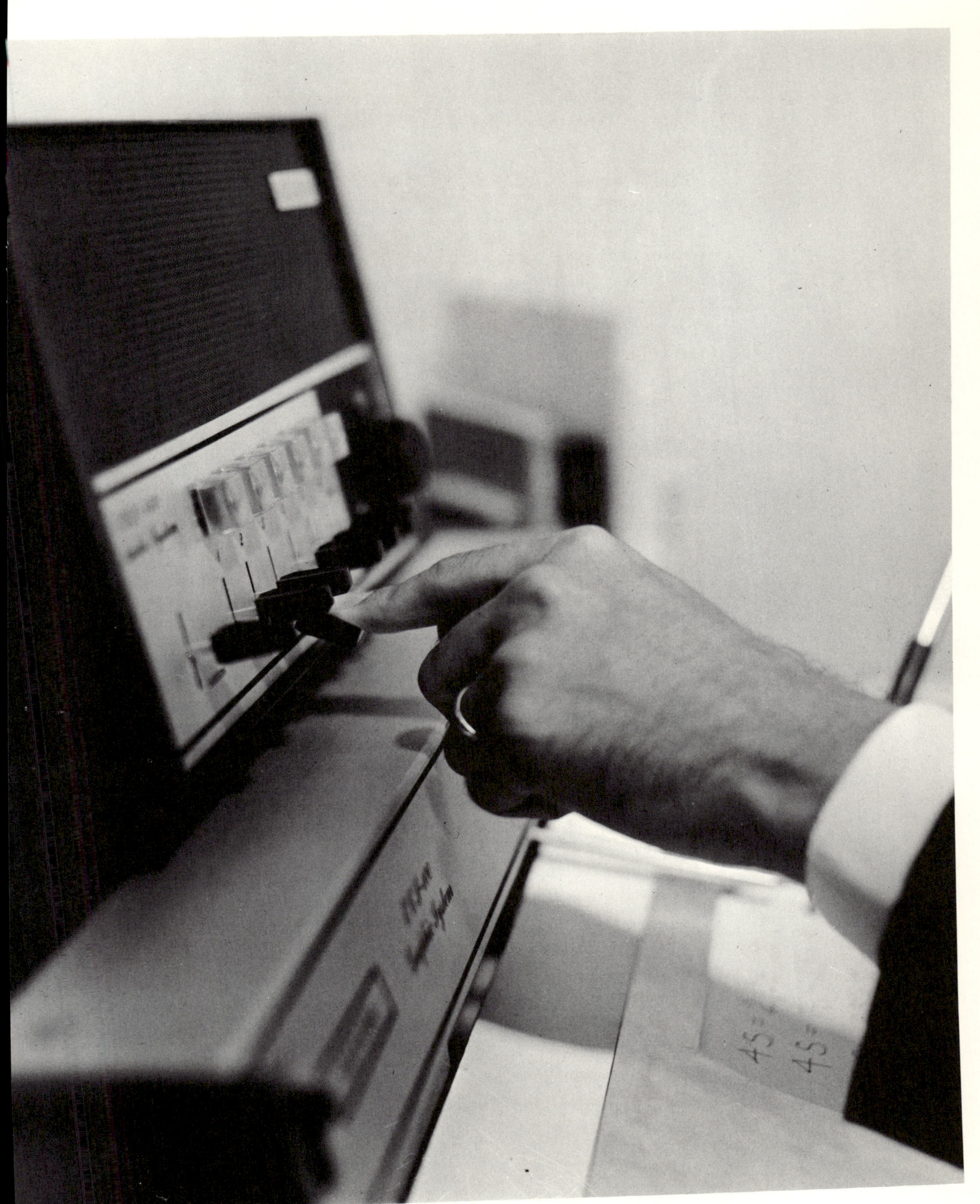

have a separate sales and advertising department for each item. The Chrysler Corporation, for instance, sells its Chryslers, Dodges and Plymouths separately.

The advertising agency

The ad agency is an organization composed of specialists. In the beginning its primary function was to create printed advertising. Three experts (or three skills) were required. First, a writer who was expert in the economical use of persuasive language. Second, an artist to illustrate the product and create a layout that would attract attention. Third, a media expert familiar with periodicals and their subscribers (age, sex, income, etc.) and the rates charged per thousand readers.

Advertising agencies exist by the thousands, and have expanded their functions until they now have large departments for research, public relations, merchandising, program production, making commercials, film distribution and so forth.

Broadcasting networks

The principal radio and television networks are the National Broadcasting Company, the Columbia Broadcasting System, and the American Broadcasting Company. The Mutual radio network is an alliance of independent stations.

Networks do not own all their stations. The Federal Communications Commission limits ownership by any single interest to no more than one AM, FM or TV station in the same territory, or more than seven FM or seven AM or seven TV commercial stations throughout the entire country. A further restriction is that no more than five TV stations may be in the Very High Frequency band.

Most stations are good money-makers, so each network owns its full limit and then augments its list by signing agreements with additional independent operators. The deal is mutually attractive because the station is guaranteed payment for a minimum number of hours each week, and the network is promised that the stations will carry its programs. Thus, networks can offer an advertiser the assurance that his program or announcement will be heard on two hundred or so stations located in the nation's principal cities.

Networks are designed to support their primary functions of (1) programming, (2) selling time and (3) engineering. Sub-departments include those for musicians, writers, producers, sound effects, lighting, makeup, research, merchandising, station relations, syndication (foreign and domestic), employee relations and others.

Radio and television stations

A broadcasting station has the twin responsibilities of serving its community and making enough money to stay in business. Its principal executives are (1) a station manager, (2) a program manager and (3) a sales manager.

Ancillary organizations

Dozens of kindred organizations function in many ways to extend and support the broadcasting function. Among them are:

Radio and TV station news services
Talent agents and managers
Independent program producers
Producers of commercials
Business film producers
Film processing laboratories
Film distributing services
Publicity services
Station sales representatives
Attorneys specializing in FCC regulations and law
Consulting engineers
Schools of broadcasting
Technical schools
Government agency, religious and various other broadcasting departments
Broadcasting periodicals: daily, weekly, monthly

Somewhere among these activities, innumerable opportunities await young Americans. Broadcasting is not for the clock-watcher or the security-seeker who treasures regular hours and fringe benefits. But for persons who have a zest for challenges, a concern for the public weal and a blind eye for the eight-hour day, it affords profound satisfactions and intellectual stimulation.

Willard E. Walbridge, chairman of the board of the National Association of Broadcasters, and one of the industry's outstanding thinkers, addressed a group of college students:

"We are waiting to welcome young people like you," he said. "You will come with your education and your ideals, and you will blend them into our industry to change it and enrich it, and make it grow to be a better servant of our society. . . .

"The mess you find this world in is the test of your aspiring spirit. You must make the choice to embrace its challenge . . . not to fall back in despair or drop out. Do you seek an opportunity to serve? I know of no better way than a life in broadcasting . . . The challenges are great—the tasks formidable. But how we, the older generation of broadcasters, envy you for what you will do and what you will see— if you want it *enough*."

What is the true concern of the broadcasting industry? It means different things to different people. To most, perhaps, it is entertainment—show business—which is surely one of its important functions. Entertainment is the unique magnet that regularly attracts the millions whose attention so many advertisers are eager to catch.

"But broadcasting's highest duty is to inform the public," says a spokesman for the National Association of Broadcasters. "This is the broadcaster's greatest challenge, and his greatest opportunity."

It is true and trite to say that our world is becoming smaller. Instantaneous awareness of events across the ocean is upon us, thanks to electronic communications. Any newscast provides testimony. We live on a scientific frontier. Man took five thousand years to progress from the sailboat to the steamboat. He took a hundred years to go from the steamer to the skyliner.

He spent forty years in moving from the air age to the atomic age.

And only twelve years to leap from the atomic age into the space age with its exploration of the moon.

Where next? Does man now turn to thought waves? Or perhaps to physical transference? The greater probability is that he will perfect his capacity to bring a "happening" into the home, so that it enters each viewer's nervous system, muscles and mind with such reality that it can hardly be separated from the original event.

As viewers know so well, the manner in which electromagnetic waves are manipulated today serves to move the event into the living room. And if we want to examine any part of it for a closer look, an engineer can "freeze" it or play it over or run it backwards.

When this is done regularly, one wonders what will happen to old patterns of thought and emotion. What new meanings will accrue to such old terms as fellowship and brotherhood? The Olympic Games of 1968 may have given us a hint. They were broadcast in twelve languages to an audience numbering hundreds of millions. As TV cameras focused on the athletes and the audience in the arena on the final evening, they conveyed a message of such warm brotherly love that a lump rose in the throat.

The Olympic Games are old, but this human experience, conveyed by electrons, is brand new. It foretells an era of international understanding more fruitful than any ever known.

Tomorrow a viewer will be involved not only in his hometown, but with whatever happens anywhere. When the jungle trails of Vietnam or the streets of Tel Aviv run through our parlors, when we can step from our easy chairs onto the Sea of Tranquillity, we become different persons. For we are there.

Are we prepared for this exposure? Or does it add to our confusion? Ed Murrow recognized this danger. In 1962, when the National Association of Broadcasters honored him with the industry's highest award, its Distinguished Service Award, he said: "A bus burning in Birmingham would be seen live throughout West Africa. A United Nations debate on the admission of Red China may be seen live throughout the Far East. A Geneva conference on disarmament and nuclear testing will go live to the country that has felt nuclear weapons, Japan. Fidel Castro will be seen as large as life from one end of Latin America to the other. And all of Southeast Asia could be drowned under a torrent of instant Khrushchev, direct from Moscow."

Sober-faced Murrow added, "A communications system is totally neutral. It has no conscience, no principle, no morality. It has only a history. It will broadcast filth or inspiration with equal facility. It will speak the truth as loudly as it will speak a falsehood. It is, in sum, no more or no less than the men and women who use it."

Reverend Billy Graham once told broadcasters: "You men and women have the power to help bring to this nation the moral and spiritual renewal that is so desperately needed. You can make America think, buy, or do almost anything. You can make us pro-Communist or anti-Communist. You can make us moral or immoral. We must come to the point where all of us together join our hands to teach moral law in a period of moral rottenness. You have a tremendous responsibility."

A career that enables a youth to share so vast a responsibility is bound to provide satisfactions. Already, a trail has been blazed by thousands of broadcasting pioneers. We are what we are today because of their programs. We become, tomorrow, the result of the learning experiences of today, from watching some part of the 22,000 hours of programming that U.S. broadcasters deliver to U.S. homes annually.

The challenge of social change confronts every citizen and every corporation. Both stations and networks are meeting it. The National Academy of Television Arts and Sciences names some of the more recent TV answers to the challenges:

"The Slow Guillotine," about pollution, was produced by KNBC in Los Angeles.

"Journey to a Pine Box," a chronicle of the life of a welfare recipient, was produced by station WRC-TV in Washington, D.C.

"New Voices in the Wilderness," a study of the relevance of religious faith to today's dilemmas, was produced by WNBC-TV in New York.

Other essays in pictures and words, concerned with local and national topics, have been "Lost Cargo," a commentary on the causes of the decline of Seattle, Washington, as a major port; "Architecture Is Rusting at the Hinges"; "Biography of a Gang"; "Front Page: Pravda"—in which Americans received an insight into what the Russian masses are told by their leaders; and "What's Wrong with Television?"

Note that each of these subjects adds size and comprehension to a current challenge. Note also that each program reached its audience and won its preeminence only because a mind or a group of minds was willing to invest time, sweat and imagination in a creative effort. For the most part, these were young minds.

Tomorrow's recruits to broadcasting will take over a delicately tuned instrument. Its entertainment satisfies, its information informs and its profits are generous. But the old structure is beginning to sag. New media are challenging. Cable TV, for instance. Fresh sensitivity is needed to formulate new policies. Remodeling is in order, for change cannot be stopped. In 1970, after fifty years, the industry stands as the richest legacy ever left to a new generation. Bright innovators can win for it new power and grandeur.

Somewhere a modern, youthful Solomon is probably settling for himself the issue of what broadcasting should begin to say to America and the world of the '80s. Each generation produces a handful of wise men. Edward Murrow was one of the elect. Listen to him again:

> "Global television will not bring more wisdom to our minds. It will only give wider dissemination to what our minds have to say. . . . You gentlemen will share the burden of what this new communication system will have to say. Around this globe there are many people who seek only to lift their lives from a crushing way of existence. There will be many with starving bellies, diseased children, and squalid hovels who will turn with but marginal interest to your new television. And what will you say to them? . . . I suggest the problem of what we are to say is one to which the broadcast world might turn its mind, and urgently."

Inevitably, all mankind will presently be united in a vast web of swift communications. The prospect is both a challenge and a dilemma, perhaps the greatest of our age. It demands unprecedented ideals, sensitivity and guts of its servants. But it offers incomparable rewards.

A CAREER FOR TOMORROW

Herewith is information that may be useful to a person desiring to become a broadcaster. Much of it is a condensation of publications of the National Association of Broadcasters, *Careers in Radio* and *Careers in Television*. Both are obtainable by writing to the NAB, 1812 K Street N.W., Washington, D.C. 20006.

Another useful periodical is *Broadcasting Yearbook*, published by Broadcasting Publications, Inc., 1735 DeSales Street N.W., Washington, D.C. 20006. It lists every network and radio and television station by call letters and location, plus officers and their addresses, and much other pertinent information. Also included are associations, broadcasting services, syndicates and so forth.

A Word About Education

Some beginning jobs do not require a college education. However, all authorities agree that a college diploma is a big help in reaching the top echelon. This applies equally to programming, sales or engineering staffs.

Scores of schools and colleges now give accredited courses in radio and television. Interested students can write for additional information to the Association for Professional Broadcasting Education, 1771 N Street N.W., Washington, D.C. 20036. Many junior colleges have also introduced excellent courses which provide ample training for beginners' jobs. If a student continues with his education at a university, most of his credits can be transferred. In recent years, many scholarships have become available. An inquiry addressed to the National Association of Broadcasters will bring a complete listing.

JOBS IN BROADCASTING

Authorities recommend that beginners first apply to stations rather than to a network. Stations come in all sizes, from those with 250 employees in large cities to smaller ones with only a dozen or so workers.

Most radio and television stations each have four general departments:

1. Programming
2. Sales

3. Engineering

4. General administration

During the '60s, hundreds of stations increased their news activities. Many of them created special news departments; in most cases, however, news is a part of the total programming operation. Small stations may even require news reporting of announcers or salesmen.

Programming

This department and its employees are concerned with a single objective—supplying a good program service to the community. The programming staff conceives and produces local programs, which range from children's shows to religious panels, from baseball games to the county fair. In the field of electronic journalism, reporters may be assigned to beats or routes where they collect news and then return to the station to put it on the air.

Outside programs are often purchased from independent producers or syndicates that offer Hollywood movies, network reruns, drama, comedy, games and documentaries. These programs are on film and can be run at the station's convenience; or in case of a radio show, they are on tape. One of the oldest syndicated shows on TV is "Truth or Consequences." One of the newest successes is "The David Frost Show."

A second type of outside program is available if a station is affiliated with a network. Most TV stations have a network affiliation, as do many radio stations. Network programs are more expensively produced and use bigger stars than a single station can afford.

The Program Director

He, along with the sales manager and the station manager, is one of the triumvirate that decides on program policy for the station. He develops new programs and improves old ones. He works with producer-directors, talent, writers and musicians to create the kind of program the sales manager can sell. If outside programs are bought, he participates in their selection. His day-to-day responsibility includes assigning his personnel to various productions, scheduling programs so they reach the right audience—and keeping his production costs within a budgeted figure. Most program directors reach the top only after working their way up from lesser production jobs. Many begin as announcers or production assistants.

The Production Manager

He is the program manager's right arm. He supervises personnel, work assignments and studio activities. What it takes to put a show on the air, he supplies.

The Producer-Director

He is responsible for producing a single program or a series. Once assigned a project, he selects material and talent, acting on his own judgment. If lighting and camera angles are involved, he makes the final decisions. If dramatic interpretations are required, he directs .them. Usually he is given a sum of money to cover production costs, within which he must work. Imagination must be used to brighten up old situations and ideas. Skill in personal relations must be employed to inspire actors to give their best performances. Authorities agree that this is one of the most demanding tasks in broadcasting.

Staff Announcer

The staff announcer is a fixture from the early days of radio. He reads commercial announcements, community bulletins, introduces recordings, tells the time of day, gives the weather forecasts. The best announcers convey warmth, sincerity and integrity. Their English is correct and their pronunciation is clear, natural and without mannerisms. In appearance, the clean-cut look is important. Though a college diploma is not essential, a knowledge of world events and cultural affairs is an asset to those who want to comment on world affairs or to present editorials. Some announcers become so popular that they are given special assignments. More than any other member of a station's staff, it is the announcer who creates the image of a station's personality.

Program Specialists

The specialist concentrates on a field of interest that usually has its own audience. The standard areas are sports, news, weather, farm, home economics, entertainment (interviewing or being a master of ceremonies). A specialist must keep in contact with community groups interested in the same subject, participate in their meetings and make speeches. Some specialists work with sponsors whose products fit naturally into an alliance, contributing off-the-air efforts to improve sales.

The News Director

Most television stations and many radio stations have a news director. His job is to supervise the selection of news stories and the amount of air time to be devoted to each. He assigns newsmen and cameramen to cover local events. He chooses items of national interest from the AP or UPI news wire and cuts or rewrites them to interest his local audience.

The Newsman

The newsman (reporter, cameraman, or both) is on the scene when history is made. When a story breaks, he has a job to do no matter what the hour. With camera, mike, tape recorder and notebook, he covers his community and frequently mingles with the principals of each big story. The pressure for speed and accuracy is great. He must be able to capture the color and action of a newsbreak in the fewest possible words. For some stations, he will not only collect the news but will report it on the air, either reading from the manuscript he has just written or playing his tapes. In a crisis, he may have to ad-lib an eyewitness account. Most radio and TV newsmen start with a college degree in journalism or have some newspaper experience. Reporters who develop administrative skills become news directors.

The Editorial Writer

An increasing number of radio and TV stations are broadcasting editorial comments on issues of local and national interest. Some large stations employ a special writer who also delivers his editorial to the camera or the mike. A few station managers like to write and deliver their own opinions. Frequently, newsmen will write an editorial on a subject on which they are expert and a staff announcer will read it.

Production Assistants

Assistants do many kinds of jobs in various departments. This is a beginner's job and a college education is rarely a requirement. Willingness to learn, to take orders, to perform frequently menial duties are prerequisites. The work varies but it all contributes toward the station's prime function of maintaining a lively program service.

The Film Director

Television introduced the use of great quantities of film. All Hollywood movies are on film. So are most commercials. So are syndicate programs. All this film must be checked (and frequently repaired or cleaned) before it is put on the air. The film director handles the screening and preparation of filmed programs. He usually has assistants, called editors, who cut, splice and clean film.

The Production Crew

The production crew is headed by the production manager, whose right arm is the producer-director assigned to a specific production. The latter usually is aided by production assistants—sometimes called "gophers"—to run errands, secure props, bring in coffee and do many small jobs that oil the machinery of production. They also learn how to be producers and directors.

Floorman

In the theater, the TV floorman would be called a stagehand. He is one of the crew that works on the studio floor arranging sets, lights and furniture. Sets are usually designed by a staff Scenic Designer, and built either by the station's own carpenters or by an outside set builder. Large stations also employ a makeup artist, a costumer and other specialized personnel.

Actors hired for work in productions or commercials are usually free lancers working from job to job. In the case of a series, they may be given a contract for a span of time or for the "run of the play."

The Continuity Writer

The basic task of the continuity writer is to write commercial announcements that will sell a sponsor's products or services, write public service and station promotional announcements and occasionally create special programs. He is a trained writer. He must have the kind of imagination that produces fresh ideas. He rarely has time for careful rewriting. Often his words are snatched from his typewriter and rushed to an announcer who is already on the air. Calmness under hectic conditions is essential.

Sales

This department sells time. The sale of time provides the flow of revenue that is the lifeblood of every commercial radio and TV station.

A station's time is sold in three ways:

1. If it is a network affiliate, network salesmen sell stipulated hours to national advertisers.

2. Every station employs a "station representative." The station rep offers a service to sponsors who need only regional or spot

advertising rather than national. Because most big advertisers are located in distant cities, the rep (who has offices in every region of the country) functions as a sort of out-of-town sales force for the local station.

3. The sale of programs to merchants or manufacturers in the station's own community is handled by its own sales force.

The Sales Manager

This executive sets general sales policy and supervises the daily activities of his salesmen. He devises campaigns to interest seasonal or regional advertisers. He works with the program director to develop entertainment of special interest to local sponsors. Most sales managers are expert salesmen and they usually have several personal accounts. More general managers of stations come from the ranks of sales managers than from any other segment of broadcasting.

The Salesman

This man is the infantryman of broadcasting, the frontline fighter who proves that time is money. He must know his station's schedule and the kind of audience drawn to each available program. He should also know about audiences and ratings on competing stations. Once he sells a sponsor a radio or TV campaign, he "services" the account throughout its duration by handling changes in schedule, copy changes, special announcements and so forth.

Most top salesmen are college graduates, but sales managers generally assert that fluency, enthusiasm and sincerity are more important than a sheepskin. A capable salesman with a scholastic background in marketing, advertising and business principles has a better chance of rising to the top. Good salesmen are in constant demand. One who has administrative ability may become a sales manager and then a station manager.

The Traffic Manager

This job is at the heart of orderly programming. Listeners rarely think of the trouble someone has taken to assure that programs go on and off the air with split-second accuracy. The traffic manager does this, preparing a log of each day's activity, using reports and orders from the sales staff, station reps, networks (if any) and the program department. Once this information is collated, with each program and each commercial assigned a time slot, it is distributed throughout the organization. In many stations the traffic manager is a woman who knows the station inside out through having started as a secretary or bookkeeper. Any person who enjoys detail work and can perform under pressure makes a good traffic manager. Many of them work up daily availability sheets for the sales department, showing all unsold time periods. Because the traffic manager is in frequent contact with other departments, the ability to work with others is of paramount importance.

The Promotion Manager

The promotion manager works closely with the sales department and the sales manager, creating ads for trade journals, producing sales brochures and whatever other material may be needed by salesmen. He also plans and directs advertising campaigns in behalf of certain programs or for the station in general. He needs ingenuity and the ability to write persuasive copy.

Engineering

The NAB booklet on *Careers* says: "In the technical nerve center of a television station (or radio), surrounded by banks of electronic equipment, the broadcast technician performs his part in bringing television to the audience, switching from the network program originating in New York to a projector for a film commercial and then to a camera in the studio for a live show. At the transmitter, other technicians monitor the equipment and adjust it so that the best possible picture is going out over the air. Others may be standing by outside the studio ready to relay a news or sports event from some part of the city.

"The engineering department is the vital link between the television station and the public. All of the work of the program and sales departments, as well as all of the other employees of the station, depends on the strength, clarity, and reliability of the signal which is sent out from the station's transmitter."

The Chief Engineer

He is the executive with an engineering degree who supervises all technical work, and his department will include a half-dozen technicians. He assigns them to various programs, sees that equipment is maintained and recommends the purchase of replacements or special devices. Usually, he has spent many years working as a technician. As a fully qualified engineer, he must have obtained from the FCC its First Class Radiotelephone Operator's license. (Information about this license can be obtained by writing the Federal Communications Commission, Washington, D.C.) The normal educational requirement for a technician is a high school diploma plus technical school courses.

GENERAL ADMINISTRATION
The Station Manager
The station's chief executive is the station manager. He runs it in behalf of its owners or its board of directors. In addition to overseeing all activities, he handles the station's contacts with the federal government, supervises finances and keeps records required by the FCC for license renewal every three years. Details of management are usually administered by an assistant called the Controller or Business Manager.

The Publicity Manager
This person's role is to promote his station's programs and its performers. He sees that they make appearances at fairs, conventions, store openings and so forth. He supplies newspapers and periodicals with information that can be turned into special feature stories. He sets up interviews with stars and personalities for journalists. In smaller stations, the publicity and promotion departments are combined.

Jobs for Women in Radio and Television
Broadcasting is probably a more fertile field for the talents of women than any other American industry. There are few jobs in broadcasting which women do not hold. They serve as general managers, program directors, salesmen, even engineers. Most beginning opportunities, however, are on clerical or program staffs doing secretarial or production chores.

Most women on the air for local stations are performers with special interests such as cooking, homemaking, fashion or child care. Many stations employ women as weathergirls and a few use them as staff announcers. Performers in the arts, such as singers or dancers, are usually hired for specific programs on a free-lance basis. Many women have enjoyed great success as script and continuity writers.

Whether they work as beginning secretaries or general managers, they are a powerful force for better community service. For twenty years, they have had their own professional association, American Women in Radio and Television, Inc. In 1960 AWRT established an educational foundation to promote international understanding through communications. It conducts seminars for women, presents forums to dramatize today's radio and television opportunities and sponsors international study tours.

250

In 1970 the American Women in Radio and Television, now 2,400 strong, held their first international convention in London, England, where President Marian Corwell Shertzer, a Ford Motor Company broadcasting executive, was succeeded by Virginia Forwood Pate, owner-manager of radio stations WASA and WASA-FM in Maryland.

Young women seeking career guidance should contact the AWRT Executive Director, 1321 Connecticut Avenue N.W., Washington, D.C. 20036.

Network Television Jobs

The glamour of network television captivates everyone who comes in contact with it. Its world is peopled with dramatic stars, playwrights, comedians, foreign correspondents, singers, orchestra conductors—all the entrancing aspects of show business.

But it is not for the beginner. Start on a local station. Learn your business in competition with others, and sharpen your skills.

Basically, a network is involved in the same activities as a station. It produces programs and sells network time to advertisers. But the competition is fierce and the demand for superior performance is unrelenting. Veteran broadcasters advise beginners to win their spurs locally before trying for the big time.

Not everyone will find satisfaction in a broadcasting career. The late Dorothy Gordon, moderator of NBC's "Youth Forum," always worried that some youngsters would be too fascinated with broadcasting to recognize their own shortcomings. "The danger," she says, "is that if they can't really make the grade they may deceive themselves for too long dreaming about success in a medium never meant for them."

Traits Contributing to Success

What qualities are most likely to make a successful broadcaster? Station managers say this:

    a. They want people who will not step on other people.
    b. They want people who can get along with others.
    c. They want people who are gracious and diplomatic.
    d. They want people who keep up their contacts with others.

So say authors George N. Gordon and Irving A. Falk in their excellent book, *Your Career in TV and Radio*. And they add that general managers always look first at an applicant's attitudes. "They can teach new skills but they cannot change attitudes," they add, "so they want persons who know how to get along with others."

These specific character traits contribute to success:

Adaptability. A broadcasting station is open seven days a week and many are on the air twenty-four hours a day. Working hours are often rotated so that inconvenient shifts are passed around. During a crisis, however, a workday may last around the clock, even twice around. One must be able to accept sudden changes of personal plans without regret and without upset.

Enthusiasm. Broadcasting is an idea business. Enthusiasm helps other persons to comprehend the novelty or the untried idea.

Sense of Public Relations. Broadcasting is a goldfish bowl and every listener is a self-appointed critic. A broadcaster, whether on the air or behind the scenes, must have a feeling for his community and the importance of the station's role in it.

Creativity. This is the special substance that attracts new listeners and cements old loyalties. But creativity must submit to discipline. Group decisions often result in new ideas being changed or shelved. Broadcasting is always a team effort.

Balanced temperament. Broadcasting is show business with a stopwatch. It demands quick decisions and fast action. Employees must often work under pressure without losing their cool.

Reliability. No characteristic is more important to an executive than the reliability of his staff. His station presents programs but it sells time. And time flies, vanishing with every tick of the clock. Deadlines must be met. Commercials must run as scheduled. Nobody plays hooky with time. As on Broadway, the show must go on, and the people who put it on are the reliable staff members on duty.

Initiative. A good worker who has learned his job never has to be told what to do next. The right kind of initiative gets things done without being pushy, bossy or bumptious.

Business sensitivity. All commercial broadcasting is supported by the sale of commercial time to advertisers. Selling time is a serious, love-it-or-leave-it undertaking. If you think of a career in broadcasting as a lark, you will not last long.

What college courses provide the best background for a broadcasting career? Many executives recommend a broad background in arts, letters and humanities. Veteran newscaster Lowell Thomas, writing in *Careers in Broadcasting*, says that he would skip vocational training. "Instead, I would concentrate on the classics, on history, both ancient and modern; plus English literature; and such scientific courses as biology, geology, astronomy, physics and chemistry, one foreign language right from kindergarten, and a second in later years. On top of that, I would add philosophy, logic and political science. As a side-line, I would devote a lot of time to public speaking."

Harrison Summers, professor of broadcasting at Ohio State University, says: "Take courses in psychology and sociology and history and political science. These fields deal with the behavior of people, and in broadcasting you're dealing with behavior in the mass and trying to influence their behavior."

On the other hand, so many universities and colleges have upgraded their broadcasting courses that much of the above is included along with technical subjects. Gordon and Falk urge a careful checkup before selecting a college. Note the number of full-time professors on the faculty, they suggest. Beware if there are too many part-timers. Make certain that its courses lead toward a degree and are fully accredited. Ask if the broadcasting department has its own studios and if its staff includes a full-time engineer. Do the professors publish their work in such journals as *The National Association of Educational Broadcasting Bulletin, The Television Quarterly* or *The Journal of Broadcasting?* In other words, make certain that the department is solidly staffed by solid broadcasting scholars.

An all-important subject is English, of course; *spoken* English. It is of importance to every person on the programming or sales side. On the other hand, technicians should ground themselves in physics, sciences, industrial arts. And for anybody, the ability to type is an asset.

How does a person go about getting a job?

Write to a station in which you would like to work, listing your qualifications. Broadcasters, especially those in smaller communities, are constantly seeking new help.

Reply to the many help wanted advertisements printed in the trade press. As before, list your qualifications.

One other tip—a most important one—make up your mind to live in a small town for a while. Most of the new stations will be built in the smaller communities and here the opportunity for jobs will be greatest. Although the salary will not be fabulous, it will be comparable to that paid by any other enterprise in the community.

The above advice comes from a survey of scores of broadcasting veterans.

A network vice president has said: "We need articulate, literate people. . . . Study what you see on your own television set. . . . Study the trade papers—*Broadcasting, Variety, Radio-TV Daily, Television* magazine. . . . Go to bat thousands of times. The more you get into the game, the better the odds. Big opportunities exist . . ."

As American society evolves, with its increasing need for more information, the managers of communications enterprises are bound to play a broader role. Some scholars predict that management men of tomorrow will work almost as hard at solving the nation's social problems as in turning a profit. Furthermore, business and government leaders will work together in ways hitherto experienced only during wartime. Our national problems will be attacked as common enemies, and solved by joint efforts.

At long last, the people themselves—the viewers and listeners —are becoming aware of the power of broadcasting and are concerned that its strength be properly applied to the American future. Raymond Gram Swing, a famous World War II broadcaster, once asked, "Who is in charge of broadcasting?" His answer was—the People.

"From them emerge men with dreams and ideas and ambitions . . . and needs and desires and hungers," he said, ". . . and out of these come conflict, from which flow the moves and countermoves which have built the United States to what it is . . . and which has built radio and television. . . . It is the democratic way, always imperfect . . . but always trying to be perfect. It is a pretty good formula."

Edward Murrow had a recipe by which he guided his own fruitful and famous career. He saw broadcasting as a whole, serving advertisers and citizens alike. "This instrument can teach," he said. "It can illuminate; yes, it can even inspire, but it can do so only to the extent that humans are determined to use it to those ends. Otherwise, it is merely lights and wires in a box."

As never before, the people are aware of their needs and of the great potential of broadcasting. As never before, the broadcasting industry understands its role in society as a partner of the people and of the federal government.

The industry, with its endless programs and its millions of sets, has climbed to a high plateau. To some, it may seem to be resting on its laurels, a bit tired after the outpouring of artistic riches that made it history's greatest industrial success. After fifty years of growth, it pauses only to prepare for tomorrow, to draw a few deep breaths and to permit a changing of the guard.

America's rate of change is without parallel. The demands for relevant programs are continuous and insistent. Only a nation that is informed and that understands will survive.

The electron has a bright and busy future.

So have the people who control it.

PHOTO CREDITS